restores one's faith in the future, in America's ability to reinvent itself, and in its most important resource: people and their ideas."

Vera Jelinek, Ph.D.
Divisional Dean, Center for Global Affairs, New York University, School of Continuing and Professional Studies

"*Making Sense of the Dollar* is a must read, fun book for anyone involved in foreign exchange markets. It is extremely topical in that it covers many of the core issues forex markets grapple with constantly. It is analytical because Marc Chandler has spent a good deal of time and research to substantiate a basically positive view of the U.S. dollar, which has its own detractors. It is extremely up-to-date and contemporaneous in that his anecdotes are very current; I loved the reference to the Taj Mahal not accepting U.S. dollars from tourists. It is perfectly timed given the critical juncture in global currency markets where the outlook for the U.S. dollar is under serious scrutiny. Given the magnitude of recent government interventions to stem the current credit crisis, it will be fascinating to see how Chandler's thesis holds up with the explosion in U.S. government debt supply ahead, concerns about what kind of burden sharing future bank re-capitalizations may require and importantly, how long this new paradigm where low interest rates actually help currencies to strengthen (witness many European market currencies where this is occurring) can be sustained."

Hari N. Hariharan
Chairman and CEO, NWI Management LP

"Against a backdrop of global economic upheaval, numerous myths have sprung up that do not reflect actual reality. Many of these myths are heard in today's economic discussions: that America is becoming vulnerable to the whims of Chinese investors; that the U.S. trade gap is turning Americans into a nation of 'sharecroppers'; that America is losing its competitive prowess in global markets; and that the dollar's standing will be in decline. Marc Chandler offers a refreshing challenge to many of these myths. This thought-provoking book discusses such issues as an obsolete trade tracking system, the dominance of America's flexible capital markets, and the importance of flexible labor markets. He explains why the dollar will maintain its premier status for decades to come. Counter to common speculation, he asserts that globalization has strengthened, not weakened, American industry and explains why the U.S. trade deficit is not a scorecard for competitiveness. Chandler's provocative challenge to many popular ideas about trade and globalization is down to earth and informative."

James Glassman
Senior Economist and Managing Director, JP Morgan Chase & Co.

Making Sense of the
Dollar

Also available from
Bloomberg Press

Hedge Hunters:
Hedge Fund Masters on the Rewards, the Risk, and the Reckoning
by Katherine Burton

The Heretics of Finance:
Conversations with Leading Practitioners of Technical Analysis
by Andrew W. Lo and Jasmina Hasanhodzic

Hedge Fund of Funds Investing: An Investor's Guide
by Joseph G. Nicholas

Investing in Hedge Funds: Revised and Updated Edition
by Joseph G. Nicholas

Bonds: The Unbeaten Path to Secure Investment Growth
by Hildy Richelson and Stan Richelson

The Only Guide to Alternative Investments You'll Ever Need:
The Good, the Flawed, the Bad, and the Ugly
by Larry E. Swedroe and Jared Kizer

A complete list of Bloomberg Press titles is available at
www.bloomberg.com/books

Making Sense of the
Dollar

Exposing
DANGEROUS MYTHS
about Trade and
Foreign Exchange

Marc Chandler

BLOOMBERG PRESS

NEW YORK

First edition published 2009

1 3 5 7 9 10 8 6 4 2

Library of Congress Cataloging-in-Publication Data

Chandler, Marc.
Making sense of the dollar : exposing dangerous myths about trade and foreign exchange / Marc Chandler.
    p. cm.
  Includes bibliographical references and index.
  Summary: "Making Sense of the Dollar explores the many factors—trade deficits, the dollar's role in the world, globalization, capitalism, and more—that affect the dollar and the U.S. economy and lead to the inescapable conclusion that both are much stronger than many people suppose"—Provided by publisher.
  ISBN 978-1-57660-321-5 (alk. paper)
  1. Foreign exchange—United States. 2. Dollar, American. 3. Balance of trade—United States. I. Title.
  HG3903.C44 2009
  332.4'560973—dc22

2009015711

For Jeannine and Nathan,
my inspiration and hope

Contents

Acknowledgments

It is customary to include in a book of this type a list of influential people who helped bring the book to fruition. In this particular case, that alone won't do. The influences are truly countless and extend beyond a quarter century. And as often as not, my own thinking proceeded as a reaction to others' arguments. Thus, many of the people who have influenced me would not necessarily recognize their contribution in the following pages.

My analysis has evolved over the years, and a number of employers provided varying degrees of intellectual freedom to explore my ideas, including Deutsche Bank, Mellon Bank, and HSBC. The book especially benefited from the opportunity provided by Brown Brothers Harriman, where I have led a team of foreign exchange strategists since 2005. Also, I have had opportunities to write for several publications, including *Foreign Affairs*, the *Financial Times*, *Euromoney*, *Barron's*, *Currency Trader*, and TheStreet.Com.

My arguments have also been "battle tested" at New York University's Center for Global Affairs; for more than fifteen years, students have been more than willing to challenge my thinking and identify the errors of their professor's arguments. Dr. Vera Jelinek, Divisional Dean and Director of the Center, has been particularly supportive and encouraging.

I have had the privilege of working with a number of people who either in their affirmation or criticism helped strengthen the arguments developed here. My colleagues on the highly regarded currency strategy team at Brown Brothers Harriman—Win Thin, Margaret Browne, and Audrey Childe-Freeman—have been helpful. Ezechiel Copic, Stewart Hall, Joseph Quinlan, David Powell, Michael Woolfolk, Rab

Jafri, Michael Casey, Renee Mikalopas-Cassidy, Angelina Yap, and Don Curry have also assisted me. Discussions about globalization and America's contribution with Laurence Norman and Chris Swann were always helpful.

Many other people have been important sources of inspiration, criticism, and support. I have a special debt to Sylvia Coutinho, who has been generous with her time, interest, and encouragement, pushing me to explore the implications of the arguments. Frank Warnock provided invaluable insight into capital flows, and Jim Glassman helped sharpen my thinking about the competitive strengths of the U.S. economy. Mark Sobel of the U.S. Treasury and Niall Coffey at the New York Federal Reserve were helpful sounding boards at important junctures in the evolution of these ideas but cannot be held accountable for any of the shortcomings of the arguments.

My greatest intellectual debt is to Professor James Livingston of the American History Department at Rutgers University. When I was an undergraduate at North Central College in Naperville, Illinois, he framed many of the problematics that I continue to wrestle with. His pedagogical roots were so compelling that I pursued a graduate degree with *his* professors at Northern Illinois University. Jim's writings, discussions, and arguments have been the single greatest inspiration. The only way such a debt can be repaid is to pay it forward, which is what I attempt to do in my own teaching.

Ann Logue, author of *Day Trading for Dummies, Hedge Funds for Dummies,* and *Socially Responsible Investing for Dummies,* provided indispensable help giving voice to my ideas. Without her help, many of the ideas would be too rarified for many readers. I would also like to recognize my agent, Marilyn Allen, and editor Stephen Isaacs at Bloomberg Press for making the book a reality.

Although the inspiration and support were broadly received, the errors, factual and judgmental, are the sole responsibility of the author.

Introduction

This book grew out of my work of more than two decades in the foreign exchange market. But anyone who wants a guide on trading currencies or advice on making a fortune in the foreign exchange market should look elsewhere. Instead, this book draws insight from the foreign exchange market and the performance of the U.S. dollar to shed light on aspects of globalization that all too often are opaque. In particular, the book focuses on how U.S. businesses have evolved a strategy that allows them to compete in an international political economy that features highly mobile capital and volatile foreign exchange prices.

Each chapter takes a piece of conventional wisdom and shows why it is either simply wrong or why reality is significantly more complicated. What emerges, I believe, is a multidimensional view of the evolutionary expansion strategy of U.S. (and increasingly other) multinational companies. It is an evolutionary strategy in the sense that it is a response to the shifting political and economic environment, much as a species responds to changes in the physical environment.

Moreover, I argue that this strategy is superior to other expansion and development strategies. Of course, I'm not saying that the U.S. strategy is the end of the evolutionary process, the way that Francis Fukuyama once argued that capitalist parliamentary democracies marked the "end of history."[1] Indeed, the global credit crisis suggests it is not yet a stable strategy. (When I use the term *credit crisis* throughout this book, I refer to the financial crisis that began in 2007 with the subprime mortgage crisis in the United States, followed with the failure of major banks, that morphed into other crises on a global magnitude and plunged the United States, Europe, and Japan into recession. At this point, there is no way to really know when the crisis will end or what form it will take next, so I am simply using this term to refer to the financial meltdown whose reverberations are still being felt now at the beginning of 2009.)

The Open Door Notes

My understanding of the U.S. expansion strategy grows out of the school of American history associated with William Appleman Williams, Walter LaFeber, Gabriel Kolko, and Martin Sklar and their students, and more contemporary scholars, such as James Livingston and Andrew Bacevich. They attach significance to the Open Door Notes, penned by Secretary of State John Hay at the start of the twentieth century. That Hay was also once the secretary to Abraham Lincoln (the man who led America's second revolution) gives him additional legitimacy.

Policy analysis is policy advocacy, and Hay well understood that. His notes were a discussion of U.S. strategic options in China and his advocacy of one in particular. With the occupation of the Philippines and a number of other coaling stations acquired in the 1898 Spanish-American War, America's long fascination with China could be acted upon. However, preoccupied with continental expansion and, of course, the Civil War, America was late to the game. China was being carved up into various "concessions" or spheres of influence by several European powers: Britain, France, Germany, Portugal, and Japan.

Hay's policy analysis discussed the various options the United States faced, such as challenging some other country's sphere of influence or grabbing its own sphere of influence. Instead, Hay advocated a bold course: challenge the whole traditional "sphere of influence" approach to foreign affairs itself. Spheres of influence as a dominating principle of international relations was terribly and tragically unstable because wars were the fundamental means by which spheres were expanded.

Hay's alternative vision was based on variable shares in the world economy, and their variability depended on economic prowess, not political concessions. Hay's understanding of national interest recognized that it was preferable for the United States to be able to compete for *all* of China, meaning that China's territorial integrity would have to be preserved.

The implication was clear. Although the immediate application was China, a broad application of the Open Door Notes provided the basis for the U.S. global grand vision and strategy: a country's share of the growth in the world economy should be determined by the competitiveness of its businesses. It is a strategy of a rising power, of an economically competitive economy. Hay was proposing nothing less than replacing the rent-seeking behavior of international economic relations with profit seeking. Another implication was in terms of an ancient dialectic, if you will, between trade-oriented, commerce-based maritime systems (consider Athens) and a more statist and egalitarian land-based system (consider Sparta). The Open Door Notes placed the United States squarely in the tradition of other maritime powers: in the Athenian tradition.

The New World Order

Nearly half a century later, post–World War II institutions such as the United Nations, International Monetary Fund, and what became the World Bank and the General Agreement on Tariffs and Trade, the predecessor of the World Trade Organization (WTO), were, in effect, the institutionalization and globalization of the Open Door. The world wars destroyed the globalization of the late nineteenth and early twentieth century that Lenin describes so well in *Imperialism: The Highest Stage of Capitalism*. The U.S.-led version of globalization would be predicated on variable shares, not fixed spheres. It was a globalism, but it was neither colonialist nor imperialist in its traditional guise.

Of course, the entire world did not embrace the Open Door, the new world order. The Soviet Union and its sphere of influence in eastern and central Europe did not. Nor did China or India, the most populous countries in the world, or other large parts of the world. Indeed, much of the world's population was really on the periphery of the Open Door world. In reality, it seemed more of an objective of how the Western capitalist countries and Japan should compete with each other.

The Open Door Widens

Another half century later, however, the bipolar division of the world characterized by the Cold War is over. Countries in what used to be the Soviet Union's "sphere of influence" in central Europe, such as the former Czechoslovakia (now the Czech Republic and Slovakia), Poland, and Hungary, are now NATO members, and much to Russia's chagrin, there are still efforts to include Georgia and the Ukraine. The number of countries that have joined the World Trade Organization and in effect

embrace the Open Door (as it has become operationalized) continues
to grow. Overshadowed by the enormity of 9/11, 2001 also marked the
entry of China, a rapidly rising economic powerhouse and significant
exporter and importer, into the WTO.

Russia is the one large economy that has not joined the WTO.
Russia's invasion of Georgia in the summer of 2008 did not cause a shift
in the balance of power in Europe; it was a reflection of the fact that the
balance had already changed. One casualty of Russia's invasion of Georgia appears to be Russia's ascension to the WTO. In fact, the process had
been previously politicized. As required, Russia had reached bilateral
agreements with all WTO members save one: Georgia.

The larger point, however, remains valid. The Open Door has become
the basis of the current globalization, and more countries and people
have been included in it. The essential service provided by the WTO
and arrangements such as the North American Free Trade Agreement
and many bilateral trade agreements is one of conflict resolution. Rather
than wars breaking out from the inevitable crises that arise as countries
seek to expand their variable spheres, there are rules of engagement and
competition. One can seek redress for grievances if the rules are vio-
lated when a competing country's variable share increases.

U.S. Competitiveness

This book looks at how the United States competes in this Open Door
world. There is, of course, the sobering possibility that the credit
crisis may mark the end of that world. This book assumes that even
though the credit crisis will most likely generate significant institutional changes and a restructuring of the financial sector in numerous countries, including the United States, financial innovation will
continue even if in a different—and more regulated—environment.
The economic contraction will be very painful for many people, and
the savings of hardworking people will be destroyed, but I expect the
insight by Adam Smith and David Ricardo will remain broadly true:
the origins of the wealth of nations lie in specialization and division
of labor, which boosts productivity but is limited by the extent of the
market. The mobility of capital, goods, services, and labor increases the
extent of the market.[2]

It is also possible, with the epicenter of the global credit crisis in the
United States, that the role of the U.S. dollar in the world economy may

be threatened. I do not think that will be the case, and part of the reason is based on understanding why the role of the dollar remains so significant even after the advent of the euro and despite the chronic current account deficits. This is explored in detail in the following chapters.

In its infancy, America was a great experiment. Traditional political philosophy maintained that one could not have a representative form of government over a large piece of territory: it would fracture and break apart. The center could not hold.[3] After a couple centuries, the United States has ceased to be an experiment. We are at the beginning of another great experiment: can there be a sustainable basis for monetary union without political union in Europe?

The Euro

The credit crisis put strains on the monetary union, revealing certain fissures that point to potential sources of future tension. Interest-rate differentials relative to the German benchmark widened considerably. That is to say that the cost of money diverged significantly in an economic region that shares a common currency. In addition, in the summer of 2008, the Bank of Spain restricted acceptable collateral to AAA sovereign paper. In effect, that rejected the use of Italy's government bonds, even though Italy is a fellow euro-zone member and European Central Bank board member. Lastly, similar to other countries that adopt or are dependent on another's currency, euro-zone members do not control the euro printing press, the currency in which their debt is primarily denominated.

Ten years after the birth of the euro, it is still little more than the sum of its parts as a share of reserve currencies—the German mark, the French franc, and European Currency Unit (ECU). Only a little more than half the euro-zone's imports and exports are invoiced in euros. The economic integration to date, including monetary union, does not appear to have boosted the region's productivity or competitiveness. In fact, the gap between the United States and many euro-zone members, including Germany, France, and Italy, on a per capita income basis, actually widened in the euro's first ten years. That the advent of the euro has not boosted the region's economic prowess should not be surprising because, at its heart, monetary union itself was an economic solution of an essentially political challenge: under what terms would a united Germany be acceptable? Some observers imply that the euro is supplanting the role of the U.S. dollar in the world economy. Many who believe this appear more enthusiastic about the role of the euro as a serious rival to the dollar than do European policy makers and most of the world's central banks. The legacy currencies (the German mark, French franc, and ECU) accounted for about 25 percent of the world's reserves before the run-up to the monetary union and only slightly more in 2008.

The Importance of the U.S. Treasury Market

One of the most important and perhaps most underappreciated factors that supports the dollar's preeminent role in the world economy is the backing of the deepest and most liquid bond market in the world, the U.S. Treasury market. In terms of size, by some measures the euro-denominated sovereign bond market rivals the U.S. market, but the sovereign bond market is simply not a unitary market like the Treasury market: there are many different issuers. Most issues tend to be small. There are different auction schedules, tax regimes, and conventions. The better comparison might be between the euro sovereign bond market and the U.S. municipal bond market rather than the Treasury market.

The breadth and depth of the U.S. Treasury market gives it unrivaled liquidity and transparency. A combination of other attributes such as political stability, rule of law, general rules that support entrepreneurship, and a military power that is second to none even when stretched plays an important role in why sovereign countries freely continue to allocate a large part of their reserves to dollars. But if it is not the euro that will rival the dollar, then what will?

China's Economic Rise and Its Currency

When I've spoken at meetings or conferences, people have often asked me if the Chinese remnimbi or yuan is not the real challenger. A rising economic power, with reserves that in late 2008 were nearly equal to its annual GDP, China has captured the imagination of many businesses and investors. Its growth has been phenomenal. By some measures, China—which tends not to follow the advice of the multilateral institutions, such as allowing more rapid appreciation of the renminbi, or does not feel obligated to adhere to best practices such as reporting the composition of reserves—single-handedly accounts for the reduction in absolute global poverty in recent years.

At purchasing power parity, China's economy is already the second largest in the world, yet its currency is of tertiary significance in global finance. It is not convertible for investment purposes. It is not a unit of measure, a store of value, or a means of exchange outside of China. China's financial institutional framework is still evolving. The renminbi as a global reserve asset is probably beyond the pale of the imagination of most Chinese officials. Its role as a regional reserve asset could follow its convertibility on the capital account and its use as an invoicing currency.

Perhaps one day China's currency may be among the global reserve assets. Maybe one day it will rival the dollar. But that day is in a distance best measured in decades, not months or years. In lieu of a clear reasonable alternative, and unless one believes the United States is about to abdicate, the U.S. dollar will remain the *numéraire*, the key metric in the world economy.

Assessing the Dollar

It is not simply that the dollar will remain the basis of the global economy, but, contrary to what passes as conventional wisdom, the United States itself is not in decline. The United States was never the hyperpower that its friends and enemies have claimed. Its ability to convert economic power and presence into political influence was always very much circumscribed.

The "glory days" were not all that glorious, and the decline in relative or absolute terms seems similarly exaggerated. Many traditional arguments cite as supposed evidence of the U.S. decline, in some kind of structural sense of its position and influence in the world, economic factoids such as the large U.S. current account deficit, low savings rate, and the deeply negative net investment position. This book explains why those metrics are inappropriate or misused.

In Chapter 1, I show why the U.S. trade deficit does not reflect U.S. competitiveness. Not one in a hundred economists seems to appreciate and incorporate into his or her analysis that roughly half the U.S. trade deficit can be accounted for by intrafirm trade or the movement of goods within the same company. Every time a good or service crosses national borders, government bean counters call it trade. I show how misleading this can be as an accounting measure.

In Chapter 2, I look at those arguments that try to explain the dollar's movements in terms of the current account balance, which is a broad measure of trade (and includes goods, services, tourism, worker remittances, and income from investments such as dividends and interest). Businesses and investors would find their burden lightened considerably if it were as simple and straightforward as that. Alas, it is not, and for good reasons. This chapter shows, for example, how capital flows far and away outstrip trade flows, and that there are other factors that influence supply and demand for currencies, especially the dollar, that swamp the impact from trade.

In these early chapters, I explore one of the essential characteristics of the U.S. expansion strategy: build locally and sell locally. It is partly a hub-and-spoke model, except the spokes increasingly interact as well. This strategy is superior to the early export-oriented strategy as the main means of servicing foreign demand. It also lends itself to global development to a greater extent than the old export-oriented thrust.

Chapter 3 picks up the topic of capital flows and investment. A basic academic course in international trade includes an introduction to what economists call an "identity" (true by definition) that the current account position is the difference between a country's investment and savings. My argument that the U.S. current account is overstated (and is a poor measure of U.S. competitiveness and a poor guide for forecasting the dollar's vagaries in the foreign exchange market) is bolstered by a corollary: U.S. savings are underestimated. I present significant examples of how. In this chapter, I also flesh out another key function that the United States has in the world economy and for which there seems no clear alternative: the United States acts as the safety valve for the world's excess savings. In effect, it acts like the world's banker. One of the consequences of this is the infamous U.S. trade deficit.

Chapter 4 stays focused on capital and suggests that U.S. capital markets are an underappreciated contributor to U.S. economic performance. Often the flexibility of the U.S. labor market seems overemphasized. Most workers experience the labor market flexibility as being hired and fired at will. Their wages do not necessarily keep pace with inflation or productivity gains, and one is responsible for one's own pension money performance under the defined-contribution plans.

Instead of the labor market mobility, I emphasize capital market flexibility, and this naturally lends itself to a discussion in Chapter 5 of the two main ways capital is distributed: banks and markets. This, in turn, leads to an appreciation that capitalism itself is no more monolithic than communism was. The communism practiced in the Soviet Union was different from that practiced in Tito's Yugoslavia, which itself was different from communism with Chinese characteristics. Similarly, different clusters of behavior and practices allow a discussion of varieties of capitalism. These behaviors involve institutions and relationships and are mutually shaped and supported by other institutions and relationships, like an organic whole rather than machines with interchangeable parts.

In Chapter 6, the focus shifts more properly to the dollar itself. I document its role in the world economy: the dollar is not just the key reserve asset but also an invoicing currency for trade that does not even involve the United States or a U.S. company. Many commodities continue to be denominated in dollars, e.g., oil, despite speculation to the contrary or the efforts of Iran and Venezuela, which in effect suffer from a first-mover disadvantage of having to bear the currency rise in periods of the dollar's strength and the euro's weakness as they try to shift away from selling their oil in dollars. Outside of a handful of countries in close proximity to the euro zone, the dollar is the key metric by which investors and policy makers evaluate a country's currency. The U.S. dollar remains the intervention currency of choice.

There are some vocal critics of the U.S. Open Door–inspired globalization. Some worry, as economics editor of the *Financial Times* Martin Wolf once put it, that through its chronic current account deficit, the United States is "well on the road to ruin."[4] Others, such as investor icon Warren Buffett and Microsoft's Bill Gates, have also expressed concern that the United States is becoming poorer because of its trade deficits.[5] In recent years, other former defenders of the Open Door vision have had a change of heart. Even the late management guru Peter Drucker did not have confidence that the Open Door, which had served the United States so well in its first hundred years, would serve it as well in the next hundred years.

These issues are explored in Chapter 7. I show how the fundamental transformations of the U.S. economy, which are often shared by other major industrialized high-wage economies, have little to do directly with the fluctuations of the dollar. The dramatic decline in manufacturing jobs in the United States cannot be a function of an overvalued dollar, as some critics suggest. Manufacturing jobs have been lost throughout the advanced industrialized countries and many developing countries, including China, which is "stealing" such jobs, according to popular mythology. The real culprit is technology. The U.S. manufacturing sector is larger than the entire Chinese economy. Before the crisis, U.S. manufacturing output had never been higher. Fewer workers were employed. It's called *productivity*.

The resilience of the American consumer is often misunderstood because observers tend to focus on debt. The fairer measure is household net worth, which is a comprehensive tally of assets and liabilities. Before the economic downturn, the U.S. household net worth would often rise in a year by more than the inflated estimates of China's annual GDP.

Simply—if crudely—put, Americans are in many ways better off than ever before. Yet rarely are these ways incorporated into economic analysis, let alone even appreciated by most observers, including many Americans themselves.

The quantitative and qualitative picture that emerges is one of a more educated American workforce that has been freed from the compulsion of physical toil, is enjoying more leisure time, and is living longer than ever before in larger and more comfortable residences. In some ways, it does not appear much different than what Samuel Gompers, founder of the American Federation of Labor once defined as socialism: More *now*.[6] This is the topic of Chapter 8.

If capitalism can be defined as a type of society in which power is derived from the ownership of productive property, then America and other industrialized countries represent something more than capitalism.

Since the mid-1990s, the United States has had a declaratory policy that embraces a strong dollar. Many economists and opinion shapers argue that this is folly. The U.S. dollar is overvalued, they say; given the chronic trade deficit, the United States should encourage an orderly decline in the dollar to boost exports and reduce the deficit over time while helping to attract foreign capital into the United States to finance the yawning deficits. In Chapter 9, those arguments are examined and found wanting.

In Chapter 10, I broadly examine the foreign exchange market itself. Although the dollar's value is often quoted now in the news and appears prominently in the financial press, in many ways, of all the capital markets, the foreign exchange market may be the least understood. Yet it is incredibly significant. The Bank for International Settlements estimated in its 2007 triennial survey that the average daily turnover in the foreign exchange market was about $3.2 trillion.[7] The turnover in a little more than two weeks is sufficient to finance world trade for a year. In less than a month, turnover in the foreign exchange market is sufficient to buy all goods and services the world produces annually. Yet the significance of the foreign exchange market outstrips its impressive size. As I illustrate, it is an important part of the return on foreign investments.

Chapter 10 also looks at the participants in the foreign exchange market. One of the insights gleaned from an examination of the players may challenge the way many readers conceptualize the market. In the back of our minds is often an informal model of the way any market operates—in this case, the foreign exchange market. Buyers and sellers, driven by the profit-maximization mandate, come together and in the price discovery process (bids and offers), a market-clearing price arises. This is too simple by far and sufficiently distorts the way the foreign exchange market works to make it unrecognizable.

The book concludes with Chapter 11, which summarizes and pulls the various arguments together. What emerges from the arguments, individually and collectively, is a more nuanced picture of how the U.S. expansion strategy works. And that is the real point: It works.

Some Preliminary Thoughts on the Implications of the Financial Crisis

It is difficult to know how the credit crisis or the dimensions of the new financial architecture will affect the constellation of political and economic forces discussed in this book. Institutional rigidity and nationalism toppled the globalization of the nineteenth century. Those same forces can effectively close the Open Door. Yet that does not seem like the most probable scenario. It is more likely that what emerges from the credit crisis are stronger and more transparent institutions. The so-called junk bond market may offer some preview. In the late 1980s, when many thought there was a high-yield corporate bond market, they were fooled. It was a rigged market that was run essentially out of one man's office. Today the high-yield bond market is a bona fide asset class, transparent and with a dedicated following on the buy side. At the same time, there are likely some evolutionary dead ends, too, such as structured investment vehicles, auction-rate bonds, and "ninja loans" (made to people with no income, no job, and no asset verification).

Just as policy makers in both the private and public sectors have managed to smooth the business cycle, the credit cycle itself now needs to be longer in time and lower in amplitude. This will likely require more and different regulations and regulators. It will require more disintermediation, not less.

As a snake molts its skin to allow itself to continue to grow, so too may the financial sector reconstruct itself post–credit crisis so as to permit the broadening and deepening of globalization in the years ahead. Pegged currency regimes largely collapsed between 1995 and 2001. They were too rigid in a world in which capital mobility intensified markedly. Similarly, the capital mobility and leveraging that was achieved—not only in Anglo-American economies but also in Europe, including Iceland, and in many emerging markets such as Brazil, Mexico, South Korea, Hungary, and South Africa—appear to have been greater than the risk-management tools and regulatory regime could cope with.

As this book goes to press, the situation is very fluid. Although the credit crisis marks the end of something, new institutions, relationships and practices are already arising from the ashes. It is possible that the eventual outcome is one that allows for the continuation of the maritime values embraced by the Open Door by placing it on more solid footing. Barring the low probability of a real Bretton Woods II, with a new fixed exchange rate regime, it is likely that more companies will adopt the evolutionary strategy of U.S. businesses. It is based on foreign direct investment and servicing foreign demand from local production and distribution centers, which in turn offers insulation from the vagaries of the foreign exchange market.

Chapter Notes

1. Francis Fukuyama, *The End of History and the Last Man* (New York: Free Press, 1992).

2. Adam Smith, *An Inquiry into the Nature and Causes of the Wealth of Nations* (New York: Oxford University Press, 2008); David Ricardo, *Principles of Political Economy and Taxation* (New York: Cosimo Classic, 2006).

3. Charles de Montesquieu, *The Spirit of the Laws* (Anne M. Cohler, Basia Carolyn Miller, and Harold Samuel Stone, eds., Cambridge Texts in the History of Political Thought) (New York: Cambridge University Press, 1989); *The Federalist: A*

Commentary on the Constitution of the United States by Alexander Hamilton, James Madison, John Jay, and Robert Scigliano (New York: Modern Library, 2000).

4. Martin Wolf, "America Is Now on the Comfortable Path to Ruin." *Financial Times*, August 18, 2004.

5. Warren Buffet has long expressed concern that the U.S. trade deficit is and will continue to undermine the dollar. See for example, Andrew Farrell, "Buffet against the Buck," Forbes.com, February 7, 2008 (www.forbes.com/2008/02/07/buffett-dollar-economy-biz-cx_af_0207buffett.html); or Dan Roberts, "Buffet Deepens Dollar Worries," FT.com, March 5, 2005 (www.ft.com/cms/s/2/14d1fb9c-8da0-11d9-a4d2-00000e2511c8.html). For Bill Gates's view of the dollar, see James Hertling and Simon Clark, "Bill Gates, World's Richest Man, Bets against the Dollar," Bloomberg.com, January 29, 2005 (www.bloomberg.com/apps/news?pid=10000103&sid=aO.Rl7JwFWy8&refer=news_index).

6. Cited in Martin J. Sklar, *United States as a Developing Country: Studies in U.S. History in the Progressive Era and the 1920s* (New York: Cambridge University Press, 1992, page 144n).

7. Bank for International Settlements, "Triennial Central Bank Survey of Foreign Exchange and Derivatives Market Activity in April 2007–Preliminary global results–Turnover," September 25, 2007 (www.bis.org/press/p070925.htm).

The Trade Deficit Reflects U.S. Competitiveness

Which car is more American: a Honda Civic sedan made in Ohio or a Chrysler Town & Country minivan made in Ontario?

A car begins with a design. An engineer imagines what it should look like and how all the pieces should fit together. Someone else mines the iron ore that will become the steel; another person mines the platinum that will go into the catalytic converter; and still another person slaughters the cow for the leather interior. The manufacturer brings all the pieces together for assembly according to the design. The car's buyer, of course, has to fill it up with gas before going anywhere. Every step is important, but some add more value than others. The slaughterhouse worker, for example, needs few skills beyond strength, and the leather that his work generates isn't integral to the finished product; it could be replaced by cloth or vinyl. The engineer, on the other hand, is key because without her basic design, there is no car. If she develops a great new body shape or an engine that uses less gasoline, then she can add a lot of value to the finished product. She can directly influence how much the car costs and how well it sells.

Although different processes add different amounts of value, the system of accounting for international trade looks at the movement of goods and services over national borders and has no appreciation for ownership. Setting aside the huge problems that the General Motors Corporation (GM) has experienced in its U.S. operations—brought on by bad choices in product design and labor decisions, etc., but that's

1

another issue—GM's basic business strategy perfectly exemplifies how a U.S. multinational company's structure interacts with the trade deficit and the dollar. When GM makes parts in the United States, sends them to Canada to put into Chevy Impalas, and then ships those Impalas back to the United States for sale, the company has engaged in two international transactions: it exported the parts and imported the car. The parts cost less than the finished car, so GM's imports exceeded its exports, adding to the U.S. trade deficit; yet all the transactions took place within the virtual walls of the same U.S. corporation. Essentially, GM is moving goods from one side of the corporate factory to the other; it's just that the forty-ninth parallel weaves in and out across the floor. (Amazingly, the movement of goods and services within the same company accounts for half the U.S. trade deficit.)

We've all heard the worries: America has turned its global supremacy over to the Chinese. Our jobs are going to China, and the Chinese are practically buying the U.S. government because they buy all our Treasury bonds. The main piece of evidence cited for this is the U.S. trade deficit. In 2008, the United States recorded an average monthly trade deficit of slightly more than $57 billion. It shows how miserable the United States has become. As Americans consume more than they produce, or invest more than they save, China is quickly moving into ascendancy.

Right?

Wrong. But that's the way too many people think of foreign trade. Too often the focus is strictly on this number called a *deficit*. It is simply understood that deficits are bad, and what's happening behind the numbers is frequently left unexamined. Americans produce ideas, and ideas can generate a spectacular amount of money. Microsoft, for example, doesn't produce much that anyone can touch or feel, but its software has changed the way that we all live, work, and play. How do we account for that? Software, drug patents, product designs, secret formulas, and desirable brand names generate huge profits from all over the world for American companies. When those companies move goods and services between their own offices, it can contribute to the U.S. trade deficit.

Trade accounting is misunderstood. It was designed for a world that no longer exists, one in which dominant nations exported and weak ones imported. Now, goods, services, and ideas flow across borders, as does investment capital. Companies can parcel out business operations not only around the globe but also within the same corporate entity.

The trade deficit is large, but it is not a sign of national weakness, nor is it a twin of a budget deficit as is often portrayed. American workers and American companies are still the envy of the world, even if it's not apparent looking at the trade deficit.

How Trade Accounting Works

At its simplest level, the trade deficit is the value of goods and services exported minus the value of goods and services imported. However, the accounting for it gets complicated. How do we value goods made and sold overseas under patents and trademarks developed in the United States? What if the basic assembly is done overseas but the finishing work is done here? What if the parts are manufactured in three different countries? What if a U.S. retailer asks a clothing manufacturer to start shipping goods on hangers instead of folded in boxes? How much value do those hangers add?

To keep track of the funds that cross borders, nations rely on a system of accounting called the *balance of payments* (BOP).

In each nation, a central agency (in the United States, the Department of Commerce's Bureau of Economic Analysis) collects data, adds up the value of all imports that come into the country during a set time period, and then compares the total to the value of all items exported. For the purposes of the argument here, we will leave aside issues relating to the bias of the data collection. There is a vested interest in documenting imports, since the government often collects a duty or tax. There are also security reasons for documenting imports. Exports are a different story. The full value of U.S. exports may not be fully captured in the official data.

The transactions are separated into three accounts. The *goods and services trade account* only includes imports and exports. The *current account* includes the goods and services trade account along with worker remittances, tourism, and transfer payments (i.e., foreign aid, charity, gifts to relatives overseas, as well as interest and profits from capital investments, royalties, and licensing fees). The *capital and financial account* includes investments made by individuals, corporations, and governments.

A country that exports more goods and services than it imports will have a trade surplus. A country that imports more than it exports will have a trade deficit—and the United States has had a trade deficit for more than thirty years. Intuitively, we know that surpluses are good and deficits are bad, but international trade is far more complicated than that. A trade surplus doesn't mean that a nation is getting ahead, and a deficit doesn't mean that it is falling behind. What matters more are the reasons for a deficit or surplus. Is a country importing because its service-industry workers are prosperous? Or is it importing because its economic base is so primitive that there are no goods to export and imports arrive almost entirely in the form of charity?

Table 1.1 illustrates the international trade transactions of the United States from 2006 to 2008, showing how Americans do business around the world.[1] The trade deficit is calculated in the current account by subtracting imports from exports (line 1 – line 2 = line 3).

TABLE 1.1 U.S. Balance of Payments (2006–2008 Data) in Millions of $

Line	(Credits +, debits –)	2006 year	2007 year	2008 1Q
	Trade account			
1	Exports of goods	1,023,109	1,148,481	317,813
2	Imports of goods	–1,861,380	–1,967,853	–528,845
3	**Trade account**	**–838,271**	**–819,372**	**–211,032**
	Current account			
4	Income receipts on U.S.-owned assets abroad	682,270	814,807	198,700
5	Other private services	189,050	223,483	60,850
6	Transfers under U.S. military agency sales contracts	17,430	16,052	4,068
7	Tourism dollars received	154,079	173,884	48,958
8	Royalties and license fees received	72,191	82,614	22,267
9	Compensation received for U.S. employees of foreign companies	2,880	2,972	757
10	U.S. government miscellaneous services	1,155	1,212	314
11	Total payments from foreign sources	1,119,055	1,315,024	335,914
12	Income payments to foreign-owned assets in the U.S.	–618,467	–726,031	–167,125
13	Other private services	–125,221	–144,375	–38,032
14	Direct defense expenditures	–31,032	–32,820	–8,783
15	Tourism dollars paid	–164,867	–171,703	–46,239
16	Royalties and license fees paid	–23,777	–25,048	–6,209
17	Compensation paid to foreign employees of U.S. companies	–9,489	–9,999	–2,561
18	U.S. government miscellaneous services	–4,021	–4,184	–1,082
19	Total payments to foreign sources	–976,874	–1,114,160	–270,031
20	**Net payments from foreign sources**	**142,181**	**200,864**	**65,883**

(continued)

Line	(Credits +, debits –)	2006 year	2007 year	2008 1Q
21	Transfer payments	–92,027	–112,705	–31,227
22	**Total current account**	**–788,117**	**–731,213**	**–176,376**
	Capital and financial account			
23	**Capital account transactions, net**	**–3,880**	**–1,843**	**–597**
24	U.S. official reserve assets	2,374	–122	–276
25	U.S. government assets, other than official reserve assets	5,346	–22,273	3,346
26	Total foreign assets held by the U.S. government	7,720	–22,395	3,070
27	Direct investment by Americans in foreign assets	–241,244	–333,271	–85,608
28	Foreign securities held by Americans	–365,204	–288,731	–38,826
29	U.S. assets by unaffiliated foreigners reported by U.S. nonbanking concerns	–164,597	–706	53,644
30	U.S. assets reported by U.S. banks, not included elsewhere	–488,424	–644,751	–218,907
31	Total foreign investment by the U.S. private sector	–1,259,469	–1,267,459	–289,697
32	Total foreign investment by Americans	–1,251,749	–1,289,854	–286,627
33	Foreign government holdings of U.S. government securities	453,582	344,367	142,568
34	Foreign government holdings of other U.S. assets	34,357	66,691	30,933
35	Total U.S. assets held by foreign governments	487,939	411,058	173,501
36	Direct investment by foreigners in U.S. assets	241,961	237,542	46,627
37	U.S. government securities held by foreigners	–58,204	156,825	68,932
38	Other U.S. securities held by foreigners	683,363	573,850	–20,115
39	U.S. currency held by foreigners	2,227	–10,675	–914
40	U.S. liabilities to unaffiliated foreigners reported by U.S. nonbanking concerns	242,727	156,290	57,185
41	U.S. liabilities reported by U.S. banks, not included elsewhere	461,100	532,813	85,746
42	Total U.S. investment by the foreign private sector	1,573,174	1,646,645	237,461
43	Total U.S. investment by foreigners	2,061,113	2,057,703	410,962
44	**Financial account transactions, net**	**809,364**	**767,849**	**124,335**
45	Financial derivatives, net	29,710	6,496	0
46	**Total capital and financial account balance**	**835,194**	**772,502**	**123,738**
47	**Statistical discrepancy**	**–47,078**	**–41,287**	**52,638**

Source: U.S. Department of Commerce.

Although the current account's traditional components are raw materials and finished goods, services are included, although the total value may be more difficult to track. Goods go through customs; at points of entry, they are tallied and inspected. But services? When a British family flies to Orlando for vacation, it's as though American companies are exporting vacation services. But just exactly how much money did the family spend on hotel rooms, amusement park tickets, food, transportation, and incidental services? Did anyone tip the hotel maid? Many of these numbers are estimates that may throw off the values in the current account (see *Figure 1.1*).

The total current account (Table 1.1, line 22) includes money as well as goods. These payments include income from U.S. businesses overseas, e.g., the profits that accrue to McDonald's from its global restaurant operations (Table 1.1, line 4). The current account includes

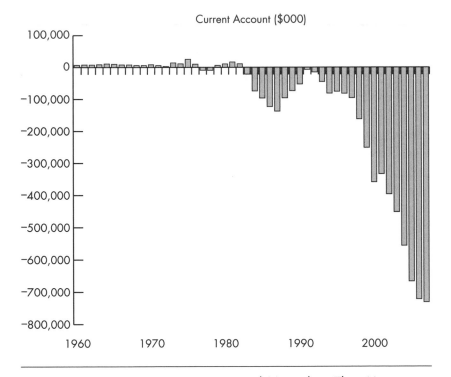

Current Account ($000)

FIGURE 1.1   Americans Have Imported More than They Have Exported Every Year Since 1983

Source: U.S. Bureau of Economic Analysis. "U.S. International Transactions: First Quarter 2008," June 17, 2008.

dividends that American investors receive from their investments in international stocks (Table 1.1, line 4), and it includes compensation earned by American workers employed by foreign companies (Table 1.1, line 17). It shows how the money flows to and from Americans, but it doesn't always capture the total economic value of what is being transferred. Does importing raw materials and exporting finished goods leave more value in the United States than importing accounting services and exporting software? Than importing profits and exporting brand names? Than importing actresses and exporting movies?

The capital account (Table 1.1, line 23) includes net transactions in nonfinancial assets, usually real estate or businesses. Capital imports are as controversial as current account imports. They include money that comes into the country when a German or Japanese company acquires a business or builds a factory here, which sometimes generates concerns about the increased role of foreign businesses in this country.

Capital can be exported, and Americans export capital all the time. McDonald's, Coca-Cola, and Procter & Gamble became household brands worldwide by exporting capital. Companies do it when they buy an international subsidiary or open a sales office overseas.

General Motors, which has been hobbled by its U.S. operations, sold more than one million cars in China in 2007, giving it nearly one-eighth of one of the fastest-growing auto markets in the world and making it the largest foreign automaker in the country.[2] None of those cars were made in the United States; most were assembled in China. That GM plant in Shanghai? It represents an export of capital that began in the early part of the twentieth century. And it's not just GM. Individuals export capital when they buy vacation condominiums in Mexico. In the first quarter of 2008, Americans exported $597 billion in capital.[3]

The balance of payments is set up as an identity equation: the current account (Table 1.1, line 22) equals the capital account (Table 1.1, line 23) plus the financial account services (Table 1.1, line 44). The financial account has two components: private assets (Table 1.1, lines 31 and 42) and official assets (Table 1.1, lines 26 and 35). Private assets are the financial investments in stocks and bonds made by individuals and businesses. Along with imports and exports of goods, services, and corporate capital, a lot of money flows over national boundaries. When the BOP was invented, it would have been unimaginable that an average American could buy software delivered over the Internet by an Indian company, let alone purchase shares in companies traded on the Hong Kong exchange simply by clicking on a button. But that's the reality. The Internet, standardized financial contracts, and an awareness of how many great investment opportunities there are around the world have whetted the American appetite for international investing. It's a simple matter to buy a global mutual fund, a developing market exchange-traded fund, or a stock of a company based somewhere else. These transactions fall into the financial account (Table 1.1, line 44).

By definition, the balance of payments has to balance. It includes so many transactions, however, many of which are estimates, that it never equals exactly zero. That's why it includes a plug factor, a *statistical discrepancy* figure (Table 1.1, line 47) that forces the calculation to balance. It's nothing more than an offset to the imbalance that has been created by the estimates themselves. However, it does not balance over several quarters even though in theory it should. (Some people think this might be a measure of smuggling, drug trades, and terrorist activities that aren't reported on customs forms or income tax filings.) It is often statistically significant. In the first quarter of 2008, for example, the statistical discrepancy was at $51.6 billion on a $176.4 billion estimated current account deficit.[4]

And that is the balance of payments.

What Do All Those Numbers Mean?

The BOP figure, which the United States publishes quarterly, was established during an era in which currencies did not float freely and capital mobility was limited. Under the Bretton Woods agreement of 1944, the exchange rate for the dollar was fixed to the price of gold and the rest of the currencies were pegged to the dollar and a fixed exchange rate. Government officials had to buy or sell securities and transferred gold to maintain the respective fixed exchange rates.

Nations that peg their currencies to other currencies, such as Thailand did before 1997 and Saudi Arabia does today in 2009, still have to do that. When Thailand suffered inflation in the mid-1990s because of a real estate price bubble, the government was forced to buy more reserves to prop up its currency. By 1997, the Thai government ran out of money and was forced to accept an international bailout organized by the International Monetary Fund. The entire process could have been avoided if Thailand had allowed its currency to float in the open market, which it has done more or less since the Asian financial crisis of 1997–1998.

Countries, including the United States, keep official reserves. Most commonly, the reserves are held in the form of gold, foreign currency, and Special Drawing Rights with the International Monetary Fund. Reserves are accumulated when a government requires converting export earnings from the nation's domestic firms through various other operations meant to insulate an economy from short-term capital flows and through intervention in the foreign exchange market.

To fund its current account deficit, the United States must be a net importer of capital. If the private sector is incapable or unwilling, resulting in downward pressure on the dollar at times and upward pressure on other currencies, foreign central banks often step into the breach. They buy U.S. dollars and sell their own currency. How willing countries are to tolerate volatile currencies (which is how many experience what the G7 euphemistically calls "flexible" exchange rates) depends on numerous factors, including: the strength of domestic financial institutions, sensitivity of exports and inflation to currency appreciation and depreciation, and the significance of the export sector to the overall economy.

That the balance of payments is calculated on a flow basis, not a stock basis, is also a source of confusion. This means that the numbers represent changes in value, not absolute amounts of value. The BOP doesn't consider inflation. It can't take into account how General Motors has steadily increased the value of its business in China by entering the country eighty years ago, writing off that investment after the Communists took power and then recovering part of it through its interest in joint ventures begun in 1999 when the Chinese economy took off. That's one reason that U.S. investments overseas tend to look smaller than foreign investments in the United States. Just about everything everywhere costs more in 2008, when international acquirers went on a buying spree in the United States, than it cost in the 1950s, 1960s, and 1970s, when U.S. companies were getting established overseas. Economists often use historic prices for valuing direct investment. Changes in the value of those operations, whether due to changes in overall prices or ongoing investment and expertise, are not marked to market until they are realized when they are sold. As that overseas business grows, it can generate funds to continue its expansion, so no more capital is exported, but the profits aren't necessarily returned here right away. GM, for all its woes in the United States, is reinvesting its Chinese profits in China. Traditional accounting undervalues the benefits that accrue over time to a global corporation based in the United States and investing overseas for the long haul.

Trade brings business into the United States. When goods are imported, someone has to get them off ships and across the country into consumers' hands. Because the United States has 300 million consumers spread out over 3.8 million square miles, storage, transportation, and marketing costs can end up being 30 percent to 50 percent of the cost of goods sold. As a proportion of the sale price, these other locally incurred costs appear to be greater in the United States than elsewhere and help explain why trade flows are not as sensitive to the vagaries of the dollar in the foreign exchange market. Those costs also represent revenues for some American companies and earnings stream for some American workers.

The Old-Fashioned World of Trade Accounting

Trade accounting reflects a very different era. In the eighteenth and nineteenth centuries, economists approached the world mechanically. Classical economists such as Adam Smith (eighteenth century) and David Ricardo (nineteenth century) thought that debits had to equal credits, gains had to equal losses, and exports had to equal imports or the world would fall into chaos. But over time, it's become clear that imbalances create opportunities. Unlike the classical view of the world, modernity embraces imbalances. Chaos theory and work with large systems seem to emphasize the problems with that old-fashioned approach. Looking only at the sum of the world's imports and exports overlooked other ways in which people did business with each other.

A modern economy is full of strains and stresses that form as businesses succeed and fail. Balance is the exception to the rule. Growth, which is the rule, means things are out of balance. When an economy expands, supply and (effective) demand are out of balance. That's good. Capitalism is not a calm pond; it is a tumultuous ocean.

Why would we expect trade to be different? We might because modern trade accounting is based on the old-fashioned notion that trade involves only raw materials and finished goods. It evolved in the 1930s by the Bank for International Settlements to manage Germany's reparations for World War I and to promote monetary stability. Even though the Great Depression raged, the United States had strong industry relative to the rest of the world, which was either underdeveloped or damaged by war. The United States almost always exported more than it imported; it showed a trade surplus under the BOP for decades. It became normal to think of a trade surplus as the way to measure America's strength relative to the rest of the world.

But then the world changed. Now, Pakistanis buy MP3 players designed in the United States and manufactured in China. They load those machines with content produced in the United States, or Ireland, or Mexico and downloaded from Web sites hosted in the United States, using debit cards branded in the United States but offered through a bank once based in the Netherlands, now owned by a bank in Scotland.

In decades past, when American companies imported oil, then pressed vinyl records, put them in cardboard sleeves, and sent them overseas, trade accounting was much simpler. But now that content is purchased electronically and paid for electronically, the old accounting system breaks down.

Although Apple Computer makes a hefty profit selling iPods, each one sold increases the U.S. trade deficit by $150.[5] Yet, the iPod sells for about twice its cost of goods, which means that $150 accrues in profit to an American company for each iPod sold. That doesn't get factored into the trade deficit. Who would argue that America would be a more competitive nation if Apple had never developed the iPod? Would it be better if a Chinese company had invented the iPod and manufactured it here? How about if a Chinese company had invented the iPod and sold it only in China?

The BOP was established when labor and manufacturing formed the basis of the U.S economy. Americans are known for high-level skills, including design, technology, financial services, and generally getting things done. These often add more value than manufacturing. The balance of payments doesn't fully account for that.

Traditional trade accounting wasn't designed for the activities of multinational corporations that don't care about borders—unless, of course, sending goods across a border means paying a tax. Modern companies want to sell to everyone everywhere, whether they are in Shanghai or Chicago. The activities of multinational corporations are tracked using an accounting system designed for a world where only some nations could do sophisticated manufacturing. In the modern era, manufacturing can be done almost anywhere. And now so can many white-collar jobs that people once thought could only be done at home—thanks to technologies that have expanded the span of command, control, and communication functions. Employers can share ideas with their employees and monitor performance without ever getting on an airplane. They can hire contractors with an assurance that the work will get done as well abroad as it would be at home. Accountants in India, customer-service representatives in the Philippines, and graphic designers in the United Kingdom can now serve American taxpayers, consumers, and businesses from their own countries, close to their own families, ensconced in their own cultures. None of this was possible two decades ago, let alone when the BOP was invented.

Offshoring, Outsourcing, and Intrafirm Trade

The BOP understands international trade as involving two parties: a buyer and a seller. That's changed.

Businesses face long chains of processes between idea and customer: inventory, design, manufacture, sales, marketing, advertising, accounting, human resources, and office management, just to name a few. The modern business was not born in its current form, like Athena popping full grown from the head of Zeus. Initially, the same company that produced the goods did not do the marketing and sales, for example. A drive to control and lower costs encouraged companies to integrate functions. A company can own the raw materials, the transportation, the office building, and even the advertising. We call this *vertical integration.* If a company is not publicly held, it doesn't even have to hire an outside accounting firm. Yet almost all businesses find it distracting and costly to do everything; instead, employees concentrate their energy on what the firm does best and then create networks of suppliers and service providers to handle everything else. Managers coordinate these relationships rather than dream up new ways to arrange the internal processes.[6] That's outsourcing.

Some companies find that it makes sense to take in house functions that had once been outsourced. They may start simply by adding accounting, legal, and human resources departments, or they may add a lot of complexity by opening retail stores, acquiring manufacturers, hiring designers, and taking on other links in the chain between concept and customer. They might do this all over the world, too.

Outsourcing is often confused with offshoring, but they are not the same. Offshoring involves exporting a business function to another country. This can be done through outsourcing—hiring an outside firm in another country to handle the work—or simply by acquiring or opening a facility in the new country and doing the work there. Of course, with so many global brands headquartered in the United States, America provides offshored and outsourced services on an enormous scale. Business operations all over the world rely on American branding, American technology, and American financial services.

Companies often outsource and offshore to save money, but they also do it to improve quality, get more flexibility, or gain local market experience. Managers have to decide if it makes more sense to build or to buy the capabilities that they need. Think about advertising. A business can create and place its own ads in-house. Maybe it can be done cheaply that way, relying on simple ideas and maybe the assistance of a clever employee or an occasional intern. But if those ads work, the company will grow larger and will want or need full-time people to create and place ads. However, it may be difficult for a manufacturing company to hire good advertising folks because it can't offer them the same career-development prospects, variety of work, or quirky office culture that an advertising agency can. The company will probably decide to outsource its advertising campaign to an agency that specializes in nothing but ads—even if it ends up costing more than hiring someone to do it internally.

Now imagine this company expands to another country. Does it make sense to keep shipping goods abroad and promoting them with the home advertising agency? Even if labor costs are higher, the company might find that opening a manufacturing facility and hiring a local advertising agency offer better returns on investment. In fact, having local operations may help the company generate much higher profits than if it relied on support from back home. Unfortunately, for getting a handle on global economic relations and competitiveness in the twenty-first-century, the BOP accounting system puts more value on costs than on profits, even though profits ultimately motivate economic activity and help American companies thrive domestically.

Outsourcing and offshoring can also give businesses and countries access to skills that may not be available locally. Politicians all over the world hire American campaign strategists who have perfected the art of winning elections. Where democracy—or negative campaigning—is new, it makes sense to bring in the U.S. experts. Even in Zimbabwe. Could the good folks drawing up the BOP have imagined a time when a corrupt African dictator would hire an American agency to help him win a rigged election?

The Current Account and Economic Risk

Changing patterns of trade between and within corporations has produced large U.S. trade deficits. It is a source of anxiety, for sure, but it is misplaced. Yet the biggest risks to the world economy in general and the U.S. economy in particular are not the imbalances, but the attempts to fix them through protectionism, which often sacrifices growth and development. Most proposed cures seem worse than the supposed illness. If the United States was forced to run a balanced trade account, as some like Warren Buffett have proposed, it would likely translate into higher unemployment, lower wages, and lower living standards for most Americans and a broad swathe of the world.[7] In no way should the U.S. deficit be seen as an automatic sign of weakness.

In a world of capital market mobility, the price of financial assets adjusts quickly (perhaps too quickly). An imbalance may show up in the currency markets, or it may appear in asset markets as companies sell expensive assets to buy cheaper ones. An imbalance can and usually does come from a combination of price adjustments in both the currency and asset markets. A century ago, the imbalances were larger and more persistent because the gulf between the few industrialized nations and the many lesser-developed economies was huge and capital was not nearly as mobile. Technology and new financial instruments have now made it possible for world financial markets to cope with larger imbalances.

The underlying concern is that America will become a weaker nation if it is not self-reliant. As a share of GDP, U.S. imports and exports are smaller than many other advanced industrialized countries, but still many chafe under developments in the past third of a century that made for greater interdependence. America is richer, better, and stronger than it was before the late 1970s and early 1980s when it began recording a sustained current account deficit and became a debtor nation again. The gap between the United States and other major industrialized countries in terms of two key measures widened in the United States' favor over the past couple of decades: productivity and GDP per capita.

The current account shows the value of goods and services that cross national borders. It doesn't show anything else. When a U.S. company sets up an office in another country to manufacture and sell its goods according to specification developed in the United States, there is no import or export to show up in the balance of trade. That local operation is treated as a local company, not as a U.S. operation. That's why many researchers would like to see a different approach to trade accounting, one that would look at who owns the goods and services rather than who buys them.

One such approach is called the *ownership-based framework* for the current account and is calculated by none other than the Commerce Department's Bureau of Economic Analysis. It is published every year as a parallel account report to the BOP—so it's clear that at least some people in government recognize the problem. It's possible that eventually this alternative will become the standard.

The most recent calculation, which was for 2007,[8] showed that the United States had exports of $2.01 trillion under the ownership framework, compared to $1.46 trillion under the BOP system. The trade deficit was *just* $466.0 billion under the ownership approach, rather than $700 billion for the balance of payments.[9] That shows just how much American companies are generating from business done by their international affiliates.

For all our complaining (which is our constitutional right), the United States has a stable government, deep and liquid capital markets, and common-law traditions that allow contract and property rights to evolve over time in a way that they can't if new statutes have to be passed every time something changes. It's an entrepreneurial approach to business that people all over the world envy. In America, people see investment opportunities that offer great returns for the amount of risk involved. That's attractive to people who live in places with economies that are fortunate to grow by more than 2 percent a year, such as Japan and Germany, or where there's tremendous uncertainty about national security, as in Russia. The current account is the difference between imports and exports. That's it. It does not capture the American business climate. An accounting equation is not an explanation or a driver for change.

Technologic Improvement (Progress) Costs More Jobs than Trade

The United States has a high standard of living. Workers expect to be paid well for their efforts, so they devote their time and talents to things that pay well. Basic manufacturing once paid really well, but not anymore.

Although no politician who hopes to be elected or reelected will admit it, not all workers add the same amount of value to the economy.

Many manufactured goods are commodities these days: highly automated production that often assembles interchangeable parts that were produced elsewhere. People in countries that have a lower standard of living will work on an assembly line for less money than Americans (though generally with lower productivity, too). Manufacturing is more interesting and pays better than subsistence farming, but it's still hard work. Far better to be the engineer who designs the products that are eventually made in some factory somewhere else. The goods that Americans produce for export are usually manufactured with fewer hands than in decades past. The United States, for example, exports more steel now than at any time in its history, but fewer workers are required to produce it.

Trade isn't the most potent threat to traditional work and life styles; technology is. Farmers, factory workers, and office workers have all seen their work change because of technology. It's hard on those who have to make the transition, but it's not the fault of foreign trade.

Despite the hand-wringing about the U.S. trade deficit and the deindustrialization of America that it represents, the United States remains the world's largest manufacturer, accounting for more than one-fifth of the world's total manufacturing output as recently as 2005 (the most recent year for which comparative figures are available). Although factory output has not been higher (before the 2008 recession), fewer workers are generating it. From a peak of around 17 million factory workers in the late 1970s, manufacturing employment is approaching 13 million workers and falling.

The key here is productivity: output per person over a unit of time, such as an hour or a year. American manufacturing productivity has risen by 160 percent over the past thirty years. The same driver of labor-saving technological advances has seen workers replaced by machines in practically all countries, including China.

The same forces are evident in the service sector. The secretary function is largely missing in action in most offices. Should we look to China or maybe Puerto Rico or Mexico for these secretarial jobs? No. Bill Gates and Microsoft Office Suite have replaced them. Where are all the bank tellers? Diebold and NEC and the other makers of the ubiquitous ATM machine have downsized them. Not India, China, or Mexico.

Reality: The Balance of Payments Is a Poor Measure of American Strength

Profits in a service economy don't come from slinging French fries: they come from the entire concept, start to finish. A group of Americans might form a company that invents a French fry recipe, designs the packaging, develops the brand, lays out the store, and writes employee training materials. Then they might offer this entire concept to someone in Asia who buys local land, contracts local builders who use local materials, hires local employees, buys local potatoes, and even uses a local printer to make the packaging. In other words, McDonald's exports a service: the ability to make its French fries anywhere. Nothing has changed hands, according to traditional trade accounting—only ideas. The related capital flows may be quite minor, limited to some licensing fee or royalty, but trade has surely taken place.

Accounting allows people to measure economic activity, but it rarely measures it exactly. When the BOP was established more than sixty years ago, its developers could not have imagined the economy in which we operate now. The old metric, the BOP and the system of trade accounting, no longer offers an accurate picture of how the global political economy works. It is based on a world that no longer exists. It undercounts the money that American companies make from global activities.

The BOP is not necessarily a fair measure of the economic competitiveness of a particular country. It does not measure the economic prowess of the United States. It raises more questions than it answers. The BOP overweights the value of finished goods and underweights the value of intellectual property. It doesn't reflect the way that multinational corporations operate, slicing, dicing, and distributing their operations around the world where it may make political and economic sense, for reasons that far outstrip comparative advantage as traditionally understood. And it causes people to make the wrong decisions that might actually hurt the U.S. economy.

Every month when the Commerce Department reports the trade balance and every quarter when the BOP data is released, the hand-wringing and chest-beating ritual is renewed. But at the same time, American household wealth has been rising right along with the trade deficit. Companies, individuals, and nations become great because they invest in the future, often using other people's money. That creates deficits. Americans borrow money for college in hopes of earning more money in the future. They borrow money to buy houses. Even after the horrible financial crisis and the associated house foreclosures, a higher percentage of Americans will live in residences they own than nearly any other country. Japanese retirees buy U.S. treasuries in order to get 4 percent interest, higher returns than they can earn in Japan. Americans buy Japanese stocks through international mutual funds in order to diversify their retirement savings. We're all managing a series of deficits and surpluses, at home and abroad, in order to find stability for personal savings, finance government spending, or generate big profits, such as by selling pharmaceuticals to people who desperately need them.

The U.S. trade deficit isn't a measure of U.S. power. During the period that the trade deficit grew, Microsoft developed technologies that changed the way we all live, work, and play. General Motors became the largest foreign automaker in China. Coca-Cola and McDonald's both entered India. Researchers studying at American universities developed commercial applications for the Internet, which has made cross-border trade and communication possible at a scale that could not have been imagined in years past. If the accounting system doesn't show that, then the accounting system—not trade—should be changed.

Chapter Notes

1. U.S. Bureau of Economic Analysis, "U.S. International Transactions: First Quarter 2008." Washington, DC: U.S. Department of Commerce, June 17, 2008 (http://www.bea.gov/newsreleases/international/transactions/2008/trans108.htm).

2. General Motors Corporation. Press release. January 11, 2008.

3. U.S. Bureau of Economic Analysis, "U.S. International Transactions: First Quarter 2008." Washington, DC: U.S. Department of Commerce, June 17, 2008.

4. Ibid (p. 8–11).

5. Greg Linden, Kenneth L. Kraemer, and Jason Dedrick, *Who Captures Value in a Global Innovation System? The Case of Apple's iPod* (Irvine, CA: University of California, Personal Computing Industry Center, June 2007).

6. This is the subject of Alfred D. Chandler's Pulitzer Prize–winning book *The Visible Hand: The Managerial Revolution in American Business* (Cambridge, MA: Belknap Press, 1993; original edition released in 1977).

7. Warren Buffett, "Squanderville versus Thriftville." *Fortune*, October 2003 (http://money.cnn.com/magazines/fortune/fortune_archive/2003/11/10/352872/index.htm).

8. The most recent numbers just came out for 2007 as this book went to press. The Department of Commerce releases the numbers once a year, so there's a lag. The 2008 numbers will be available in January 2010.

9. U.S. Bureau of Economic Analysis, "An Ownership-Based Framework of the U.S. Current Account, 1998–2007." *Survey of Current Business*, January 2009 (Vol. 89, No. 1).

The Current Account Deficit Drives the Dollar

Money is good for more than just keeping score.

Money has a price, and that price can be measured by exchange rates and interest rates. If the price of money goes up, is that good or bad? If the price of the dollar rises against another country's currency, is that good or bad? If the dollar goes up against the euro, has it increased in world status? If the dollar goes down, is the U.S. economy losing?

The price of money, like the price of other commodities, is driven by supply and demand. Because the current account shows the demand for imports and exports, many people think that it signals demand for currency. However, exchange rates reflect the international supply and demand for all uses of money, including direct and portfolio investment, hedging, intercompany loans, worker remittances, tourism, and speculation.

Capital flows are larger and more important than trade, making measures that exclude capital flows, such as the current account, a distortion of international economic relations. Moreover, the causal relationship between current account position and exchange rates is not as clear-cut as is often suggested. In particular, correctly forecasting the direction of the U.S. current account deficit in advance does not allow one to predict the direction of the dollar. Nor does forecasting the direction of the dollar allow one to more accurately anticipate the current account balance.

Unfortunately, policy makers who focus on the trade balance all too often misunderstand the very forces they are trying to master.

The United States is a large, open economy. The American currency is accepted all over the world and the exceptions, like the Taj Mahal in 2008 (which refused to accept dollars), prove the rule. Imbalances that might cause economic problems in smaller, less-diversified nations such as Iceland or Indonesia can be accommodated with grace in the United States. The foreign exchange market is the largest and most liquid in the world because money is used for investment, savings, and speculation as well as for trade. The falling dollar doesn't necessarily help the trade deficit because the dollar is used for so much more than simply the goods and services moving in and out of the country. That is one of the basic reasons why there is so little relationship between the value of the dollar on world markets and the size of the U.S. current account. The price of the dollar needed to bring into balance trade may be different than the one needed to bring the capital market into balance.

Currency Supply and Demand, Version 1.0

Workers deposit their paychecks into their bank accounts. When they go to a store, they present a little piece of plastic. Then the bank transfers money out of their accounts and into the merchants' accounts. Nothing changes hands, but money has been traded.

Anything anyone desires is available for a few pieces of greenish paper or a little piece of plastic. The plastic has value because a large company owned by many banks promises that it will give a credit that can be traded for those green papers. The green papers can be traded for the needed goods and services. But why do those green papers have any value?

In earlier ages, trade was barter driven and borders were often fuzzy. Cattle made a fine currency because they could walk themselves to the market, unlike grain, which had to be transported. Over time, objects that had more value per pound than cows did, such as precious metals, were traded for goods. But that wasn't always practical, because those valuables had to be transported and kept safe. Eventually, people started using documents that represented ownership in the underlying metals, with the gold and silver held in national vaults. Over time, the paper took on its own value and was supplemented by negotiable contracts such as checks or by electronic accounting.

To help stabilize the world's economy after World War II, the Bretton Woods agreement of 1944 tried to reestablish, given the changed circumstances, an international monetary regime based on gold and fixed exchange rates. The dollar-gold standard also provided a discipline on policy makers who would pursue policies that risked inflation, resulting in the debasing of one's currency. As Keynes noted, "There is no subtler, no surer means of overturning the existing basis of society than to debauch the currency. The process engages all the hidden forces of economic law on the side of destruction, and does so in a manner which no one man [sic] in a million is able to diagnose."

By 1972, the Bretton Woods agreement was dead. Though some astute economists had argued in the late 1950s and early 1960s that the Bretton Woods system was not sustainable, they were not heeded.[1] In hindsight, it seems inevitable that Bretton Woods was too rigid an international monetary regime. It was based on the power relations (including gold distribution) that existed in the immediate aftermath of WWII, which could not last long as Europe and Japan rebuilt. It was also too rigid to support the kind of expansion programs that the political elite pursued such as "guns and butter" in the United States and "cradle to grave" protection in Europe.

If a currency is tied to an underlying asset, then the economy is constrained by how much of that asset it has. One of the drivers of the age of exploration was the need for more gold and silver to support growing European economies. Ferdinand and Isabella didn't really care about the shape of the planet, but they did want Christopher Columbus to bring home more gold in less time.

Also, if a currency represents the value of something else, many people would rather hold it than the paper. Hence, when currencies are tied to gold and silver, people hoard metals, and that keeps market forces from setting currency values. It takes a lot of trust to make a paper currency work.

Currency that is not tied to an underlying asset is called *fiat money*. Businesses and creditors accept it as payment because the sovereign, the government, declares it legal tender. U.S. paper money clearly states, "THIS NOTE IS LEGAL TENDER FOR ALL DEBTS, PUBLIC AND PRIVATE." As long as we believe that our government is secure, then we believe that our currency has value. If everyone on the U.S. border uses Canadian pennies as they do American ones, then Canadian pennies magically take on the same value as American pennies. If folks in war zones are willing to trade food for cigarettes, then cigarettes are as good as cash.

At its simplest level, the price of currency is determined by how much and how enthusiastically one person wants to exchange money for another kind of money. It seems so simple, until we go to the next step of figuring out what all the different drivers of supply and demand are across the entire world. Every money changer's reason for buying euros and selling dollars, or selling dollars and buying yen, or buying yen and selling sterling becomes one of the myriad of signals that economists, investors, and policy makers study for insight into the global economy.

An American store buying boots from England needs to change dollars for pounds, and the English manufacturer buying rubber from India needs to exchange pounds for rupees. However, there are other reasons money is exchanged that overwhelm the trade channel. That's why trade between nations explains only some of the changing supply and demand for currencies. An American company opening an office in England will need pounds, as will an Indian investor looking to put money into U.K. bonds. These reasons also affect supply, demand, and exchange rates.

Currency Supply and Demand, Version 2.0

Trade in goods and services is important, but it's not the main influence on the value of the dollar. The foreign exchange market is the largest and most liquid financial market in the world, and investors are likely to show even more interest in it as other assets suffer. Every three years, the Bank for International Settlements coordinates an authoritative survey of the market for foreign exchange and the currency derivatives market. As of April 2007, it reported that daily turnover in the currency markets was $3.2 trillion,[2] an increase of 71.0 percent from the last survey.

There's no gross domestic product for the world separate from the sum of all of the gross domestic products of all the countries in the world. The dollar value of all the goods and services the national economies generated stood at $65.6 trillion in 2007.[3] Over the course of a month, there is more turnover in the foreign currency market than the total amount of goods and services produced by all 6.7 billion people in the entire world for a full year. Prices in the currency market may reflect fundamentals, but based on capital market considerations rather than trade positions.

One such capital market consideration is the decline of what economists call the "home bias" of many investors. For a long time, Americans associated international investing with risky investing, but that stigma has lessened and, due to financial innovation and some types of deregulation, the barriers to entry have eased. Americans chased the plump returns of overseas markets for several years until well into the credit crisis. In 2007, the Investment Company Institute reported that $1.7 trillion—14 percent of U.S. mutual fund assets[4]—were invested in international mutual funds. This is an approximately 20 percent increase from $1.4 trillion—13 percent of U.S. mutual fund assets—in 2006.[5]

Currency is popular with speculators, too. Many day traders have given up on tech stocks and moved to foreign exchange. It's not just George Soros playing the currency market, it's the next-door neighbor, hooked up to his PC, hoping to make a quick buck. More investors are realizing that international investing isn't just an add-on for the richest and most sophisticated but is instead a way of making money in a changing world.

The supply and demand for currencies in general and the dollar in particular is also strongly influenced by some participants who are not necessarily profit maximizers in the currency market. Corporate treasurers view the fluctuations of foreign exchange values as a risk that needs to be hedged, rather than a profit opportunity. Equity fund managers also often view foreign exchange as a necessary vehicle to make a foreign investment rather a source of independent return (what market professionals call *alpha*). Bond-fund managers often swap or sell the currency, which effectively neutralizes the effect of foreign exchange movement on the foreign bond being purchased.

Another Look at the Current Account Deficit

As noted in Chapter 1, the current account deficit is the difference between the value of imports and the value of exports broadly understood. The result is a number, not a score for the economy. By definition, the deficit will widen if imports increase by more than exports. Likewise, it will narrow if imports decrease more than exports decrease. The U.S. current account deficit was a hefty $174 billion in the third quarter of 2008.[6] But it's not the amount that matters so much as why it changes from quarter to quarter. That's often not a simple matter to determine.

Exchange rates matter, of course, but if politicians are obsessed with the trade deficit, then they may pursue policies that generate negative outcomes elsewhere and not necessarily resolve the trade deficit. That can wreak havoc with other sectors of the domestic economy and with key sectors in international trade, especially international direct investment and financial services.

If the dollar is weak, then U.S. goods might cost less for people using other currencies, depending on a host of decisions made on the business level such as hedge strategy, competition, and elasticity of demand. A weak dollar might help U.S. exports. But the best thing for U.S. exports is strong foreign demand. U.S. exports were indeed strong in the middle of this decade when the dollar was weak, but U.S. exports were also strong in the second half of the 1990s when the dollar was strong.

Foreign demand for U.S. goods is more sensitive to a country's growth than the level of the dollar. And, if the dollar is weak, imported goods may become more expensive for people paying with dollars, so Americans might buy fewer imports. However, the reduction of demand for imports tends to correspond to what economists call "demand destruction" or, more broadly, economic weakness. Often it is difficult to separate the impact of weaker growth (e.g., lower interest rates) from a weaker dollar for narrowing of the U.S. current account deficit during recessions.

The U.S. current account deficit improved sharply in the 2006–2008 period, but most Americans were worse off. The world was worse off by almost any economic metric one chooses, including growth and employment. That the world was more in balance is hardly a sufficient offset.

Instead of focusing so exclusively on the current account, we need to look at the overall economy. The strength or weakness of the currency and the size of the current account are just pieces of the puzzle. For example, U.S. retail prices don't fluctuate much with the dollar because so much of the selling price of a product is incurred on the ground here: transportation, distribution, marketing, and sales.[7] A Chinese seamstress may be making less than a dollar an hour, but the American Teamsters who get shirts from the dock to the store, and the salespeople at the mall, are making quite a bit more.

The Trade Deficit and the Budget Deficit

The U.S. economy has grown and household net worth (which nets assets and liabilities) has risen while running a trade deficit for more than three decades. Often the trade deficit is confused with the budget deficit. One does not necessarily lead to the other, though some economists talk about the "twin deficits." Sometimes not only are they not related but also they don't even know each other. The United States had a budget surplus and a trade deficit when Bill Clinton was president. Japan has a trade surplus and a budget deficit, and Iraq has a budget surplus and a trade surplus. Should the United States emulate either one?

Figure 2.1 shows the folly of using the trade deficit to keep score. Note that the U.S. trade deficit has widened over the years even while GDP has grown.[8] How can this be? Well, Americans offer the world high-value skills that can be applied to production elsewhere.

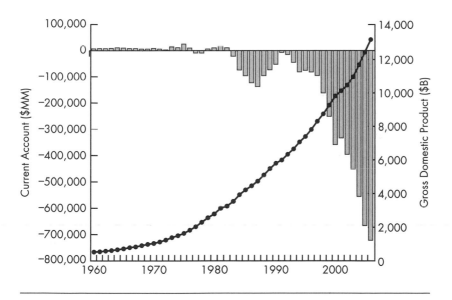

FIGURE 2.1   U.S. Current Account versus GDP

Source: U.S. Bureau of Economic Analysis. "U.S. International Transactions: First Quarter 2008." Washington, DC: U.S. Department of Commerce, June 17, 2008 (http://www.bea.gov/newsreleases/international/transactions/2008/trans108.htm). *The Economic Report of the President, 2008*, Table B-1, Gross Domestic Product, 1959–2007.

We're generating income to spend on imported goods. Some of our key imports, such as oil, have low engineering value but high usefulness to the economy. It means that American companies are benefiting from overseas capital and financial investments rather than trade in goods.

The federal deficit, meanwhile, is very much a function of social and political choices. Tax cuts could lead to less government revenue even as the GDP grows. The government is committed to several entitlement programs, and it pursued an expensive war in Iraq. None of these situations is related to trade per se. *Figure 2.2* shows how the U.S. trade deficit has steadily grown while the budget deficit has gyrated.[9]

Nevertheless, trade is a key component of the economy. Americans buy imported goods to save money and get things that aren't produced here. They export in order to reach a foreign customer base. Trade, as we have seen, is a function of the globalization of production and distribution and decisions made on the corporate level.

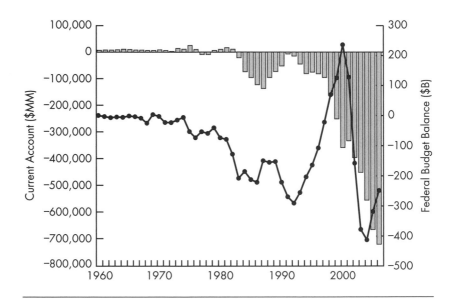

FIGURE 2.2   U.S. Current Account versus Federal Budget Deficit

Source: U.S. Bureau of Economic Analysis. "U.S. International Transactions: First Quarter 2008." *The Economic Report of the President,* June 17, 2008.

To the extent that trade is based on a division of labor, it may allow people to do what they do best. Lawyers don't have to sew their own clothes or grow their own food, and tailors and farmers don't have to negotiate their own contracts. With trade, they can all be better off. This is true whether trade happens within a town or all over the world.

Economists say an *absolute advantage* exists if one party does something better than another. Adam Smith was concerned mostly with absolute advantage. David Ricardo complicated the story, by considering *comparative advantage*. A developing country, for example, produces neither computers nor furniture more efficiently than a neighbor, but perhaps it makes furniture a little more efficiently than it does computers. Therein, economists say, lies its comparative advantage, and that is what the developing country should specialize in.

Comparative advantage is based not on doing what one does relatively better than a potential trade partner (that is, *absolute advantage*) but rather on doing what one does not as poorly as something else. It's entirely possible to have a comparative advantage but not be fully competitive.

Imports and exports aren't always based on the lowest price. The law of comparative advantage comes into play. Let's say a lawyer is billing out at $300 per hour. She is also a word-processing expert—how else did she get through law school? She hires a secretary for her practice, but he is kind of slow at Microsoft Word—way slower than she is. But he is paid $16 per hour. Should she fire the secretary and do the typing herself?

No, she shouldn't, because even though it takes him longer, the cost per finished document is still cheaper if the secretary does that than if the lawyer did it. In fact, by having him do the typing, she has freed herself to work on the higher-value legal projects.

The law of comparative advantage carries over to goods as well as services. Now, let's say that an American manufacturer makes snow globes. His U.S. workers generate snow globes with almost no defects, but they get paid $10 per hour. In Hungary, half the workers' output will be too shoddy to sell, but those employees get paid only $7.50 per hour. Should he send his manufacturing overseas? Clearly no. In this example, the lower productivity is not enough to offset the significantly lower labor costs. This frees his high-quality manufacturing workers to work on projects in which the quality stakes are higher than they are with snow globes.

Under the law of comparative advantage, people, businesses, and countries should focus on those things that they do best. When it comes to economics, the thing that someone does best is the thing that earns that person the most pay. (There may be plenty of bad orthopedic surgeons who are great cooks at home, but if they survive the struggle through school and residency, they'll make more money setting bones than making dinner.) They can then use the money they get to buy those goods or services that they do not specialize in.

The employee at the Hungarian snow globe manufacturer will leave work, have dinner at McDonald's, then go home and watch *The Simpsons* on television. We are all better off if borders are open so that economic activities can flow to those who can perform them best. At some point, those snow globe makers will get more productive and demand higher wages, and so at some point, the absolute and comparative advantages may change, but that's another book.[10]

What a nation does best in the world is not always producing goods and extracting natural resources for export. When an economy is growing, it may have more imports than exports because businesses need materials and equipment. It may have more imports than exports because the citizens have money to spend. It may be doing the development work at home, contracting the manufacturing elsewhere, and then bringing the finished goods back home. There's no reason that a trade deficit stands opposed to economic growth.

Likewise, an economy that's shrinking might well export more than it imports. Maybe it's dumping the last of its natural resources to generate cash for future projects. Maybe its people are so poor that they can't buy anything, thus making meager exports look huge in comparison. Maybe the country's output is enormous relative to the size of its population, even if that output is small on a world scale. The current account balance remains a statistic but not a score for the overall economy.

The Current Account and Currency

Knowing that a team won last night doesn't tell how it will do today. And knowing the current account position today doesn't show what the exchange rate is, where the exchange rate is going, or how to make money trading it or investing financial assets denominated in it.

An exchange rate is nothing more than the price of one currency expressed in the value of another. If a dollar buys more pesos than it did a year ago, then the dollar is worth more and the peso is worth less.

But think about the prices paid for things every day, everywhere. They tend to increase over time, but not always. Over time, an item may actually cost less if there are economies of scale in production or increased uses for it. At an extreme, computer equipment becomes more powerful and less expensive all the time. In 1965, Gordon Moore, the founder of Intel, stated that the number of transistors on a computer chip would double every two years, which would indicate more power at a lower cost. This relationship, known as Moore's law, has held.[11] When a new PC costs less and does more than the one it replaces, it isn't declining in value. If anything, the new PC may become more important than the one it replaces because it can store more, process more, and stream more data.

Is it the same with money? To a certain extent, yes. The price that people pay for money is a statement on its relative value but also a reflection on the quantity and usefulness of that money. If a currency is easy to exchange—what economists call "convertible for current account and capital account purposes"—and its government pursues stable policies, then the currency may be sounder than a country whose currency is not convertible. Currencies whose values are determined in the foreign exchange market typically adjust continuously, whereas fixed exchange rate regimes often see fewer but larger adjustments.

The basic determinants of the value of money are supply and demand, the same as for any product or commodity. The supply and demand, in turn, are influenced by broader economic factors but not always in orderly or predictable ways. If interest rates are high, then savers in other countries may want to buy bonds to benefit from those rates. They may demand more of the currency and bid up the price. But if the high interest rates are due to concerns about economic stability and inflation, then they may sell their holdings in that currency to invest elsewhere. Which effect dominates? It depends. It is always contextual; rarely can it be deduced from first principles.

Because there are an imponderable number of influences and the weightings of those influences often change, it's impossible to simply look at a given set of exchange rates and say that they are good or bad. Just as with the current account, an exchange rate is a number, but it's not a way of keeping score.

Although Americans may be selling currency to buy imported goods, someone else is on the other side. They are buying the currency for something else. Why do they want our dollars? Maybe they live in an unstable country and want to invest in a safe currency to get them through tough times. Maybe they want to buy real estate or businesses here. Maybe they want to invest in the U.S. stock market because they see growth opportunities in American companies. Maybe they want to use those dollars to conduct business in a third country where dollars are preferred to the local currency. (An American dollar will go a lot further in Zimbabwe than Zimbabwe's own dollar will.)

The U.S. money supply stood at $7.7 trillion as of August 2008,[12] more than half the amount of annual trade in the United States. Because any one dollar is used several times a year as people buy and sell things, this is more than enough to finance U.S. trade. But the dollar's role is even greater because it is used as a means of exchange, a store of value, and a unit of account for many people and countries.

Nearly all U.S. imports and exports are priced in dollars. No other country has this luxury or privilege. A study by the European Central Bank estimated that countries using the euro in 2004 priced about one-third of imports and exports in dollars. In Asia, about 80 percent of exports and 60 percent of imports were priced in dollars.[13] Only about one-quarter of Japan's imports and about 38 percent of its exports are invoiced in yen.[14] Because oil is traded in dollars, any nation that imports it will need to use U.S. currency. That alone shows how the supply and demand for dollars in world markets has little relationship to the current account.

The Capital Account and Currency

The trade account grabs the headlines, but that's not the account to watch. Investors and policy makers should instead train their eyes on the capital account. The factors that affect capital balances explain more market developments and foreign exchange prices than trade balances do. For example, for more than the first half of this decade, the Japanese yen had been weak relative to the currencies of most of its trading partners. There were fundamentally good reasons for the weakness of the yen, all of which outweighed its trade surplus and its longest economic recovery in modern times, according to the hundreds of thousands if not millions of people and institutions that voted with their pocketbooks. The low exchange rate for the yen reflected investors' expectations that Japanese interest rates would remain relatively low.

It is admittedly difficult to prove this thesis true, but consider how Copernicus proved that the earth went around the sun. The short answer is, he didn't. But by assuming that the earth went around the sun instead of the opposite, Copernicus was able to explain other facts—in this case, observations. Similarly, if we assume that the foreign exchange market is being driven more by capital account considerations than trade factors, a number of other developments are more understandable.

Because everyone watches the current account with such awe, policy decisions designed to narrow the deficit often have unintended repercussions elsewhere in the economy. One of the unintended consequences of Ronald Reagan's success in getting Japan to agree to "voluntary export restrictions" on auto exports to the United States was to encourage Japanese automakers to export higher-profit-margin vehicles, moving up the value-added chain, and opening another front on their competition with U.S. producers. It also encouraged Japanese and other producers to locate production facilities in the United States, within the protectionist walls. This has served to exacerbate regional disparities in the United States and may have hastened the demise of Detroit as a center for vehicle manufacturing and assembling.

The obsession with keeping score using the current account ends up affecting the investment and financial accounts. The threat of a campaign to depreciate the dollar would likely send interest rates higher, whether domestic economic conditions warranted, as investors, both domestic and foreign, seek some protection from heightened currency risk. It may discourage portfolio investment flows into the United States. A weaker dollar also makes U.S. real assets cheaper, a virtual fire sale to investors with foreign currencies to invest, which is what many protectionists and "American First" supporters who want policy makers to "fix" the deficit don't get. For an American company with overseas investments, a weak dollar may encourage them to keep more profits with their foreign affiliates. Until the dollar stopped falling. After all, those profits will be worth more when they are converted back into dollars, giving companies a quick revenue boost.

One of America's strengths is the entrepreneurial drive of its people. Everyone, it seems, has an idea to get rich. Dorm-room businesses range from word processing (and term-paper writing) to Microsoft. Americans have taken their love of launching ventures all over the world. When an American executive sees a new customer base in another country, increasingly the impulse isn't to export but to start a new operation.

Those new businesses overseas, though, don't contribute much to the export line of the current account, so they aren't the focus of investors or policy makers. Sure, it's nice that Johnson & Johnson has operations in Canada, but wouldn't it be better if skin cream made here were exported there? Yes, if your concern is short-run changes in the current account rather than the long-term health of a major corporation or of the national economy.

Over the long haul, though, an American overseas expansion strategy based on foreign direct investment—produce and sell locally—is impervious to exchange rates. It is an evolutionary strategy that helps protect them through numerous channels of diversification and against the swings in the currency markets. Businesses that want to expand will do so. The exact rate of expansion and mechanism for financing might vary from year to year, depending on the relative cost (which is, of course, a function of exchange rates, and some of which can be hedged), but the trends change slowly. One can cut orders for parts made overseas and shift to U.S. sources when the dollar is strong; it's a lot harder to shut down an overseas subsidiary when the dollar is strong and reopen it when it's weak again in the interest of maximizing dollar profits.

The Financial Account and Currency

Consider this: Americans buy Chinese goods and Saudi oil. The Chinese and Saudis then take our money and use it to buy stock in American companies and bonds issued by the U.S. government. Through the myopic glasses that give the current account deficit a significance beyond justification, it may look like America itself is becoming colonized by foreign investors, many of whom do not have representative forms of government.

But looked at in the ways outlined in this book, there is no reason to be particularly anxious or paranoid. People in other countries are interested in American ingenuity, American entrepreneurialism, and American stability. The way to play those isn't measured in the current account; it's measured in the financial accounts. This includes U.S. ownership of foreign assets and foreign ownership of U.S. assets. In turn, these assets may be equities, bonds, bank accounts, and direct investments.

Moreover, economists and the media often fail to appreciate the extent of U.S. ownership of foreign assets. On a current cost basis, Americans owned $17.6 trillion in foreign assets at the end of 2007,[15] an increase of $3.3 trillion from 2006, more than the GDP of all but a handful of countries. In fact, the falling dollar increases the value of American overseas investments.

Over its two centuries of existence, the United States has been a safety valve for the world's excess people, excess goods, and excess savings. Until World War I, the United States had more or less open immigration, attracting the world's tired, poor, and huddled masses yearning to breathe free.[16] Even as recently as the 1980s and 1990s, nearly a million people a year made their way to the United States. After World War II, the United States became a safety valve for the world's excess production as the government encouraged imports from Europe, Japan, and emerging markets to help them rebuild (and avoid a return to a depression or the spread of communism).

Since about 1980, the United States has been the safety valve for the world's excess savings, which for various reasons the countries generating it cannot or will not absorb. Indeed, rather than the current account driving the capital account, it appears that the capital account drives the current account. It is not *just* a chicken-and-egg story. Given the relative size and significance of the market for capital relative to the market for goods and services, it appears that importing foreign savings allows the United States to buy foreign-made goods, even if from affiliates of U.S. companies.

That the United States would open itself to the world's excess savings was itself an attempt to resolve the economic challenges that had produced the most significant downturn since the Great Depression (until the credit crisis that began in 2007). Absorbing the world's surplus savings required larger trade deficits and was part and parcel of a larger effort to boost capital mobility and innovation. The credit crisis, in part, grew out of the excess of the strategic solution to the last major capitalist crisis and makes finding a new structural and strategic solution all the more challenging.

Reality of the Current Account and Currency

The United States was born in an age of empires and always fancied itself a global player. In modern times, it has been "the indispensable country" as Madeleine Albright once awkwardly called it. But this is not reflected in the current account position or in the movement of the U.S. dollar.

The current account deficit is not a measure of America's economic strength because it shows, in part, that the nation is rich and large enough to promote global growth by absorbing other countries surplus goods and savings. The evolutionary expansion strategy of American companies encourages international development by setting up operations in other countries, preferring to import profits rather than export goods (though it is still among the leading exporters).

To be sure, this is not an argument of American exceptionalism. It is partly a function of scale. The 2007 gross domestic product of $13.8 trillion was the largest in the world; the second-largest economy, Japan, had a GDP of just $4.4 trillion.[17] Its sheer size means that America can incorporate trade within its foreign economic strategy in very different ways from the rest of the world, making its economy even richer—and the world better off. The argument is that international growth and development is not necessarily the zero-sum game that the focus on the current account suggests.

Of course, the role of capital markets in trade and exchange rates throws politicians for a loop. "We have better capital markets!" doesn't generate national pride the same way that slogans like "We make the best cars!" or "We have the most productive people!" do. But it's reality in the modern world. The current account doesn't show America's strength, and it does not predict the price of the dollar. Instead, the value of the dollar is a function of all of the reasons why people want to buy and sell the dollar, whether for trade, business expansion, or investment.

Chapter Notes

1. See, for example, the essays during this time by Robert Triffin and Jacques Rueff.

2. Bank for International Settlements, "Triennial Central Bank Survey of Foreign Exchange and Derivatives Market Activity in April 2007—Preliminary global results—Turnover," September 25, 2007 (http://www.bis.org/press/p070925.htm).

3. *CIA World Factbook,* 2008.

4. Investment Company Institute, *2008 Investment Company Fact Book* (http://www.ici.org/pdf/08fb_letter.pdf).

5. Investment Company Institute, *2007 Investment Company Fact Book* (http://www.ici.org/pdf/07fb_letter.pdf).

6. U.S. Census Bureau, November 2008 (http://www.census.gov/indicator/www/ustrade.html).

7. Linda Goldberg and Jose Campo, "Exchange Rate Pass Through into Import Prices." *Review of Economics and Statistics*, November 2005.

8. U.S. Bureau of Economic Analysis, "U.S. International Transactions: First Quarter 2008." *The Economic Report of the President,* June 17, 2008.

9. U.S. Bureau of Economic Analysis, "U.S. International Transactions: First Quarter 2008." *The Economic Report of the President,* June 17, 2008.

10. Thomas Friedman, *The World Is Flat,* 3rd ed. (New York: Picador, 2007).

11. Intel Corporation (http://www.intel.com/technology/mooreslaw/index.htm).

12. Federal Reserve, "Money Stock Measures." Statistical release, October 2, 2008.

13. European Central Bank, "The Euro as Invoicing Currency in International Trade." ECB Working Paper 665, August 2006.

14. Linda Goldberg and Eleanor Wiske Dillon, "Why Dollar Depreciation May Not Close the Trade Deficit." *Current Issues in Economics and Finance* (Federal Reserve Bank of New York), June 2007 (Vol. 13, No. 5) (http://www.newyorkfed.org/research/current_issues/ci13-5.pdf).

15. U.S. Bureau of Economic Analysis, "U.S. Net International Investment Position at Yearend 2007." June 27, 2008 (http://www.bea.gov/newsreleases/international/intinv/intinvnewsrelease.htm).

16. Emma Lazarus, "The New Colossus."

17. International Monetary Fund, *World Economic Outlook Database,* April 2008 (http://www.imf.org/external/pubs/ft/weo/2008/01/weodata/index.aspx).

MYTH 3

You Can't Have Too Much Money

Money is just a tool. It can be put to good profitable use,
or it can be wasted if not used properly. Like other inputs,
its supply can outstrip its effective demand.

Money is paper with no value other than what society assigns it. It is a social construct. Still most people seem to want to have more money, but just how much more? Enough to buy groceries or enough to play the slot machines at a casino, guilt free? If someone has a little extra money—not enough for a fabulous vacation or a sleek little sports car, but a little extra—he might just put it in the bank to save for a trip or for possible repairs on his current car. If the bank doesn't see a good demand for loans or doesn't want to use the deposit for other purposes, then the funds just sit there—unproductive and worth little more than the paper they are printed on. The bank offers the saver low interest rates because it can't charge higher rates to borrowers without cutting off the weakened demand.

Interest rates stayed low in the United States throughout the 1990s and well into the 2000s, even though Americans don't save money as economists traditionally define savings. (For example, two important aspects of American savings that are not included in the traditional measures are the return on retirement savings, such as 401k plans and IRAs, and vast sums spent on higher education, which are considered consumption.) That would indicate that there was a supply of funds coming from somewhere else—but where? In 2005, Ben Bernanke, as a junior governor on the Federal Reserve Board before he became chairman a couple of years later, gave a speech in which he suggested a solution to the so-called Greenspan conundrum—why long-term interest rates remained relatively low despite the tightening of Fed policy and a reasonably strong economic expansion. The answer, Bernanke declared, was a global savings glut. People elsewhere were saving money far in excess of its practical uses in their domestic economies.[1] He noted that many developing and emerging market countries had become net capital exporters.

The fact is that too much money is as bad for an economy as too little. The way that nations equalize their internal supply and demand for cash is by borrowing and lending overseas. The extent to which capital is mobile, it can be deployed to places that have a greater effective demand. The Japanese, for example, with too much money relative to their productive outlets for it, can (and do) export it by buying foreign bonds such as U.S. government securities and Australian and New Zealand dollar-denominated bonds. This chapter discusses the surplus savings problem that Bernanke identified and looks at some of its implications.

Banks and the Money Supply

Banks are not the natural habitats of money. Instead, banks are way stations—intermediaries, if you will—as money moves from place to place. The big vault is just for show because the bank doesn't make money on the cash left in that vault. As any other retailer, it has to move the inventory. Instead of soap and shampoo, though, a bank trades in money. In fact, retail banking generated such poor returns that many banks sought to free themselves from their deposit roots to concentrate on investment banking and insurance businesses. The credit crisis has called such strategies into question.

Like other businesses, a bank's inventory is not fixed. The supply of money is flexible. It changes as the supply and demand adjust to changing business and investment conditions. Here's how it works under the conditions of a marginal reserve system: If a person deposits $1,000 in his bank account, the bank will keep a percentage of it on hand, determined by the central bank, so that it can meet withdrawal requests, whether from him or from other customers. The rest of the money will be loaned out. If 25 percent of that $1,000 is kept on reserve, then $750 can be loaned to others. The depositor still has a $1,000 balance in his account, and the borrower now has a balance of $750. As long as the loan is put to productive use and paid off, everyone is happy, which is what happens in the vast majority of cases. Even during the credit crisis, the overwhelming majority of mortgages and loans continued to be serviced in a timely fashion.

If the bank did not intermediate between the saver and borrower, the saver would still have his $1,000 if he put it under his mattress instead of opening a bank account, resulting in no new economic activity. His money wouldn't be put to productive use. Not only does he miss out on interest but also the disappointed prospective borrower misses out on an opportunity to create consumption or expand a new business.

A bank may not have much use for extra money, and it signals that by offering a low interest rate on deposits. Maybe there are no borrowers where the bank is located, but there are plenty in other parts of the world. The depositor decides to put his extra $1,000 on account in another country. The economic activity that his deposit supports will take place there, not here, even though he'll be able to take the profits back here. It is still a non–zero sum exercise. Everyone is better off: someone gets much-needed capital, and the depositor receives interest on his savings.

Economies need money, as people need blood and oxygen. Do not think of money as just the tangible coins and notes in circulation, but as all those other forms that money can take in the modern economy. If it is cheap enough for long enough, it will be wasted in speculation, excessive risk taking, or what economist Hyman Minsky called "balance sheet engineering."[2] When a bank or business has an excess of funds, it might take risks that it would not otherwise, and there are countless examples in numerous countries that have come to light during the credit crisis.

If the bank doesn't have enough money to lend, the distribution of the scarce resource might exclude prospective borrowers with good projects. The hopeful homeowner may be willing to make a 30 percent down payment and have income four times greater than the annual mortgage payment, but if the lender has no funds or no appetite for such risk, then no loan will be written and no house sold, leaving no commission, no need for a moving van, and no new paint job. Less money moves around, and the economy contracts, as we have witnessed with a synchronized recession in the advanced industrialized countries in the 2007–2009 period.

Furthermore, a bank that's not making loans has no income for depositors' interest. The depositors take their money elsewhere, further constricting the amount of money in the economy. Even keeping cash in a mattress beats having to pay a slew of service charges. Will Rogers once reportedly quipped that sometimes the return *of* your money is more important than the return *on* your money. And that is what we saw at certain points during the credit crisis when investors were willing to accept barely negative interest rates on short-dated U.S. Treasury bills, seemingly preferring a guaranteed minor loss instead of taking a risk for an unknown potentially ruinous loss. Even as late as the second quarter of 2009, the Swiss National Bank sold three and six month bills with no yield.

Where in the World Is the Capital?

Before the financial crises in the last half of the 1990s, emerging market countries in Asia and Latin America were net borrowers from global capital markets, drawing $80 billion in 1996 alone.[3] This changed after a series of crises that rippled through the emerging markets, from Mexico in 1994 to the Asian financial crisis in 1997–98, Russia in 1998, Brazil in 1999, and Argentina in 2002. These crises led to a sharp drop in these countries demand for investment funds, which boosted the pool of available capital seeking attractive opportunities. Domestic demand in the crisis-stricken developing countries slowed sharply, leaving a surplus of goods to be exported, depreciating currencies, and new surpluses that needed to be deployed with underdeveloped local financial markets.

Savers across the world put their excess savings in the United States, which then profitably redeployed the capital. It functions as the banker for the world. The Federal Reserve, then, is not just America's central bank; it's very much the banker to the world, and that role appears to have been enhanced during the crisis through several measures, including making an unlimited amount of dollars available through swap facilities to a number of major central banks, including the European Central Bank, the Bank of England, and the Bank of Japan. Several developing countries, including Mexico, Brazil, South Korea, and Singapore, were offered more limited currency swap lines.

The U.S. economy is safe enough that many foreign countries hold their reserves at the U.S. Federal Reserve. The Federal Reserve offers such accounts custody services and, along with money supply data, issues a weekly report of the activities of its custodial clients in aggregate. It handles investments in Treasury bonds, other securities, and gold for 250 nations, totaling about $2.4 trillion and representing half the world's U.S. dollar-denominated reserves.[4] Naturally, the Fed charges fees for these services but not enough to make a dent in the federal deficit, of course.

Any discussion of the size of foreign official holdings of U.S. Treasuries raises the issue of what would happen if these national investors sold part of their U.S. Treasury holdings? Well, some nations do sell from time to time to manage their own trade accounts, national budgets, financial obligations, and reserve management objectives. It has not been enough to create any disruption in the ability of the federal government to keep borrowing and spending. Rare is the month, though, that foreign central banks are not net buyers of U.S. Treasury securities. To be honest, the truly fickle investors in U.S. Treasuries are hedge funds and American investors themselves.

Still, there's always the possibility of major sales. However, before any nation could sell, it would have to have some place to put the funds. There isn't a mattress big enough to hold $2.4 trillion. No other nation has sufficiently broad and deep capital markets that can absorb the capital. The United States, with the world's largest economy, also has the world's most liquid sovereign-bond market, making it an ideal market for the world's surplus capital. Some countries may be diversifying the current inflow of new reserves by buying non-U.S. bonds in addition to U.S. Treasuries. They don't have to sell Treasury obligations to do it.

One lesson of the credit crisis is that the world economy is dangerously volatile, requiring greater reserves rather than less. Such national efforts will likely be complemented by increased cooperation via the creation of multinational reserve pools and networks of swap arrangements. During periods of reserve accumulation, there is another non-zero sum opportunity. Central banks around the world are accumulating reserves denominated in dollars and euros (and, to a much lesser extent, other currencies such as sterling).

Despite the near-constant wailing of the alarmist claims, there is no evidence that central banks as a whole have reduced their holdings by a single dollar through the middle of 2008. In the second half of 2008, some

Asian countries intervened to support their currencies, and this may have reduced some national holdings of Treasuries. Russia lost a third of the nearly $600 billion in reserves it held in early August 2008 over the next six months. Some sales of Treasury holdings would not be surprising. Nevertheless, in early 2009, the Federal Reserve's custody holding of marketable Treasury and Agency securities for foreign officials accounts had never been higher.

Economies, the Money Supply, and Savings

Money affects the health of the economy. Too little, and there won't be any capital investment. Too much, and investors will be incentivized to take larger risks. It's not just the absolute amount of money floating through the system, but how fast it flows, that matters. That measure is "velocity", and it tells how often a single dollar turns over. If you go out to dinner on your Friday payday, your money will be put to work faster than if you go home and raid the fridge. If the waiter takes his tip money and stops for groceries on the way home from work, then that money will turn over faster than if he puts it in his savings account. If the grocery store pays its distributor on Monday morning, then the money will keep moving; if the bill isn't paid for another week, then it won't.

The more velocity the money supply has, the less money is needed to support economic growth. With too much velocity, though, everyone is too busy spending to do anything else. During the credit crisis, measures of the U.S. money supply continued to expand, being force-fed by the Federal Reserve, but the velocity (GDP divided by money supply) appeared to collapse as nominal GDP contracted sharply.

From Money to Capital

A form of money that is particularly interesting is that component of money that is available for investment and savings. Reading the press and listening to the talking heads, one would conclude that there is insufficient savings and investment in the U.S. But, just as under conditions of global warming, where some parts of the world are likely to experience colder weather, so too, despite what many regard or experience as a dearth of money or savings, an underlying problem of capitalism is the surplus of capital it generates.

One of the first American economists to examine the problem of surplus capital was Charles Conant, a journalist and banker who wrote about the global economy in essays published between 1893 and 1903. He analyzed the problems of modern industrial capitalism that led to half the years between 1865 and 1900 being characterized by depression, panic, or crisis. These spectacular booms and busts took place during the period in which the United States took its first and only colony, the Philippines, and the world was becoming globalized on a scale that had never been seen before and, because it was followed by two world wars, a scale that was not seen again for more than fifty years.

Conant believed that the United States' frequent economic crises were part of modern capitalism itself and, ultimately, a consequence of the mechanization of production. As productivity and output surged beyond what people dared to imagine, too many goods were produced. The mechanization process raised businesses' fixed costs relative to variable costs. In turn, this provided powerful incentives to businesses to continue to produce, even at a loss, rather than to shut down production. This let them better service such fixed costs as debt, but it also created surplus capital until supply exceeded effective demand.

For every nation with a surplus of savings, there's another one with a shortage, at least a shortage of investment capital. The ability to move capital around the world may prevent booms and busts in places where the accumulated supply of capital is different from the demand. Otherwise, Conant said, the rate of return on capital will fall; if not arrested, this would have potentially far-reaching political and social consequences. Conant recognized that modern capitalism was producing surplus far in excess of what could be reasonably absorbed through increases of domestic consumption and investment, and not just in the United States but also in the other industrialized countries. The solution was to export the surplus savings.

When a sufficiently profitable opportunity becomes apparent, capital rushes in, Conant observed, creating redundancies as competing pools of capital build capacity to exploit the opportunity. It's exactly what happened more than a century later when increased productivity from the technological revolution led to too much money. To absorb the supply of capital in the United States, money flooded the residential real estate market, and too many bad loans were written.

Redundant investment can produce a general decline in prices. At first blush, falling prices might seem to be a good thing, but they are not. Deflation occurs when the supply of money greatly exceeds the uses for it. As businesses and consumers watch prices fall, they wait to see where the bottom will be before they commit to making purchases. Think about holiday sales: the Saturday before Christmas is usually the biggest sales day of the shopping season, and not just because some people procrastinate. Instead, smart shoppers are waiting for the best sales to be announced, and they know that as the merchants become more desperate to book revenue, they'll start cutting prices. Deflation causes the same effect, only economy-wide and without a December 25 deadline.

Debtors are typically helped by inflation. They are, in effect, paying back their debts with less-valuable dollars. Deflation, however, cuts the other way. Debtors are paying back with dearer dollars. Consider the impact on interest rates, the cost of servicing the debt. If real interest rates equal the nominal rate minus inflation, then in an environment of rising prices, real rates are below nominal rates. However, during a general decline in prices, real interest rates are higher than nominal rates, exacerbating the hardship of servicing the debt.

Disaccumulation and Net New Capital Investment

Savings are critical in the early phases of economic development when infrastructure is being created. Businesses require investment capital for property, plant, and equipment. As businesses grow and expand, their retained earnings provide the lion's share of their new investment capital, allowing them to rely less on external sources such as household savings. One of the hallmarks of an advanced capitalist economy is that the basic infrastructure has already been built. Sure, it still needs to be maintained, modernized, and updated from time to time, but what economists call "the capital broadening process" has generally occurred. On a household level, the same is true when one considers the penetration rate of white goods. Early in the twentieth century, households acquiring the new consumer durable goods of the era—including indoor bathrooms, refrigerators, stoves, electric lights, and washing machines—fueled U.S. economic growth to a large extent.[5]

Some American historians such as Martin J. Sklar and James Livingston suggest that there was an important break in the economic pattern early in the twentieth century. During the first period, the driving force was capital accumulation. In order to produce more goods and services, more hours of work were required. New investment in capital equipment was necessary. Consumption had to be deferred so a country could amass sufficient savings to finance the required investments (under conditions of limited international capital mobility).

Those conditions were not permanent. Businesses and technology unleashed and harnessed people's unfathomable productive capacities. If human society was historically plagued by a scarcity of goods, then the problem increasingly became a surplus of goods early in the twentieth century. It was a consequence of Conant's surplus savings problem. Starting around World War I, increased industrial output was being achieved without a commensurate increase in hours worked. Rather than needing to defer consumption to promote investment, consumption had to be expanded. Traditionally, people produced goods so they could consume. The juxtaposition in modern society is that people consume in order to sustain production.

To maintain high levels of consumption, developed countries have to varying degrees decoupled the ability to consume from work. This is achieved through transfer payments and entitlement programs, which in the United States was one of the most important sources of the increase in household income in recent years. Large businesses generally freed themselves from reliance on external sources of capital for investment in property, plant, and equipment. Retained earnings cover the vast majority of investment. In fact, most of the borrowings by large U.S. companies in the year before the onset of the current financial crisis in the second half of 2007 appear to have been used to finance stock repurchase programs.

Another force is at work. Each year, businesses take charges for depreciation to reflect the eventual decline in value of their capital investments in property, plant, and equipment. Depreciation shows up as an expense on the income statement, but no cash is spent. Eventually, the depreciated items have to be replaced. When that happens, the company will probably find that the new replacement is technologically superior to the worn-out item. New heating, ventilation, and air-conditioning systems may be more energy efficient. New computers may handle more data faster. New trucks may be more fuel-efficient and easier to load. All these little changes add up and help the company improve without increasing net new investment (net of depreciation)—and without a need for external funds.

The noted economist Harold Vatter called this the "atrophying of net tangible investment." Replacement investment embodies technical progress.[6] It is both labor saving and capital saving. It allows companies to produce greater output with smaller new outlays of fixed capital. The lack of U.S. household savings, as it is officially measured, did not and will not retard economic growth. Other advanced industrial countries such as Germany, Japan, and Switzerland, with higher savings and investment rates than the United States, do not, as a rule grow faster. Disaccumulation and the "atrophy of net investment" is both the consequence of and exacerbates the surplus savings problem Conant identified.

Large American companies have more than enough funds for their domestic activities, and many of them have exported part of their surplus abroad. Rather than only making goods for export, they set up operations abroad, exporting capital. Likewise, Conant recognized that the central drive of accumulating capital for investment in one's own resources and enterprises had reached the point of diminishing returns. Exporting capital (in addition to goods) was necessary to relieve the congestion at home that was putting downward pressure on returns.

The challenge in a modern economy is not accumulating capital; it is finding productive uses for it. An international monetary regime that embraced capital mobility increases the field of operation. In the process of exploring those opportunities, the export of capital can and has led to the development and modernization in other parts of the world in a way that the traditional goods export focus did not.

Capital and Developing Economies

Although household savings weren't the key to American economic success over the last few decades, they still are important in developing nations. Early in the development process, household savings are still needed to finance investment in the capital broadening process. Muhammad Yunus, an economist who won the 2006 Nobel Prize for Peace, saw that poor people in Bangladesh wanted to work and make money, but they had no way to get started because they had no money to buy agricultural equipment, hand tools, or shop inventory. Yunus began making small loans from his own pocket, which led to the formation of Grameen Bank, a microfinance institution that has loaned out

$7.3 billion dollars with a 98.08 percent repayment rate.[7] Yunus's own household savings launched that growth.

Shortage of investable capital is a significant challenge in developing countries. Some leaders in developing countries insist on condemning their people to relatively short and miserable lives (e.g., high rates of infant mortality and illnesses that have inexpensive cures and known preventions) through poor policy choices and corruption. Unless a government supports incentive structures and institutions that encourage investment, it is difficult to envisage how there can be a sustained improvement in living standards.

And poor people have surprisingly significant assets. In fact, the wealth in many poor countries dwarfs aid received from foreign agencies. Worldwide, poor people have assets forty times greater than foreign aid received since 1945. In Egypt, the assets of the poor are about fifty-five times more than that nation's total foreign investment, including financing for the Suez Canal and the Aswan Dam. In Haiti, the poorest nation in the Western Hemisphere, poor citizens own about 150 times more than all the foreign investment received since Haiti became independent from France in 1804.[8] To put that in perspective: Haiti received $515 million in economic aid in 2005 alone, which was about 10 percent of its gross domestic product.[9]

So what's the problem? If these people have wealth, why are they so poor? Well, most of this wealth is held informally and improperly. Houses may be built on land where the ownership rights have not been adequately recorded. Unincorporated businesses may have undefined liabilities. Savings may be worn as jewelry, which is difficult to keep safe. The result is a cash-poor economy that can't support much economic growth, and budding capitalists can't find the rules to the game.

Although many developing nations have little enforced regulation, they are not free market paradises. Capitalism works best when the government wields a strong hand to ensure property rights are broadly understood. To paraphrase William Seidman, former head of the Federal Deposit Insurance Corporation and the first chairman of the Resolution Trust Corporation that was created to resolve the savings and loan crisis, regulations help ensure that capitalism works like a prize fight rather than a barroom brawl.[10]

Development of property law is critical. It gives people title to what they own. It's a powerful tool for ensuring economic development. If rights to possessions are not adequately documented, then they can't be sold, borrowed against, or otherwise turned into capital. They can only be traded within a tight circle of people who know and trust each other. The informality of property leads to informality of trade and finance: black markets, pervasive organized and unorganized crime, and flagrant disregard of the law. With no records to back up any claims, poverty lingers. The lack of structure makes poverty worse. Deeds, titles, receipts, and stakes enable wealth to be quantified and transferred.

Without recorded property, trade will be sloppy. That's why the International Finance Corporation, an arm of the World Bank, tracks just how easy it is to record and transfer property in different parts of the world. In the United States, it takes twelve days and four procedures to register property at a cost of 0.5 percent of the item's value, on average; transferring title on a house, licensing a new car, or clearing a stock trade doesn't take very long. It's not nearly as easy in other parts of the world. Brazilians go through fourteen procedures over forty-two days, spending 2.7 percent of the property value. The Chinese have four procedures taking twenty-nine days and costing 3.2 percent of value. In Egypt, the average property transfer takes seventy-two days, involves seven procedures, and has costs totaling about 0.9 percent of value.[11]

Property law embraces the best *and* worst of human nature. As James Madison noted in Federalist Paper No. 51, if people were angels there would be no need for government. Put somewhat differently, property laws operationalize Ronald Reagan's maxim to "Trust, but verify." By contrast, many traditional economies are built on trust: people deal only with people they know, and families will enforce contracts to make sure that their reputation remains high. In developed nations, for all the free market rhetoric, trust is very low. Markets need extensive information and someone to enforce contracts if they are to function.

Making More Capital More Mobile

Modern capitalism is a Western development, based on individual property ownership, secular oversight, and an Enlightenment approach to calculating risk. The centuries-long assumption was that the world wanted to operate on a Western model. But that's not acceptable to all investors or to all who need capital; not everyone aspires to Adam Smith's views of the world.

Even people who disapprove of the way capitalism has evolved still need capital. Good thing that the world's financiers are incredibly creative. Give them some cash needs, risk measurements, and a list of constraints, and they'll invent new securities to meet the need. Whether it's Grameen Bank's style of microfinance on a small scale or *sukuk* (an asset-backed certificate used to finance deals in accordance with Muslim law) to build skyscrapers in Dubai on a big scale, the markets will rise to keep capital moving.

And the capital has to move. Here's a reality about international investing: not all nations have the same level of safety, and they do not present the same range of opportunities. That leads to imbalances. People in one country may be suffering through low investment returns because there are so few opportunities where they live, whereas people in other countries may be languishing economically because there isn't enough money to fund ideas and opportunities there. The financial markets help those with extra money get it to people who need it.

The capital markets allow the more flexible allocation of capital than banks, the other primary means by which capital can be distributed. The free flow of capital across borders can make everyone better off. It helps people match their risk and return preferences better, but it's a relatively new phenomenon. Investors have traditionally shown a preference for their own markets. This is perfectly understandable. After all, professional investors often advise people to invest in what they know best, and the average American probably knows more about a company headquartered in Chicago than one based in Shanghai.

That home country bias is starting to change. With better communication, investors are learning more about other parts of the world. (Even professional investors who bought stock in international markets once had to wait a few days for the delivery of foreign newspapers; now they are online in real time.) With the liberalization of capital markets, it's easier to buy and sell in other countries, and investors have found that they can often get better returns.

The biggest changes have come from two of the world's largest economies, Japan and the United States. For a long time, investors in both countries tended to be insular. Now the Japanese have embraced U.S. and European bonds as alternative investments offering higher returns than domestic bonds and deposits. As American investors become more comfortable with international mutual funds and exchange-traded funds, they are exporting an increased proportion of their savings and diversifying globally their savings, too.

New businesses, with no credit and no revenue, often need to find sources of investment capital to bring new ideas to the market. American investors understand that type of risk; the willingness to invest in unproven ideas is what made Silicon Valley and other technological revolutions succeed. Early stage companies from all over the world come to the United States to raise funds. Of the thirty-six initial public offerings priced in the United States in the first half of 2008, for example, four were companies based in China and four were based in Europe.[12]

Asia's developing nations have traditionally underdeveloped capital markets, and this remains true today. The inability of the regional capital markets to absorb the vast savings and export earnings forces the adoption of Conant's capital export strategy. At the very least, this exacerbates the global imbalances; at worst, it is a significant cause of the imbalances. The deepest, more liquid, and transparent markets are in the United States and the U.S. dollar. They receive the bulk of the world's excess savings.

In Conant's time as now, China's market fired the imagination of businesses and financiers. As late as 1820, China was the world's largest economy and among the technological leaders. It accounted for about one-third of the world's economy. At the end of the century, the United States didn't have designs on the Philippines simply for its own sake in the Spanish-American War, but as part of a string of coaling stations needed by the U.S. naval and commercial fleet if it were to participate in a meaningful way in the economic opportunities associated with China.

China's capitalist experiment has taken place in the midst of underdeveloped financial institutions. When Chinese companies need to raise money, they often turn to capital markets in other countries. And when Chinese capitalists want to protect their profits, they move their funds to countries with longer traditions of respect for individual property rights and stable finances.

People and businesses from all over the world come to the United States to raise investment and risk capital, but business is conducted on terms that developed primarily in Europe and the United States. It is based on a distinction between finance capital and industrial capital or debt and equity. Debt does not confer the rights and obligations of ownership that equity does. The credit crisis appears to be calling into question the viability of that stark distinction, but it clearly doesn't work for one group that is growing in both population and wealth: Muslims.

Although Asia's savings in excess of its ability to absorb it has been widely commented on (China, for example, had a 2007 current account surplus of $360.7 billion), excess savings in the Middle East is relatively greater, thanks to the flood of petrodollars. In 2007, Saudi Arabia had a current account surplus of $100.8 billion, Kuwait a current account surplus of $52.7 billion, and the United Arab Emirates a surplus of $41.3 billion.[13] These are tiny countries with enormous funds—far too much than can be absorbed at home—that have to be invested abroad. Although Conant recommended direct investment rather than simply portfolio investment, cross-border investments are primarily in bonds and deposits.

However, oil exports and the challenge of recycling the petrodollars are dominated primarily by nations that have majority Muslim populations and, in many cases, governments that are explicitly Islamic. Muslim law, known as *shariah,* has requirements for investments and business dealings that differ from European and North American practices. These have also discouraged the development of domestic capital markets in the Middle East. The best-known law is the prohibition on *riba,* usually interpreted to mean paying or receiving interest. It's intended to keep business partners equal with similar interests in the success of the venture—both have skin in the game. No matter the reason, religion matters to many people, so they look for ways to accommodate it in their daily life. Christians were forced to develop business practices along similar lines when a medieval pope ruled usury an offense that could lead to excommunication.

The prohibition on interest affects other aspects of conventional capital markets. As it has been interpreted, Muslim law prohibits not only borrowing and lending but also some types of insurance, interest-rate swaps, and such conventional derivatives as futures and options, credit-default swaps, and forward-exchange transactions. In addition, devout Muslims do not gamble and will not invest in businesses involved in charging interest or other prohibited activities, including banks, casino companies, pork processors, tobacco companies, and alcoholic beverage producers. Muslim law limits the number of acceptable finance and investment vehicles.

However, shariah does not mean that Muslim countries are locked into a predevelopment stage. Historically, the people of the Middle East have been traders and played an important role between merchants in Europe, Asia, and Africa during the Middle Ages. In recent times, these prohibitions have not prevented entrepreneurial activity or the development of contracts and property rights. Commerce goes on, but the rules are different. Instead of loans, financing is obtained through revenue sharing, lease-to-own, or other contracts that give business people the capital they need and provide the financier with compensation for the opportunity cost without structuring the compensation as interest.

Capital markets have long adapted to changing needs. The dizzying array of derivatives that are off-limits to Muslims were practically unknown forty years ago. As long as there is a need in the market and a way to price the risk, a new security will develop. There is no reason why the Western model of finance has to apply to everyone. It would not be surprising if some shariah-compliant structures that have been developed inspire a new generation of investment products that converge the distinction of creditors and owners.

Islamic financial products may increasingly be regarded as a special type of investment vehicle in an already wide array of financial instruments. Non-Muslim investors will increasingly have to learn to value these contracts or miss out on the profit opportunities of this rapidly growing asset class. Non-Muslim borrowers may find that they need to structure contracts differently in order to attract capital from Muslims with money to invest. In fact, it might be better to think of these as *new* securities rather than *Islamic* securities because anyone will be able to use them. In some ways, this parallels the growth of commodity trading, which developed to create markets for farmers but quickly presented hedging and speculation opportunities for people who wouldn't know how to start a tractor or what a soybean seed looks like.

The Reality about Money and Development

Economies need money to grow, but that money has to come in the right form—and it doesn't have to come from inside that economy. When money is in a liquid, tradable form, it can be put to work quickly. It can move across borders to provide funds where they are most needed.

People in China who need a safe place to put their money can buy U.S. government bonds, and American investors looking for bigger profits than they can get at home can buy into the initial public offerings of Chinese companies.

Businesses in developed countries don't need much external investment capital because their retained earnings are largely sufficient. Technological progress means that equipment purchased to replace worn-out items brings with it efficiency advantages *and* cost savings that let companies grow their productivity without increasing the dollars allocated to net new capital investments.

The United States has become a manager of the world's surplus capital in addition to the largest manufacturer of goods. Because many countries are developing with only the shakiest of financial services, those with liquid savings want to move the money elsewhere. China may be known for making cheap consumer goods, but it's not known as a safe haven for savings. That honor goes to the United States, and its role is likely to not only be retained but enhanced by the credit crisis as the depth, breadth, and liquidity of its markets enjoys greater appreciation in the time of need.

Chapter Notes

1. Ben S. Bernanke, "The Global Savings Glut and the U.S. Current Account Deficit," March 10, 2005. Transcript at http://www.federalreserve.gov/boarddocs/speeches/2005/200503102/default.htm.

2. Hyman Minski, *Stabilizing an Unstable Economy* (New York: McGraw-Hill, 2008).

3. Ben S. Bernanke, "The Global Savings Glut."

4. Federal Reserve, Statistical release, September 18, 2008.

5. James Livingston, *Pragmatism and the Political Economy of Cultural Revolution 1850–1940* (Chapel Hill: University of North Carolina Press, 1997).

6. Harold G. Vatter, "The Atrophy of Net Investment and Some Consequences for the U.S. Mixed Economy." *Journal of Economic Issues,* March 1982 (Vol. 16, No. 1), pp. 237–254.

7. Grameen Bank at a Glance (http://www.grameen-info.org), August 2008.

8. Hernando De Soto, *The Mystery of Capital: Why Capitalism Triumphs in the West and Fails Everywhere Else* (New York: Basic Books, 2000).

9. *CIA World Factbook, 2008.*

10. Quoted by Jo Becker, Sherly Gay Stolberg, and Stephen Labation, "White House Philosophy Stoked Mortgage Bonfire," *New York Times,* December 20, 2008 (http://www.nytimes.com/2008/12/21/business/21admin.html?pagewanted=1&em).

11. International Finance Corporation, *Doing Business 2009.*

12. See http://www.ipohome.com.

13. International Monetary Fund staff estimates, *IMF World Economic Outlook Database,* April 2008.

MYTH 4

Labor Market Flexibility Is the Key to U.S. Economic Prowess

The flexibility of the U.S. labor market is often heralded as the key to the United States' competitive edge over other countries and regions. It is exaggerated. The key is capital market flexibility.

Democracy and capitalism work best with the active engagement of people making decisions about their destinies. The United States has been a grand experiment in assimilation and democracy, accepting workers from all over the world and turning them into the richest, most productive workforce on Earth. Some want to know how to duplicate the American magic. Some think the elixir lies with the flexibility of the labor market.

Although American labor is flexible, that flexibility is not an unalloyed good. It can harm relationships between employers and employees. The labor and social mobility is not one-way, and the downside creates instability in families and communities. Businesses often are not as flexible as workers, either. Many people have to leave the workforce because of family responsibilities that preclude full-time employment, and the relationship between health insurance and employment often causes people to stay in jobs they don't like, avoid certain types of employment, and put off starting new businesses.

Multinational corporations don't need to rely on the workers in any one place. Instead, they can—and do—move the goods to the workers to take advantage of differing levels of skill and pay. The amount of intrafirm trade can be enormous, but it is not as if U.S. multinationals produce abroad to import back into the United States. In 2005, trade of goods and services between U.S. parents and their foreign affiliates contributed a *mere* $961.1 million[1] out of a total trade deficit of $716.7 billion.[2] Yet the significance of intrafirm trade raises questions about the conventional understandings of trade and exchange rates. Instead of the flexibility of labor, the real driver is the flexibility of capital.

Labor Mobility

In traditional societies, work was specific to a place. With limited transportation and technology, all work was physical labor. That's still the case in many developing nations. And if people can't find enough work where they live, then they have to move.

In a modern society, a lot of work is specific to a place, but not all of it. A farmer has to live where the land and climate are suitable for the crops he wants to grow. A factory can be located almost anywhere. A waitress has to be at the restaurant where she works. At one time, a commodities trader had to be on the floor of an exchange; now he can work from anywhere that has access to a high-speed Internet connection.

In practice, labor market flexibility means that it is relatively easy for employers to manage their workforce, hiring and firing relatively easily and cheaply. Workers can also leave businesses to secure better pay, work conditions, or benefits. Without a caste or formal class system, American workers can advance through corporate hierarchies. It may not be as common as the national mythology would have us believe, but it is possible to start at the bottom and end up running the show, as Ronald Reagan's, Bill Clinton's, and Barack Obama's inspiring examples illustrate on the political stage. The hallmark of the American job market is a highly skilled workforce, with little unionization and vacation, a defined-contribution pension scheme, and a relatively light basket of goods provided by the state in the form of health care or generous unemployment benefits, for example.

America has also been one of the world's foremost importers of labor. For most of the nation's history, the country has more or less welcomed immigrants. Until World War I, the United States absorbed the world's surplus people. Many of the new arrivals provided cheap, docile labor that allowed the Industrial Revolution to happen. (Of course, the workers didn't stay cheap or docile for long.) People came here to work, sometimes at great personal cost; as much as they wanted the job, they didn't necessarily want to give up their family and culture back home. They'd often re-create life at home as best they could when they got here, making the United States a diverse, interesting place that attracted even more immigrants.

Although most Americans are descended from immigrants, the nation has not always welcomed them. And often people don't always want to move to another country if they can find good economic activities and a prosperous life, broadly defined, at home. When it became possible to do more jobs remotely, the workers stayed put, and this appears to have adversely impacted the U.S. trade balance. If a computer programmer moves from India to the United States, then his work is all part of the U.S. gross domestic product. If he stays in India and sends his code to a developer in San Jose, then his work is part of India's gross domestic product: services exported to the United States increase the amount of American imports, making the current account deficit wider.

Technological progress has entailed replacing human effort with machines. The labor-saving nature of these advances is an important— even if faceless—source of instability in the workforce. New processes need to be constantly learned; otherwise, one becomes obsolete as a worker. Individuals can invest in developing a skill set only to find that a technological advance means the once important skill set is no longer required. The ubiquitous PDA and personal computers have replaced secretaries and voice mail receptionists.

Intrafirm Trade

ThyssenKrupp, a global steel manufacturer based in Germany, has been expanding in the Western Hemisphere. The company refers to it as its "NAFTA Strategy," after the North American Free Trade Agreement. In Brazil, ThyssenKrupp is building a slab mill projected to produce 5 million metric tons of steel a year beginning in 2009, using iron ore mined in that country. Some of the slabs will stay in Brazil, where the growing economy needs basic steel products. The rest will be shipped to ThyssenKrupp's production facilities elsewhere in the world. One of those is a rolling mill being built in Calvert, Alabama; the plant, scheduled to open in 2010, will turn some of those slabs into high-quality flat steel used in cars and appliances. It will turn other slabs into rolled coil that will be used to make stainless steel at ThyssenKrupp's San Luis Potosi, Mexico facility.[3]

This strategy lets ThyssenKrupp take advantage of the different resources, worker skills, and market demands throughout the Americas, where free trade agreements make the movement of goods economical. When the trade accounting is done, this strategy will increase Brazil's exports, increase both imports and exports in the United States, and increase imports for Mexico, yet all the steel stays within the same corporate boundaries. This is how business is done in the modern multinational corporation.

Intrafirm trade plays a crucial role in the operations of multinationals. It creates opportunities for cost savings, improved distribution of goods, the secure acquisition of inputs, and better integration of production. In the modern economy, intrafirm trade may be cheaper and more expedient than human migration. It is easier to move the goods to take advantage of different skill levels and wage rates. It is easier to make parts in one place and ship them to another for assembly than to move the assembly workers, who will ask pesky questions about language training and moving expenses and tax differentials.

Globalization means a great deal more than outsourcing. Trade has become "in-sourced." The movement of goods and services within the same company but across national borders is a critical but often overlooked feature of the modern political economy. The logistics of managing supply, production, and distribution around the world is exceedingly complex. Modern multinational corporations have internalized trade. The United Nations estimates that trade among related parties accounts for as much as one-third of global trade. It appears to be higher in the United States, which makes sense given that it is the headquarters for so many global corporations.

Unlike most trade figures, intrafirm trade numbers are not reported on a regular basis. The most recent data shows that, in 2005, affiliated exports accounted for nearly 28.8 percent of all U.S. exports and nearly one-third of all U.S. *goods* exports. In the same year, imports from affiliated parties accounted for more than one-third of all U.S. imports and 36.5 percent of all U.S. *goods* imports. In 2005, intrafirm trade accounted for $302.9 billion of the $666.3 billion current account deficit recorded by the United States.[4]

Some of the increase in intrafirm trade in recent years is due to more free trade agreements that make it easier for companies to spread their production processes across many countries, such as the North

American Free Trade Agreement, and some of it was due to the policy response to the 1997–98 Asian financial crisis. At that time, the newly industrialized nations in the region were forced to sell assets and devalue their currencies, which made it cheaper for foreign companies, including American, to own local production and distribution facilities.

The intrafirm trade data include transactions between U.S. companies and their overseas affiliates as well as between foreign companies and their U.S. affiliates. Usually, intrafirm exports by U.S. multinational companies to their foreign-based affiliates appear to be largely for additional manufacturing. Intrafirm U.S. imports by affiliates of foreign multinational companies, on the other hand, appear mainly for marketing and distribution purposes.

Sometimes, intrafirm trade by U.S.-based multinational companies actually produces a small trade surplus. This trade surplus in 1993 stood at $36.5 billion, even though that year the United States recorded an overall trade deficit of $70.2 billion. The surplus generated by intrafirm trade of U.S. multinationals consisted of a $16.7 billion surplus on goods trade and a $19.8 billion surplus on service trade. A decade later, in 2002, the surplus had fallen to $9.3 billion. This reflected a deficit in goods trade of $25.3 billion and a $34.6 billion surplus on services. The swing into deficit on the goods trade appears to reflect the vertical integration of the North American economy under NAFTA.[5]

In contrast, intrafirm trade between U.S.-based affiliates and their foreign parents have consistently produced significant trade deficits. In 1993, the overall deficit by this type of intrafirm trade stood at $104.9 billion, almost 50 percent larger than the overall U.S. trade deficit that year. It was not until 1998, in the aftermath of the Asian financial crisis, that the overall U.S. trade deficit was larger than the trade deficit created by the intrafirm trade of U.S.-based affiliates and their foreign parents. By 2005, intrafirm trade of U.S.-based affiliates and their foreign parents produced a deficit of $302.9 billion, which was a little less than half the $666.3 billion overall U.S. trade deficit that year.[6]

Some forces are pushing in the opposite direction. Some corporate restructuring has involved U.S. companies outsourcing nonessential business functions to other companies, often overseas. This has contributed to the growth of the U.S. trade deficit, although not to the growth of intracompany trade. For example, a U.S.-based company that once owned factories making running shoes in East Asia may have sold the factory to someone else and then outsourced its production to the new owner. This lets the company reduce its fixed costs, giving it more flexibility in managing its inventory. Trade that once took place within the firm now takes place between legally unrelated parties. Yet the larger point remains valid: intrafirm trade has contributed to the growth of the U.S. trade deficit.

Capital and Exchange Rates

There are good reasons to suspect that trade between related parties may respond differently to changes in the general economic environment, including foreign exchange prices, than trade between unrelated parties. For example, a sharp appreciation of the yen might not deter a Japan-based car parts supplier from exporting components to a U.S.-based affiliate, at least not in the short or medium term. In this respect, the significance of intrafirm trade might contribute to making the U.S. trade deficit less sensitive to currency fluctuations than policy makers and businesses would like or economists would anticipate.

Trade within a company may not respond to economic forces or exchange rates in the same way as trade outside of a company. Because of other considerations, including access to substitutes, corporate organization, and fixed capacity utilization, it might make perfect sense for a company to ship components from an overseas division to the United States, even if the dollar weakens. Businesses engage in long-term contracts and build relationships, such as product codevelopment, that make it difficult to change suppliers in short order.

Intrafirm trade doesn't require the kind of external financing associated with trade between unrelated parties. Normally, their banks ensure that both parties pay in full and on time, which is more complex when national boundaries and different currencies are involved. If the trade happens within a company, though, no external financial institutions are involved. The accounting staff will make accounting entries on the books of the affiliates doing the trading, but no funds actually need to be transferred. No market event needs to take place. A sale is recorded for trade purposes when the customs documents are completed, but no actual sale took place. To put it another way, the capital and financial accounts of the balance of payments aren't financing our trade deficit but showing surplus capital transactions made for investment reasons.

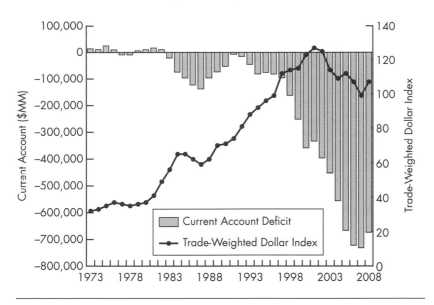

FIGURE 4.1   U.S. Current Account versus the Trade-Weighted Dollar Index

Source: U.S. Bureau of Economic Analysis. "U.S. International Transactions: First Quarter 2008." Washington, DC: U.S. Department of Commerce, June 17, 2008. Federal Reserve Bank of St. Louis Trade-Weighted Exchange Index.

The significant role of intrafirm turn may help explain why the movement in the U.S. trade deficit is a poor predictor of the movement of the dollar. There appears to be little statistically significant correlation between the U.S. trade position and the direction of the dollar, as illustrated in *Figure 4.1.*[7]

Savings and Investment

Economics recognizes an identity or truism that the difference between a nation's savings and investment is equal to the current account deficit. The argument presented here is that traditional metrics such as the U.S. current account deficit are overstated; one implication is that savings, in turn, may be understated. This seems to indeed be the case.

Consider the problem of measuring retirement savings on a national level. The United States has the most developed defined-contribution pension system in the world. Employer contributions are counted as income, as they should be. However, the payouts to retirees are considered consumption. Yet the payouts, which are not registered, are inflated by capital appreciation. The total amount of money that the worker had in the account (it is hoped) increased between the day that the money was taken from the paycheck and the day that it is cashed out of the retirement fund, but none of the real increase in wealth is included in the savings rate as it is calculated.

Furthermore, wealth created by rising residential real estate prices and stock price appreciation is not included in many measures of savings, which probably served to understate the wealth effect of the 2002–07 expansion and rise in asset prices. Most years, real estate appreciates at the rate of inflation, and such U.S. market indexes as Standard & Poor's 500 Index tend to increase at a rate well above inflation. This represents a steady increase in the value of assets owned by American households, but it does not show up as savings. Because equity and home ownership are more widespread in the United States than in most other countries, it represents a bigger distortion in our household savings rates than it does elsewhere.

Savings measures overlook another form of American investment. Households save up money, but what for? One big goal, in the United States, is college education. The American university system is academically rigorous and, through community colleges and evening programs, accessible to almost all. The payoff of a college degree is a higher salary: over a lifetime, a white worker with a bachelor's degree will earn $1,902,033, whereas the same person with just a high-school diploma will earn $1,070,692. With an advanced degree, that worker would bring in $2,663,080.[8] The difference more than makes up for the cost of tuition and lost wages while the student is in school. People with a college education qualify for higher-paying jobs and have more flexibility in a changing economy. It's an investment that people make in their future.

However, college expenses don't show up in GDP accounting as investments. Instead, they are tracked as consumption. A college student doesn't invest money in his future when he plunks down hundreds of dollars for textbooks. Instead, from an economist's perspective, he's out shopping, the same as if he spent those hundreds of dollars on a suit, golf clubs, or a flat-screen television. This key piece of American savings and investment is not included in official measures even though it may be the most important, if not the biggest, investment that households make. It does show up in America's high per-capita income and GDP, which continue to grow despite our low recorded-savings rate.

Instead of regarding savings as the residual of income minus consumption, it might be more accurate to consider the ratio of household net worth to disposable income. In addition to household savings, the national savings calculation includes corporate savings and the government's fiscal position. U.S. corporate savings stand near the highest rate in decades. However, the conventional measure probably under states the amount because the official definition of savings and investment does not include research-and-development expenditures. Even though investment in new ideas and technologies is one of the keys to innovation and wealth creation, the government regards it as consumption. Surely it is an investment that, like other investments, ought to be counted among the nation's savings.

The definition of savings has changed before, and maybe it should again to reflect the investments made by American workers out of their income. It was not until 1999 that software expenditures by business and government began to be included in the U.S. definition of investment, savings, even though those investments made it possible for workers to do far more work in less time. Because the United States is among the most modern capitalist nations, with an extensive and a relatively quick dispersion of new technologies, and because it spends more per capita on higher education than other major industrialized countries, the antiquated definition of savings penalizes America the most.

In addition to workers investing their own fruits of labor into retirement plans, equity mutual funds, and new houses, the capital markets have ways to trade labor, and not necessarily in a form that Marx would recognize or appreciate. English singer David Bowie famously sold the rights to the income from his pre-1990 works through bonds issued in 1997; similar bonds are now known as Bowie bonds, even though new issues are tied to the works of other artists. When she was fourteen, tennis player Ana Ivanovic received backing from Swiss businessman Dan Holzmann, who agreed to pay for her coaching in exchange for a cut of her winnings when she hit it big, which she did in 2008 when she won the French Open. Two U.K. hedge funds, Hero Investments and Sports Asset Capital, are negotiating similar arrangements with up-and-coming soccer players.

Trade and Aid

In his 1949 inaugural address, U.S. President Harry S. Truman announced a plan to help the world recover from war. "We must embark on a bold new program for . . . the improvement and growth of underdeveloped areas," he said. "More than half the people of the world are living in conditions approaching misery. . . . For the first time in history, humanity possesses the knowledge and the skill to relieve the suffering of these people."[9]

And that is what Truman and several of his successors tried to do. After World War II, the United States and other nations embarked on a plan to elevate less-developed nations into modernity. Instead of people having to move to the United States (or Canada or Australia) to make their fortunes, they could stay where they were and benefit from a changed society. The U.S. government encouraged American corporations to invest overseas and to set up trade in order to help rebuild war-torn economies. The relative strength of the dollar provided a powerful economic incentive. At the same time, American workers were freed to work on projects that added more value to the economy, especially in communications and technology.

Some nations—notably India and China—have shown dramatic improvements, but much of the world remains stuck despite foreign aid and increased school enrollment and other panaceas offered by well-meaning people.

Many people live in poverty because their government officials simply do not care about the public good. In these places, the highest returns are earned by lobbying the government. It's not what you know, but who you know that matters, whether it's a K Street lobbyist dispensing political action committee funds or a fixer who can help you win the contract in exchange for a suitcase full of cash. It's what economists call *rent-seeking behavior.* Rent-seeking activities reallocate resources, like money, but they do not create wealth or help raise living standards the way growth does. Rent seeking takes place in developed and developing countries and everywhere undermines the rule of law and entrepreneurship while fostering corruption and cynicism.

In some developing countries, rent seekers rather than profit seekers have captured the foreign exchange market. Maybe the government has a fixed exchange rate, which was the foremost orthodoxy in capitalism's history. It prohibits trading in foreign currencies, and its currency is undervalued, which in this country feeds quickly through into domestic inflation. That creates profitable opportunities for trading foreign exchange. Skilled people will lobby the government for access to foreign exchange so that they can sell it for a hefty profit in the black market. Will those people be the prime minister's friends and relatives? No matter who those folks are, their activities do not contribute to GDP and simply redistribute income.

Education can be a center of corruption, too, especially if millions of dollars of foreign aid is flowing into it. Administrators may be hired for their connections to the people in power rather than their pedagogical expertise. Teachers, in turn, may receive low salaries, and not enough money may be spent on textbooks, paper, or pencils—at least not after accounting for any enticements paid to vendors associated with the government.

In Pakistan, politicians disperse teaching posts as patronage; three-quarters of teachers could not pass the exams they administered. The language taught in schools is Urdu, but the working language in that multilingual society is English. In other countries, education can create a supply of skills for which there is no demand, and so the skills go to waste, whether in the form of highly educated taxi drivers or administrative assistants with masters' degrees in art history.

Development, Labor, and the Flexibility of Capital and Labor

It's easy for a person to move between labor and ownership if it's easy to start a business. In the United States, the process involves about six procedures and takes six days. In Egypt, it takes six steps over seven days. In India, though, it takes thirteen processes and thirty days. In China, it takes fourteen steps and forty days. And in Brazil, the prospective entrepreneur has eighteen tasks to perform over 182 days.[10]

Another measure of labor-force flexibility is how long it takes to dismiss workers. Whether the employee is a shirker or the economy is sliding into recession, there are perfectly valid reasons for letting workers go. But it's not always easy to do, and not just because of the human component. In some countries, laws and customs make it difficult and expensive to fire people. In the United States, it's pretty easy to hire and fire, with no required cost to the company. In Egypt, a company has to pay a fired worker 132 weeks of salary as compensation. In India, it's fifty-six weeks; and in China, it's ninety-one weeks. Brazilians aren't so fortunate; they receive just thirty-seven weeks of salary as severance.[11]

It may seem counterintuitive, but another measure of the strength of a nation's business climate is how long it takes to close a business. If a company isn't doing well, shutting it down lets the owner rescue capital to put somewhere else. But it's not easy to close a business everywhere. If entrepreneurs think that they will lose most of their capital in the event of a business failure, then they will be less willing to commit it in the first place.

In the United States, closing a business takes a year and a half from start to finish and costs about 7 percent of the business assets; unsecured creditors recover an average of 76.7 percent of the assets in case of bankruptcy. In Brazil, it takes four years and costs 12 percent of assets. In case of failure, the creditors typically recover just 17.1 percent of the assets. In Egypt, it takes 4.2 years and costs 22 percent of assets, and the recovery rate is 16.8 percent. In China, it takes 1.7 years to close a business, at a cost of 22 percent, and has a recovery rate of just 35.3 percent.[12]

Many of these costs of "doing business" cannot be laid at the feet of geography, demographics, terms of trade, or exploitations. Making it easier and cheaper to start a business, register property, hire and fire workers (the United States need not set the standard here, but three years of compensation seems excessive), and have reasonable bankruptcy laws is well within the reach of most countries at little or no cost.

The Reality of Labor and Trade

With technology, farms require fewer people to operate. The corn still grows in Illinois, but it's hybridized, chemically enhanced, and mechanically planted and harvested. The farmer doesn't have to live on the land because the farmer is probably a major agribusiness conglomerate using hired hands who commute to the job. The same process has been repeated in manufacturing and appears to some extent to be taking place in some service-sector functions as well.

Technology changes the relationship between the work and the place. People who once could find work where they lived now have to move, whereas others who once would have had to move to pursue a chosen occupation can stay put.

The United States had open borders for much of its history, and it's always been open internally. With its vast geography, the fed-up city dweller can move to a quiet rural hamlet while the bored small-town kid can pack up for the bright lights of Manhattan. That's not true everywhere; in China, for example, people need government permission to change their place of residency. That mobility certainly helped American economic growth, but it isn't the secret.

If you can't move the people, you can move the work, and that's easier than ever because of fast and inexpensive transportation, improved information and communication technology (which transports data), and reduced barriers to trade. A company can have intricate supply chains and a complicated production process spread out over long distances. The design and marketing may be done in the United States, but the accounting can be handled in India and customer inquiries out of Canada. A finished good and the services associated before and after production and sales are an amalgam of tens, hundreds, or thousands of different processes that come together at the very end.

Because so much trade takes place within a corporation's walls, the size of the trade deficit and the amount of capital needed to support trade may both be overstated. Furthermore, the contributions of American workers to the nation's growth end up being understated. Their investments in education are ignored, although that spending explains much of the skill of the American workforce.

In the narrative often told of America's economic prowess, economists—many of whom hold tenured posts at universities—emphasize the flexibility of the U.S. labor market. Yet most Americans experience the flexibility of labor as being hired and fired at will, as wages that don't keep pace with inflation, as having a defined-benefits pension program swapped for a defined-contribution scheme in which one's own economic and consumer knowledge is paramount.

American workers are highly productive, and it is their productivity, rather than their flexibility, that explains the nation's economic success. Moreover, that productivity appears to be enhanced by capital market flexibility.

Bank lending is often a binary decision. The terms have to be negotiated. The capital markets have money for anyone: bankrupt businesses, innovators and inventors, and even musicians who want to be paid now for royalties to be earned in the future. The extensive development of the capital markets and what appeared to be the disintermediation of banks has been challenged by the credit crisis to be sure, but the resolution will likely be more transparency, more disintermediation, and stronger and different regulations. The credit crisis will not mark the death knell of financial innovation, although it may shape the direction that future innovation takes. The credit crisis also reveals the need for new metrics for measuring and monitoring risk.

Workers in developing countries have the same potential as workers in the United States, but they need to have an institutional infrastructure that can be integrated into the world economy. Property rights need to be created and enforced, business procedures need to be streamlined, and capital from investors in other countries has to be welcomed in order to bring in the money and ideas needed to get the economy rolling. International corporations, looking for new markets and for workers who can handle different facets of their business can often act as agents of change.

Chapter Notes

1. U.S. Bureau of Economic Analysis. *Survey of Current Business*, January 2008 (Vol. 88, No. 1).

2. U.S. Census Bureau. "U.S. International Trade in Goods and Services—Annual Revision for 2005," 9 June 2006 (http://www.census.gov/foreign-trade/Press-Release/2005pr/final_revisions/).

3. See http://www.thyssenkrupp.com/en/nordamerika/mexiko/index.html (accessed September 20, 2008).

4. U.S. Bureau of Economic Analysis. *Survey of Current Business*, January 2008. U.S. Census Bureau. "U.S. International Trade in Goods and Services—Annual Revision for 2005," June 9, 2006 (http://www.census.gov/foreign-trade/Press-Release/2005pr/final_revisions/).

5. Ibid.

6. Ibid.

7. U.S. Bureau of Economic Analysis. "U.S. International Transactions: First Quarter 2008." Washington, DC: U.S. Department of Commerce, June 17, 2008. Federal

Reserve Bank of St. Louis. "Trade-Weighted Exchange Index" (http://research. stlouisfed.org/fred2/series/TWEX/downloaddata/TWEX.XLS).

8. U.S. Census Bureau. *The Big Payoff: Educational Attainment and Synthetic Estimates of Work-Life Earnings*. Washington, DC: U.S. Department of Commerce, July 2002 (http://www.census.gov/prod/2002pubs/p23-210.pdf). Numbers are in 1999 dollars.

9. Inaugural Address of Harry S. Truman, January 20, 1949 (http://avalon.law.yale. edu/20th_century/truman.asp).

10. International Finance Corporation, *Doing Business 2009* (http://www.ifc.org/ ifcext/media.nsf/Content/Doing_Business_2009).

11. Ibid.

12. Ibid.

There Is One Type of Capitalism

It's not us versus them; it's more like the American League versus the National League. We may be on the same side, but we're not on the same team.

The opening up of China's economy begun in the late 1970s, and the collapse of the Soviet bloc a decade later acknowledged that there was no real alternative to capitalist development. Yet capitalism as it is practiced varies greatly. The size and role of government varies greatly. Capitalist countries have different regulatory regimes, and this has been made clear in the credit crisis. The basket of goods and services—things such as health care, family support, education, public transportation, and civil liberties—differ as well. So do the responsibilities of the citizenry: in some countries, voting is mandatory, as is military service.

The world's many capitalists are playing the same game but using different rules. Some countries are providing support for different parts of their economies, which makes even the fairest of free trade agreements a little less than perfect. Whether they cover government manipulation of interest rates, currency regime, nationalized health insurance, or limits on lead for toys, these rules can affect competitiveness and international trade.

Three of the four countries to which the investment bank Goldman Sachs gave the now ubiquitous "BRIC" (Brazil, Russia, India, and China) label were regarded as socialist for many years. Russia, India, and China practiced what they called "socialism" for years, although they practiced different forms of it. Brazil was the capitalist exception, but was often dominated by rent-seeking behavior.

This stands to reason. As a historian and economist, Karl Marx had envisioned that socialism would first appear in Germany or Great Britain, where capitalism was the most advanced. Instead, the Bolsheviks tried to graft socialist principles to a largely agrarian, preindustrial country. In China, Mao Zedong gave communism Chinese characteristics to match the needs of China as well as his own interests. In his interpretation, the People's Liberation Army turned peasants into soldiers and soldiers into proletariats and the proletariats into comrades. India, meanwhile, wanted to use collective resources to improve the lives of its desperately poor people, but it also wanted to give them a voice in government that had been denied under British rule. From three different forms of socialism emerged three different types of capitalism.

Capitalism does not mean that markets control everything, nor does socialism mean that the state controls all. Capitalism simply means that the assets of production are privately owned and operated for profit. In earlier times, power often was based on might or divine right, but in capitalist societies, power emanates from the ownership of private property. That's it.

Exactly which assets are privatized and how they operate in pursuit of that profit varies from Ohio to Alabama, and it varies from France to Vietnam. Capitalist countries, for example, have stock markets, where corporate securities can be bought and sold. However, while forms may be similar, the function is not. In the United States, the equity market is where businesses can raise capital, and risk can be broken down into palatable packages (shares) and distributed. In contrast, the stock market in Japan was traditionally a place where companies could solidify corporate alliances and interlocking ownership.

The role and extent of the governments' activities vary in ways that neither Adam Smith nor Karl Marx could have anticipated. With a better understanding of the varieties of capitalism, people can make more nuanced decisions about trade than they can using the tired right–left or free markets–socialism simple dualisms.

Capitalism arose from within the feudal system. Once, someone owned the land; through reciprocal rights and responsibilities, the peasant would grow a crop and surrender part of it to the feudal lord in exchange for a place to live, a role on the manor, and other protections. Under capitalism, someone owns the shops, the factories, and the ships and gives the workers cash money in exchange for their labors. To Marx, capitalism was an exploitative system but was superior to feudalism and other premodern social organizations. Marx wrote (or maybe it was really his collaborator, Friedrich Engels) for the *New York Tribune* during the American Civil War. There is no doubt that, as opposed to capitalism as he was, Marx clearly favored the capitalist North over the slave-owning South.

The Forms of Capitalism

Leaders in capitalist nations don't open a copy of Adam Smith's *Wealth of Nations* and start checking items off a list. Instead, capitalism in each nation evolves from a base of private ownership and profit generation along with traditions, social structures, and needs unique to the country. The size of the country matters, too. Capitalism means something different in Iceland than in the United States, which has a thousand times more people and far more land and natural resources than Iceland does. The United States can be more flexible in a crisis for this reason. Yet there are some similarities in types of capitalism within all this diversity.

The world's established capitalist nations can be loosely sorted into three categories: liberal market capitalism, which is associated with Anglo-American economies; the corporate market capitalism typical of Asia; and coordinated market capitalism, sometimes called the *Rhine model,* which marks the modern social-democratic European economy. Each style has advantages in some types of markets and disadvantages in others.[1]

Market-led capitalism is what people usually associate with Anglo-American economies. Under it, the highest values are innovation and entrepreneurship. The idea is that the market is the most efficient mechanism for the production and distribution of goods and services. To borrow from American political scientist Harold Laswell's definition of politics, market mechanisms and the price discovery process provide better answers to the question who gets what, when, and how than such alternatives as a lottery, a government bureaucrat, or a commissar.[2] The market encourages ideas, innovation, and individual initiative. Meanwhile, the purpose of government in liberal market capitalism is to establish and enforce the rules of competition and provide services that the markets may fail to deliver or are socially desirable even if unprofitable, including education, health care, transportation, infrastructure, and, of course, national defense. Yet the state's role is comparatively small. This is the style of the United States, many former English colonies, and, to a lesser extent, modern Great Britain.

Under corporate capitalism, large businesses—often growing out of kinship ties—set the tone. A handful of conglomerates, frequently family controlled, manage all phases of production and distribution. Workers have long careers with the same employer because they can move among many different divisions; the company can take profits from successful business units and invest them in research and development. Shareholders, often employees and their families, hold their position out of loyalty. The corporation, not the government, becomes the protector of the welfare of the workers. This style is typical of Asian capitalism, marked by the Japanese keiretsu and the Korean chaebol.

Social-democratic capitalism, common in Europe, is sometimes viewed as more socialist than capitalist, but market forces remain strong. Workers have the power to negotiate as partners with businesses and the government. Taxes tend to be high because the government provides an extensive basket of goods and services to its citizenry: support for health care, education, child care, retirement, and cultural institutions. It may not be as flexible as other forms of capitalism, because employers have to comply with onerous mandates and the governments often seem more concerned with welfare than with commerce. But it also tends to create a stable society with little or no poverty and less economic inequality. Sometimes known as the Rhine model, it emphasizes collective achievement and public consensus in the hope of achieving both economic efficiency and social justice.

Within these models, the citizens determine how to allocate resources. The larger the nation, the more resources and the more choices different groups within it can make. Japan, with 127 million people, has more flexibility than South Korea, which has about one-third the number of people, even though both countries use a similar model of capitalism. Although Canada has far more land and natural resources than the United States, it has only about a tenth the number of people, almost forcing a less-diversified economy than in the United States even though the capitalist style is broadly similar.

In addition to the differences caused by the absolute size of the nation, the size of the government relative to the economy also varies.

Governments provide the infrastructure that makes commerce possible: defense, property rights, and contract enforcement; roads, communications, and airports; education and basic health care. Some governments provide more services than others. Some government policies help businesses, and some hurt them.

One way to measure the differences among capitalist countries is to look at government spending as a percentage of gross domestic product (GDP). The Organization for Economic Cooperation and Development (OECD) compiles this data for a range of developed capitalist nations. As illustrated in *Figure 5.1*, in 2007 the U.S. government spent an estimated 37.4 percent of GDP compared to the average for OECD member nations of 40.4 percent.[3] The French government spent 52.4 percent of that country's GDP, the highest percentage in the sample; the lowest is Korea at 30.7 percent.

Although the relationships are not perfect, Asia's developed capitalist nations are to the left on the graph in Figure 5.1, with relatively little government spending because large corporations provide the

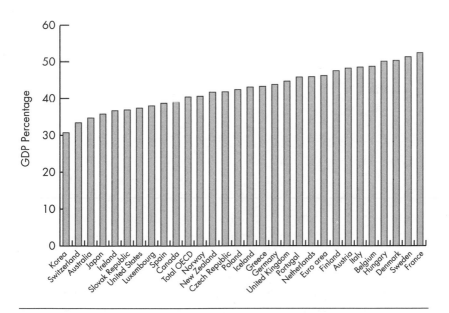

FIGURE 5.1   Government Spending as a Percentage of GDP, 2007

Source: "Table 25. General Government Total Outlays." *OECD Economic Outlook No. 83—Annex Tables.* Paris: OECD, June 2008.

safety net. The former English colonies of the United States, Australia, Canada, and New Zealand, are mostly clustered to the right of the Asian nations, with the government providing more support to business than in Europe but with a heavy reliance on the private sector. The United Kingdom and most other European nations dominate the right of the chart with greater government support. (Note that the U.K. government spends relatively less than many of its European neighbors, showing its Anglo-style capitalist roots.)

Switzerland is an outlier, spending far less of its GDP than any industrialized nation but South Korea; the United Kingdom is a big spender, but it still spends less than many other nations in Europe. Switzerland and the United Kingdom have something else in common. Both nations kept their own currency rather than join the Economic and Monetary Union (EMU) and convert to the euro. (The United Kingdom belongs to the European Union, but Switzerland does not.)

The EMU has been an ongoing experiment in linking the economies of nations with very different cultures without political union. Although the cultural and historic differences between France and Belgium may not be as great as those between South Korea and Sweden, they are real. Recent research sponsored by the European Commission found that monetary union reduced income equality in Europe, although part of the hope for the euro and its predecessor, the European currency unit, was to foster greater economic integration on the continent and reduce the stark regional inequality. From 1977 to 2003, income disparities among European nations declined but remained at twice the levels of the disparities among U.S. states; within countries using the euro, income inequality increased.[4]

No matter where it takes root, capitalism grows on the soil of existing institutions, even if it modifies them and spawns new ones. These are organic, reflecting the culture and the needs of the people and the businesses. And they are not transferable; grafting an educational, religious, or cultural institution that works in one country on to another doesn't mean that it will thrive elsewhere. Nor can an institution be changed in isolation. The American liberal education, for example, is a function of the political economy: it needs workers who have a broad background to learn new skills because capital is flexible and jobs and industries change often. In Japan, the complexity of the language means that the educational system emphasizes memorization; without it, few people could be truly fluent. In Scandinavia, the countries are so small that the people almost have to learn foreign languages so they can interact with others. These differences affect how Americans, Japanese, and Swedes approach business. Although there's a risk of stereotyping when discussing cultural issues, the culture influences the way that people operate. It makes global business far more interesting and nuanced than simply going to different restaurants.

China, India, Russia

Three nations have recently embraced capitalism: all are large in terms of land and population, poor in terms of per-capita income, and new to the modern era of global trade. China, India, and Russia all spent portions of the twentieth century under self-declared socialism. China and Russia had communist-led revolutions; India was never communist, but the nation flirted with socialist economic practices early in its independence. These new capitalist countries look to conquer the market under very different political systems, abandoning socialism in very different ways. China remains officially communist, India is the world's largest democracy, and Russia appears to be slipping into autocracy.

China is unabashedly capitalist and unabashedly Chinese. Modern China is hardly a democracy, and it may not be one anytime soon. Russia, by contrast, had a brief burst of democratic fervor before settling back into a more authoritarian government that maintains only the appearance of democratic mechanisms. Some of the old elite in the Soviet Union managed to remain in power, but now as capitalists instead of communists. They exploited the nation's resources, especially oil and gas, for power and profit throughout Europe. Russia may be wealthier now than under communism, but it's not clear that the realm of freedom or liberty has increased. Birthrates are low, emigration is high, and longevity has fallen.

In India, the nation's open society has helped its development. It has a diverse population, and many people have worked or studied abroad. The Indian diaspora creates the basis for global networks with nodes (contacts) all over the world to help them build connections to grow business at home. Many entrepreneurs have built on the language of the colonists, English, to provide outsourced technical support to American and European countries that ranges from accounting to

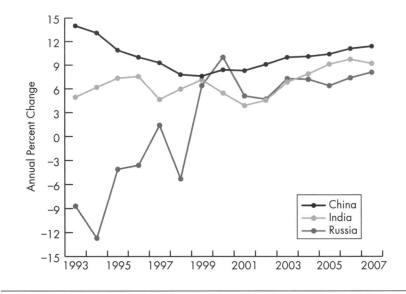

FIGURE 5.2   GDP Growth of China, India, and Russia, 1993–2007

Source: International Monetary Fund.

catalog customer service. But India is still poor, and it still has a culture of petty corruption.

Since 1993, China, India, and Russia have all been growing their economies. As shown in *Figure 5.2*, Russia's trajectory of GDP growth has been fitful, in part due to its debt default in 1998. China's growth has often been at double-digit levels. India's growth has been a bit steadier and still higher than levels experienced in more developed nations.[5] By any measure, the gains are impressive and show that capitalism is building these nations' economies.

Which of these approaches to capitalism is best? The question makes no sense because no matter what is proven to work in Russia, China, or India, the knowledge might not be transferable. The cultural and demographic differences between the nations are great: China had centuries of dynastic rule; India is brilliantly polyglot and long colonized; Russia has a history of strong, central leadership.

There is no such thing as the best capitalism in the abstract. It is contextual. What works in one country may not work or be acceptable in another country. What works is a function of country-specific context: geography, endowments, institutional relations, inertia, composition, and governing coalitions. The use of temporary workers, expectations that office workers will eat lunch at their desks, and two-week standard annual vacations may be unobjectionable or the norm in one country but not in another. What is best is reflective of certain cultural values. A society that is culturally or ethnically homogenous will have different norms than one that's diverse. Culture matters.

An economy structured so that it is relatively easy to get a job—and relatively easy to lose it—will have a set of institutions and investment incentives different from one in which it is hard to get a job but hard to be fired once hired. The first will have more resources dedicated to training and career development, for example, but less loyalty between employer and employee. The latter may need more resources for labor relations because employee and employer are expected to spend so much time together. But both approaches to employment can be capitalist.

Capitalism and Capital Structure

Under modern globalization, when production tends to be capital-intensive (equipment and technology), the way in which it is accessed and distributed is a key difference among the different capitalisms. Whether they are banks, pension funds, the government, or the entrepreneur's relatives, investors expect to make a profit from their investment. Expectations are influenced by the amount of risk being taken and the alternative uses for their money. Stocks are riskier than bonds, so stock investors expect a higher return than bond investors. And stocks are easier to trade than bonds are, and are unsecured creditors if the company fails, so equity investors may be less patient with poor performance than bond investors.

Some differences in capital structure can be explained by the cash flow characteristics of different industries. Utilities, which have predictable cash flows, are more likely to use bonds for financing than technology companies, which prefer the flexibility of equity. Capital structure will also be influenced by the distribution of industries in a particular country.

American companies get much of their capital from the capital markets, which tend to be more fickle than banks, the other main source of investment capital. European and Japanese companies tend to have more long-term or patient capital, especially from banks and bondholders. Debt securities can be traded, but often the secondary market in Europe and Japan is notoriously light. Lenders prefer a nice, steady stream of interest payments rather than collecting capital gains. Companies that rely on such debt don't have to worry as much about short-term earnings fluctuations, provided there is confidence in the overall strategy.

Although this seems straightforward, there are important consequences. An American (or, for that matter, British) company experiencing a sharp appreciation of its functional currency would be likely to pass a greater part of it on to its customers in order to maintain earnings performance. The incentive structure is such that companies need to maintain profit margins or face a higher price of capital. In essence, they are willing to sacrifice market share for earnings.[6] A Japanese or continental European company, with access to the more patient capital, may accept some compression in profit margins in order to preserve market share, which is the key to the enterprise's long-term strategic viability. Indeed, the different competitive modes may help explain why the pass-through from dollar depreciation is limited, which in turn reduces the impact of a falling dollar on the U.S. trade balance.

The European Union's BACH Database tracks financial data for manufacturing companies in several EU nations, the United States, and Europe. As illustrated in *Figure 5.3,* in 2005 the average U.S. manufacturing company had a balance sheet that was 58 percent debt and liabilities, 42 percent equity. France, Japan, and Germany had significantly more debt and less capital.[7]

Equity holders don't demand steady cash flow, but they can get out of an investment easily. That, in turn, can hurt a company's ability to make acquisitions, upset employees who received stock as part of their compensation, and raise anxiety about potential layoffs and frighten customers concerned about the company's long-term viability.

A privately held corporation, managed by its owners, may follow the whims of those owners even if they do not lead to profits. The interest may instead be to maximize pay, afford a private jet, increase community visibility, or follow some quixotic interest. Profit may not be

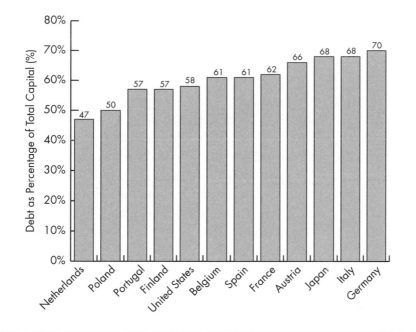

FIGURE **5.3**   European Union BACH Database of Harmonized
Company Accounts, 1995–2007

Source: European Committee of Central Balance Sheet Data Offices.

the driver at all; the owner–managers answer to themselves and define
value in their own way. That makes it the most patient of all capital. It's
also the most constraining, because few companies can become significant players without external financing.

A company that takes on outside shareholders, whether in the public or the private market, becomes accountable to someone else. If the
new investor is a private investor or private equity firm, then it will
probably expect the management to make progress toward high profits.
A public shareholder will probably want consistent earnings per share
growth to support a high stock price. If the company turns to debt
instead of equity, it will not be accountable to a new owner. However,
it will have to generate enough funds to pay principal and interest on
schedule. That may restrict the type of projects that can be sanctioned,
creative projects, or risky new ventures that might threaten the steady
cash flow needed to service the debt.

Broadly conceived, the environment that the business is operating in provides incentives for the capital structure. There is a role for culture; people in some places feel more comfortable with risk. Financial and demographic considerations are also important here as well. If a nation's investor population skews toward retirees, then investors may not be interested in taking much risk with their investments. In some nations, the tax structure favors capital gains from equity over interest from debt, a situation that is reversed in other places. Companies, meanwhile, may find debt more advantageous to issue than equity if corporate tax rates are extremely high. And the state of regulation and stage of market development may lead to more of some types of securities in an economy than others.

A country where commercial banks provide investment banking services may have less flexible capital rates than one where commercial and investment banking are separated, because the former will have less competition than the latter. If a company has ties to one bank for both debt and equity, then it will have to work harder to maintain that one relationship than if it has many relationships.

Even where a market relies on common equity holders for the bulk of the capital, different groups of shareholders have different preferences that affect how the company sets priorities. An individual investor may be patient and feel some loyalty to the company, holding on to the stock through bad times. An institutional investor may care more about performance than anything and thus be quick to sell on bad news. The average mutual funds in the United States have portfolio turnover rates that near 100 percent. A government shareholder may be patient but also have interests not related to profitability, such as employment or technological innovation. A sovereign wealth fund may be interested in profit, but it also has to be cognizant of the effects of its purchases and sales on diplomatic relations and may not seek to influence corporate policy as much as its investment could warrant.

Differences in capital preferences can cause companies to look for lenders and investors in other countries. Cross-border movement of capital could impact the two dimensions of the price of money: interest rates and exchange rates. European and Asian companies often come to the United States for venture capital because American capital structure, institutional arrangement, and culture provide incentives for risk taking. During the second half of the 1990s' technology boom, for example, this demand helped keep the dollar strong. European investors, looking for higher interest rates, lent money to people in emerging nations during the 2000s. This ended abruptly in 2008 when the borrowers proved to be riskier than many lenders had assumed. Many European banks may not have mispriced risk in lending to subprime borrowers as U.S. banks did, but they did misprice the risk of lending to emerging markets and corporations. This was among the considerations that weighed on the euro's exchange rate in the second half of 2008 and in early 2009.

Capitalist Government Priorities

Nations have governments. The culture and the capitalists may set the tone, but the government is heavily involved in how business operates. No matter how free the market, government choices about security, fiscal and monetary policy, and intellectual property protection affect how companies trade in world markets. Even though these are basic levels of government involvement that all but the most anarchic of free traders would accept, they are often overlooked in debates about broader regulation and social welfare.

One form of security is military strength, but another is the structure of the government. Some capitalist nations have little or no democracy, so businesses do not have to worry about periodic about-faces in government priorities. Democratic nations hold elections on different schedules, some more frequently than in others, some on more predictable schedules. All of this affects how much stability companies have in local markets, and that can influence how much energy and enthusiasm go into international trade. Elections lead to uncertainty, even in established democracies with a history of orderly governmental transitions. Investors hate uncertainty and surprises.

Although a few countries outsource their monetary policy by pegging their currency or closely tracking another country's currency, such as the dollar, most conduct their own monetary policy with admittedly varying degrees of freedom. That means figuring the proper quantity (money supply) and price (interest rate) of money. That puts government squarely into the middle of the macroeconomy as officials try to manage inflation, interest rates, GDP growth, and employment.

The Central Bank's Role

Central banks come in various forms, differing mandates, and mixes of policy tools. The way that the central bank is organized affects how it makes decisions, and that in turn may influence the coefficient placed on the variables in the policy-making equation. In the United States, the Federal Open Market Committee holds eight meetings a year. Its members include the seven governors of the Federal Reserve System, the president of the Federal Reserve Bank of New York, and four of the eleven different regional Federal Reserve Bank presidents, who serve one-year terms on a rotating basis. Hence, the Washington-based Board of Governors, which outnumbers the other members of the Open Market Committee, strongly influences the direction of policy. This division of labor became more significant during the credit crisis when many of the Fed's innovative steps, such as creating numerous lending facilities, were results of decisions made by the board while the FOMC, where the regional presidents are represented, was increasingly marginalized.

At the European Central Bank (ECB), the setup is different. The governing board consists of the six members of the ECB executive board and each of the fifteen governors of the central banks of the nations on the euro. Because the core group is small, it could theoretically be outvoted by the governors, who may be more sensitive to the economic conditions in their own country rather than the region as a whole.

Although this risk has not materialized in the ECB's brief history, it is interesting to note that regional Federal Reserve banks, especially the New York bank, at one time dominated the Fed decision making, leading to new institutional arrangements that gave the board a clear majority. As more countries join the EMU, the sheer number of members may make the governing board increasingly unmanageable. There are two ways that the management challenge can be addressed. The first is to limit the size of the governing board in absolute or relative terms. The second is to take a page from America's James Madison's Federalist Paper No. 10 and appreciate that the region is sufficiently economically diverse as to prevent a permanent majority that could challenge the authority of the ECB's executive board.

The institutional and cultural context in which the ECB operates as well as its structure seem to be more significant than the differences that observers typically emphasize. Often the ECB's single mandate for price stability is contrasted with the U.S. Federal Reserve's two mandates: price stability and full employment. The ECB focuses on headline inflation, whereas the Federal Reserve often has cited a preference for a core measure of prices changes of personal consumption expenditures (PCEs). The ECB has adopted its own formal definition of price stability: to keep consumer prices rising around 2 percent. In contrast, the Federal Reserve has an informal target, expressed as a "comfort level" of below 2 percent on the core PCE deflator.

These differences are more apparent than real. The Fed tends to operate as though full employment is only possible when prices are stable. Operationally, the two mandates are not really fundamentally different from the way the ECB has interpreted its single mandate.

Although the ECB has an explicit inflation target, its formality is not so different from the Fed's informal target. The ECB has rarely met its own self-defined inflation measure and rate with no consequences. In contrast, for example, if the Bank of England fails to keep inflation within a specified range around the target given to it by the Chancellor of the Exchequer, it must write a letter explaining itself. Even this level of accountability of a formal inflation target seems quite mild and, outside of some embarrassment, does not appear to be substantively different from the Fed's informal target.

Similarly, observers may exaggerate the significance of core rate of inflation to the Federal Reserve. Although a number of Fed officials have cited the core rate as their preferred measure, they clearly take into account headline rates, too. This is seen in their citation of the breakeven on the Treasury's inflation-protected bonds and inflation expectations picked up in surveys such as the University of Michigan's. Fed officials and ECB officials have both cited the five-year and five-year forward measure that essentially takes the five-year forward rate of the second five years of a ten-year inflation-linked bond to get another reading on long-run inflation expectations.

The most important difference between the Federal Reserve and the European Central Bank may lie more in their organization and the political, cultural, and institutional context in which they operate rather than the more discussed differences such as mandate, inflation measures, and formality of the inflation target. Part of that contextual difference is that the ECB often explicitly warns against wage demands, or what it calls "second-round" impact of higher prices. It was precisely that logic that compelled it to hike rates in early July 2008 in the middle of a historic credit crisis, within a couple of weeks of the end of the euro's multiyear uptrend, and at the end of an incredible boom in commodity prices. Many at the time were critical of the ECB's decision, and history may make a similar judgment.

Intellectual Property and Capitalism

Intellectual property drives capitalism, too. Governments have to protect creators' rights through patents, trademarks, and copyrights, or they will have no incentive to innovate. If the government is too protective, though, it will be difficult for ideas to evolve. How well a government protects ideas can affect how eager companies are to do business there and how much new technology is created. It has long been forgotten that Charles Dickens refused to allow *A Christmas Carol* to be published in the United States because various publishers were violating Dickens' copyrights. In fact, Dickens came to the United States to campaign for international copyright laws. Of course, as the new nation developed its own portfolio of intellectual property, the owners sought greater protection of such rights. China might make a similar transition itself.

The different types of capitalism generate different types of innovation that can be seen in the patterns of patent applications. In the United States, for example, patents are more likely to be issued for radical changes than for incremental innovations. That pushes researchers to focus on big, new ideas. In Germany, the patent office is willing to support small changes in materials and technique, which creates a tendency for subtle improvements in form and function. Neither is necessarily better, only a function of a whole host of institutional arrangements and cultural preferences.[8]

If intellectual property is not protected, then companies will be reluctant to become involved in a country. This is especially important in developing economies, where consumers may want brand-name products but be unable to afford them. The Indian government demanded that Coca-Cola turn over its secret formula as a condition of entering the country, which kept Coke out for decades until the government acquiesced.

Reality: American Capitalism Is Not the Capitalism of Its Competitors

Capitalism isn't a singular doctrine followed uniformly. It comes in several varieties that are affected by a nation's culture, history, and institutional context. Capitalism's many forms lead to very real differences in the way that capitalist countries trade. Even with free trade, some nations will have advantages that others won't because of the different sources of capital that businesses rely on, the different forms of government support, and the cultural milieu of the people who work. The form of capitalism is reflected in how much risk companies take, and when; how managers respond to changing markets; and what workers and consumers expect of corporations and of governments.

Anglo-American-style capitalism and liberal-market economics are driven by entrepreneurial ideas, a strong profit motive, and flexibility throughout the political economy. There is not much government support, which creates its own trade-offs. The credit crisis highlights the weakness of too light a regulatory environment. Once hailed as the maestro, Alan Greenspan delivered a mea culpa in testimony before Congress in October 2008, admitting that his deregulatory bias was based on a mistaken belief that institutions, especially financial institutions, would look after the long-term interests of shareholders.

What an incredible career trajectory; in many ways, it tracks America's own evolution and illustrates its essential pragmatism. In the 1950s and 1960s, as the Great Society was erected, Greenspan moved in the milieu of Ayn Rand, the Russian-born novelist who advocated raw individualism and minimalist state. In essays Greenspan wrote with her, he advocated the return to a pure gold standard and the abolishment of the central bank. He first distanced himself intellectually from Ayn Rand, who was there as his guest when he was first sworn in as President Gerald Ford's chairman of economic advisors in 1974. Even as chairman of the Federal Reserve, Greenspan was encouraging a light regulatory regime. A little more than twenty years after becoming chairman, he was admitting he was wrong and that there was an important role for government after all. The credit crisis will likely result in a permanently larger role for government and in greater regulatory oversight.

The reality is that modern Americans would not recognize nor truly want only market solutions to the distribution of scarcity, nor would they recognize or accept pure socialism. Simply because China, or India, or Russia are embracing more capitalist practices does not mean that any of those countries will necessarily become allies. They still have their own national and strategic interests; capitalist interests are not inherently American interests. A better understanding of the range of capitalist styles around the world can help U.S. companies compete better without infringing on our basic political beliefs. But it is not only competitive elements that will be enhanced; a greater appreciation of the different trade-offs may suggest a greater range of choices domestically, and may also help generate greater understanding, less unreasonable demands, and improved relations with U.S. trading partners and hosts of U.S. direct investment.

Chapter Notes

1. See Peter Hall and David Soskice, eds., *Varieties of Capitalism: Institutional Basis for Comparative Advantage* (New York: Oxford University Press, 2001).

2. Harold Laswell, *Politics: Who Gets What, When, How* (New York: Meridian Books, 1964).

3. Organization for Economic Cooperation and Development, *OECD Economic Outlook No. 83—Annex Tables* (Paris: OECD, June 2008).

4. Guiseppe Bertola, "Economic Integration, Growth, Distribution: Does the Euro Make a Difference?" In *Growth and Income Distribution in an Integrated Europe: Does EMU Make a Difference?* Conference proceedings, Brussels, October 11–12, 2007.

5. International Monetary Fund, *World Economic Outlook Database*, April 2008 ed. (http://www.imf.org/external/pubs/ft/weo/2008/01/weodata/index.aspx).

6. Linda Goldberg and Jose Campo, "Exchange Rate Pass Through into Import Prices." *Review of Economics and Statistics*, November 2005 (Vol. 87, No. 4, p. 679–690).

7. European Union, BACH Database of Harmonized Company Accounts, 1995–2007.

8. Hall and Soskice, *Varieties of Capitalism*.

The Dollar's Privileged Place in the World Is Lost

If the dollar is weak, wouldn't the Chinese rather own euros?

In March 2008, Iceland's leaders thought that the country would be better off if it adopted the euro as currency and jettisoned its krona. They knew that the nation needed a stronger currency—not just in terms of price but also and especially in terms of stability. With the support of the government, two Icelandic banks asked the European Central Bank (ECB) for permission to conduct their accounts in euros—and they were rebuffed. The Icelandic government itself floated the idea of simply tying the krona to the euro, much as Saudi Arabia and China peg (fix the currency's exchange rate) theirs to the U.S. dollar.

Ever since the euro was introduced in 1999, observers and pundits have warned—and some even appeared to have hoped—that it would replace the dollar as what economists call the *numeraire*—the currency benchmark for the world economy. Before, and even at the beginning of the credit crisis, there was much ink spilled over how the numerous central banks were diversifying reserves away from the once mighty greenback and how sovereign wealth funds were buying nondollar assets.

As the euro made new record highs in the first part of 2008, the demise of the dollar was trumpeted far and wide. It even entered the popular culture: a Brazilian supermodel reportedly asked to be paid in nondollar currencies and a few shops in the United States accepted euros. The dollar's decline was the subject of commercials, videos, and television skits. In early 2008, the Director of U.S. National Intelligence, Michael McConnell, told Congress that the weak dollar was a threat to national security.

Is this the euro's moment? Most definitely not. Not only did the ECB refuse Iceland's request, but it also issued a revealing statement saying that it would not encourage others to try to peg to the euro. Eurozone officials show no inclination whatsoever to rival the dollar. Being the world's numeraire may have greater rights of seigniorage, but, as in so many things, there are trade-offs. As trade and capital flows increase, for example, there is a need and desire for more of the reserve assets. Economist Robert Triffin pointed out more than a decade before the collapse of Bretton Woods that there was a fundamental dilemma with having a national currency, like the dollar, yen, or sterling, used as a reserve asset. Demand for the currency would increase over time, and supplying enough to meet the market would require larger and larger current account deficits, which would undermine confidence in it.

Foreign exchange, by its very nature, is unique. One can sell shares and buy a bond, or sell a bond and buy gold, but when one sells a currency, one has to buy another currency. Foreign exchange is the price of one currency expressed in terms of another. Every country's currency value is expressed in terms relative to other currencies, or basket of currencies. This does not mean, of course, that all currencies are equal. Some countries currencies may be a better store of value, or more acceptable as a means of exchange, such as for invoice purposes, or a more universal metric for accounting purposes.

Some countries chose to peg their currency to another currency. Under Bretton Woods, the dollar was pegged to gold, and all other currencies were pegged to the dollar. Although Bretton Woods collapsed in the early 1970s, it took the 1997–98 Asian financial crisis before most of the countries in the region were forced to abandon their currency pegs to the dollar. A few years later, Brazil and Argentina had to ditch their pegs, too. Several continue to peg their currencies to the dollar, notably many of the Persian Gulf states and Hong Kong. The United States, on its own and through the G7, has encouraged countries to adopt more flexible currency regimes rather than maintain the pegs.

It is ironic then that some observers, such as Craig Karman, author of *The Biography of the Dollar*, cites the fact that many countries have heeded this call as evidence of the dollar's demise.[1] Surely it is more complicated than that. At Bretton Woods, the United States saw its national interest best served with an international monetary regime of fixed exchange rates. The pressures generated by the rebuilding of Europe and Japan and their economies "catching up," the Vietnam War, and the expansionary domestic agenda prompted the United States to unilaterally break the link between the dollar and gold, ushering in the era of fiat currencies whose value would be determined by a host of supply-and-demand considerations, rather than by the government or central bank. Grudgingly, the United States accepted floating exchange rates as the least bad alternative. Later, America's knack for making a virtue out of a necessity called for others to liberate currency prices and turn the setting of their relative value to the markets.

When a nation chooses to peg its currency to another, it turns its monetary policy over to someone else. Its citizens have to live with a currency that goes up or down in value depending on what is happening elsewhere in the world. But without a peg, a currency fluctuates based on the supply and demand in the market. For a small nation like Iceland, that makes for a highly volatile exchange rate. That might be great fun if you are a currency trader, but not if you export fish. The European Central Bank isn't interested in becoming the currency of nations large and small that don't want to confront the forces of the market. The United States retains that role, perhaps partly because of inertia, partly because many commodities remain denominated in dollars (matching many countries exports), and partly because of some unique characteristic of America, such as its security, political stability, the depth and breadth of its U.S. Treasury market, and its status as a superpower.

Currencies take on an aura of privilege when they are readily convertible and relatively stable. Then they become desirable for both trade and savings. The U.S. dollar is the world's leading currency. It is not just the key reserve asset but also an invoicing currency for trade that does not even involve the United States or a U.S. company. When the dollar is weak, though, people sometimes wonder if it will still be the world's favorite currency—and if the United States will enjoy the power and privilege that goes along with that.

Many commodities continue to be denominated in dollars, such as oil, despite speculation to the contrary, or the efforts of Iran and Venezuela, which effectively suffer from a first-mover disadvantage of having to bear the currency rise in periods of dollar strength and euro weakness. Outside of a handful of countries in close proximity to the eurozone, the dollar is the key metric by which investors and policy makers evaluate a country's currency. The U.S. dollar remains the intervention currency of choice. It will likely continue as the world's premier currency for decades to come.

Reserves

The purpose of reserves has changed as the international political economy has transformed. Under a regime of fixed exchange rates and limited capital flows, a country needs reserves to cover trade flows. Three or six months worth of imports was often thought to be sufficient, just as a household is advised to have several months of rent or mortgage payments in a savings account for a rainy day.

When a country pegs its currency to another, as Argentina pegged its peso to the dollar in the early 1990s, its dollar reserves are often thought of relative to measures of its money supply. If everyone who has a peso wants U.S. dollars instead, does the central bank hold a sufficient amount of dollars that would ensure the peg would be guaranteed?

In the 1997–98 Asian financial crisis, economists and investors began thinking about a country's reserves relative to the amount of short-term foreign debt obligations of the private sector. The question was, did the country have enough foreign currencies to guarantee the repayment of largely private-sector short-term debt obligations? In the credit crisis, capital flows continued to dominate trade flows as the key metric of reserves, but the emphasis shifted to equity flows. For several years before the crisis erupted, a great deal of foreign capital flowed into emerging market equities. During the crisis, those capital flows went into reverse. As the money flowed out, reserves, especially in Asia, were used to absorb the local currency being sold by fleeing foreign investors.

Reserves also provide countries with the wherewithal to intervene in the foreign exchange market should they choose to help the market adjust to changing supply-and-demand pressures. Some countries, especially emerging market countries that are rapidly being integrated into the global capital markets, may accumulate reserves as they seek to insulate their domestic economy from what could be short-term portfolio capital inflows. This type of intervention is a smoothing operation rather than a protest of market developments and an attempt to reverse the trend. At the same time, it may help slow a currency's appreciation and help maintain the export-oriented development strategy.

Some central banks, such as the Reserve Bank of Australia, frequently operate in the foreign exchange market as chiefly an exercise as part of its market surveillance function. Norges Bank, the central bank of Norway, regularly enters the foreign exchange market to shift its oil and leasing revenues into its sovereign wealth fund.

The type of coordinated intervention meant to reverse the market's direction is rare and has a mixed track record. Coordinated intervention such as the Plaza Agreement in 1985 to drive the dollar down, action in 1995 to stop the dollar from falling, and the intervention in October 2000 to strengthen the euro are regarded as among the more successful operations. Bilateral cooperation has also taken place, such as between the United States and Japan to cap the dollar against the yen in 1998.

Unilateral intervention has a generally poor track record. In late 2003 through early 2004, the Bank of Japan engaged in large-scale intervention, buying several hundred billions of dollars as part of a program to arrest the deflationary forces that had gripped the economy. The dollar fell throughout the intervention period and only began recovering when the intervention stopped.

Before leaving the topic of intervention, a few strategic observations may be useful. First, size does not seem to be the key determinant factor in the success of intervention. The United States possesses relatively few reserves. When it intervenes, it appears to use its market intelligence and finesse. Japan's intervention often seemed to be an attempt to overwhelm the market with size. U.S. intervention is rare, though every president since the end of Bretton Woods, except George W. Bush, has authorized it. When the United States does intervene, it appears to try to time the intervention with an appreciation of market psychology, which may include key charts points and speculative positioning.

Second, it may be best to consider intervention as an escalation ladder. The early rungs of the ladder are verbal in nature. Officials singularly and then maybe collectively express concern about the volatility of the foreign exchange market. Sometimes they may object to the continuation of an existing trend, such as indicating, for example, that further euro losses would be counterproductive to reducing global imbalances. Officials do not typically intervene out of the blue, and yet a successful operation often has an element of surprise.

Third, the odds of a successful intervention operation appear to increase if it signals or is backed up by a change in policy, such as interest rates. This is not always possible and sometime gives the impression that the intervention is meant to buy time—to steady or slow the market's movement until macroeconomic developments adjust.

Lastly, intervention by the G7 nations risks confusing or diluting its strategic call on other countries to let market forces determine currency values. Besides sounding hypocritical, it may reflect insensitivity to the hardships that rapid currency movements have on smaller and less-developed countries with weaker financial institutions and practices. When the G7 calls for "flexible" currency regimes, it's experienced as "volatile." As many have learned, the only thing worse than short-term speculative capital inflows overwhelming a country's asset markets, distorting economic signals, and fueling bubbles, is when the money flows out.

The credit crisis may transform some of the ideological arguments about the role of reserves. Before the crisis, much was written about the excess reserves that were being accumulated. Some countries, such as China and Japan—which, between the two of them, account for a full third of the world's reserves in 2009—held excess reserves. However, the lesson to be drawn for other countries is that they will need not only to replenish their war chest of reserves that may have been run down during the crisis but also to continue to accumulate more reserves as they become more integrated in global trade and capital flows.

Moreover, those reserves often need to be complemented with swap lines with other key central banks as a way to access different currencies. Among the largest of the emergency facilities that the Federal Reserve established during the credit crisis were extensive swap agreements with a number of major central banks and several emerging markets. The provision of dollars via swap lines may have helped temper the dramatic appreciation of the dollar as the crisis became more acute in the second half of 2008. The Fed was not alone. In November 2008, for example, the Swiss National Bank agreed to provide a euro–Swiss franc swap line to the Polish Central Bank that would allow the Polish bank to provide banks in the country with funding for their own foreign exchange activities.[2]

Managing Reserves

Reserves are managed just as any another investment portfolio whose primary objective is safety. No central bank wants to tell its citizens that the nation's reserves were lost by speculating on emerging-markets currencies. The value of reserves is almost always expressed in dollars. The value of the reserves is affected by purchases and sales as well as by the shift in the price of assets when converted into dollars. The dollar's decline from around 2000 into mid-2008 against the euro and the general increase in government bond prices because of falling yields helped boost the reported value of reserves. Similarly, the dollar's rise and the decrease in bond yields will contribute to a decline in reserves, as will some countries' intervention activities.

The most authoritative source on the currency composition of reserves is the International Monetary Fund. Its COFER (Currency Composition of Official Foreign Exchange Reserves) report consistently demonstrates that the U.S. dollar is the most popular reserve currency, followed by the euro and the yen.[3]

For all the fear of a supposed decline in global influence, the dollar became a larger part of allocated world reserves between 1995 and 2007 (see *Figure 6.1*). And contrary to popular belief, the euro didn't take a share from the dollar. The euro and its predecessors maintained a more or less constant share of allocated reserves over the same period. The currency that instead had the biggest change as a portion of global reserves was the Japanese yen, which gave up more than half its share.

Vast quantities of money have been earmarked for reserves. Foreign central banks held approximately $3.3 trillion worth of U.S. assets at the end of 2007[4] in official reserves and other investments. Central banks increased their position by acquiring $411 billion in assets during the same year.[5] Even with this bump up in foreign central banks' U.S. dollar holdings, they still represent just a quarter of gross domestic product. They aren't taking over the United States.

It is no surprise then that the central banks' investment in the United States is heavily concentrated in U.S. Treasury and government-sponsored debt instruments because the banks have a clear and understandable preference for the least risky and most liquid securities as reserve assets. U.S. Treasury and agency securities are a modest part of the overall U.S. securities market and a small part of the overall

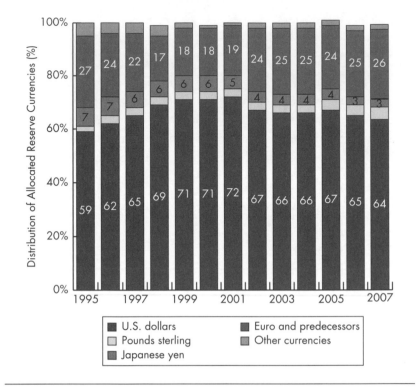

FIGURE 6.1   Distribution of Allocated Reserve Currencies,
1995–2007

Source: International Monetary Fund, COFER database, updated 30 September 2008

capital inflows into the United States. A look at the Treasury Department's Treasury International Capital (www.ustreas.gov/tic/) monthly
portfolio flow report illustrates this point. This data series is not rec-
oncilable with the U.S. quarterly current account reports or the U.S.
Bureau of Economic Analysis's net international investment report, but
it is nevertheless revealing, and the financial markets, especially the
foreign exchange market, pay close attention to it.

For the twelve months ending in August 2008, the total increase
in foreign holdings of long-term U.S. securities was $798.2 billion, of
which $172.5 billion was purchased of government issues by foreign
government entities. At the same time, U.S. investors cut their holdings of foreign securities by $34.8 billion, reducing their exposure to
overseas markets.[6]

The role of the dollar as the key reserve asset was supposed to be weakened by the deterioration of its international balance sheet and challenged by the advent of the euro. Various central banks from Asia to eastern and central Europe to Canada have diversified their reserves, but they haven't been selling dollars to do it. Instead, they had been selling yen, buying pounds, and adding a few miscellaneous holdings.

In addition to currency reserves, many nations use surplus wealth generated from their current account surplus to make risky investments. These funds, known as *sovereign wealth funds*, were initially encouraged by the International Monetary Fund to help countries preserve and manage their wealth for the future when they may lose their export advantages. This is what Norway has done. Or consider Kuwait: it has become a wealthy nation selling a commodity with a finite supply. By investing some of its excess now, it will be able to cushion the effects of a dwindling oil supply. Other nations, especially those that do not have sovereign debt, invest surplus funds abroad to support old-age pension programs. These funds have become players in international business, especially in propping up troubled financial services companies; their investments include Citigroup and Morgan Stanley.

Although the U.S. government does not invest its funds in private businesses (the 2008–09 financial bailout notwithstanding), the United States is a player in the world of sovereign wealth through such state investment accounts as the Alaska Permanent Fund. Others would add the California Public Employees Retirement System (CalPERS), which manages the pension money of state employees. Just as Americans sometimes are anxious and ambivalent about the involvement of the Abu Dhabi or South Korean sovereign wealth funds in their business affairs, some Japanese companies have been less than thrilled by the attentions of CalPERS.

The motivation of sovereign wealth funds isn't global domination; it's pure risk-adjusted profit. That these nations want to invest in the United States is generally a good thing. America was built with foreign capital. Sovereign wealth funds can be long-term patient investors. In their investments, they have rarely sought a seat on the board or to influence a company's policies. CalPERS is a notable exception in this regard, insofar as the fund has sometimes been aggressive about forcing companies to improve their corporate governance.

Central banks have many options for how to hold their surplus and reserve funds. They can be held as gold and cash in a vault, bank deposits, Treasury bills, short- and long-term government securities, and other types of securities that could be exchanged for cash quickly. As the trade, capital flows, and economic integration increases, nations will need to accommodate more types of reserve holdings. The asset and debt managers may need to find new ways to attract reserves, bond buyers, and investors. That could entail developing new securities.

Shariah

What if the United States wants to create more options for Middle Easterners to hold their currency reserves here? Under Muslim law, known as *shariah*, it is forbidden to make or take on a loan for interest. Instead, shariah recognizes as legitimate financial securities that derive the rate of return from the performance of real assets, for example, from a share of profits. Devout Muslims still need to access and invest capital, so financial instruments called *sukuk* have been created. Sukuk are asset-backed certificates that carry ownership rights and risks.

Other shariah-compliant securities include special-purpose vehicles that acquire a financial asset and then issue financial claims on that asset. The claims represent a proportionate beneficial ownership for a defined period. The shariah has been interpreted in such a way that it appears to be flexible enough to change over time.

There is a wide array of shariah-approved financial instruments that have been issued and that duplicate many of the functions of conventional financial products. These include instruments with fixed and floating rate payoffs, forwards, futures, and swaps. Just as the surge in oil revenue in the 1970s was a catalyst for development, so too is the current deluge of petrodollars spurring further development. An estimated 240 financial institutions in forty countries are shariah-compliant, managing about $400 billion in assets.

Muslim financing is primarily a niche market, although the World Bank has issued sukuk to raise capital for its activities. So have a German state and a U.S.-based oil company. Deep and broad Islamic capital markets are arguably in the U.S. economic and geostrategic interests. They promote economic development and, through economic development, foster stability. They help integrate the region and its people into the world economy, giving them a greater stake in the world's prosperity. Developed Islamic capital markets would also help avoid repeating the potential destabilizing imbalances in Asia. The U.S. Treasury should consider constructing a dollar-denominated bond that would be shariah-compliant. There are various forms that it could take. It would signal respect for Islamic law and people and would recognize the limitations of military and political strategies. It would recognize the real battle, as always, is for the hearts and minds of the people. Because it would be an asset-backed security, it could translate into a low interest rate for the Treasury and U.S. taxpayers.

One doesn't have to be Muslim to invest in sukuk. Many conventional fund managers have begun embracing sukuk as a separate asset class that helps diversify the overall portfolio. Fund managers in the growing socially responsible investment space may also be attracted to the high ethical standards that shariah demands.

And ongoing innovation is what makes the United States a world financial center and an attractive place to invest. Many U.S. officials had expressed concern that New York City was losing its leadership role in global finance. When Gordon Brown was the U.K. chancellor of the exchequer before becoming prime minister, he said he wanted London to be the global center for Islamic finance. Why should it be London instead of New York? Sharia-compliant Islamic banks have been chartered in the United Kingdom. In its supervisory and regulatory roles, the Federal Reserve is likely preparing for the day when an Islamic bank applies for a charter to operate in the United States.

Invoicing Currencies

The IMF's COFER data on global reserve holdings cited earlier in this chapter are measured in U.S. dollars. In fact, most global economic data is maintained in dollars. Duty-free stores in the Mexico City airport price their designer scarves in dollars, as does OPEC when it sets the price of oil. Businesses that trade internationally find that using the dollar as a standard currency reduces complication and risk. An American buyer or seller doesn't have to be involved for the dollar to be.

In the United States, 90.3 percent of 2003 imports were priced in dollars. (That's the most recent year that data are available.) In Japan,

68.7 percent of imports were billed in U.S. dollars. In France, the dollar was used for 46.9 percent of imports, a higher proportion than were in euros, 45.3 percent.[7] Four years after the advent of the euro, the dollar still dominated world trade, even in many parts of the eurozone. That acceptance means that, contrary to the naysayers, the dollar's role in the world economy remains second to none and largely unchallenged in another dimension. Those that argue that the sun is setting on the dollar rarely discuss the use of the dollar as an invoicing currency. Moreover, this is one element of the dollar's role that does not appear affected by its fluctuations in the foreign exchange market.

Possibly, the popularity of the dollar for invoicing is due to the U.S. status as the world's banker and significant trader. Imports and exports may not be remarkable relative to the total U.S. gross domestic product, but in dollar terms and relative to the size of most other countries' GDP, they are substantial.

The United States imported $2.34 trillion of goods and services in 2007. In the same year, it exported $1.65 trillion of goods and services. Being a net importer is not necessarily good or bad. Some economies import goods because there isn't enough local production. Others bring in raw materials in order to make finished goods. And some purchase low-value products so that their workers can concentrate on developing and manufacturing higher-value ones.

Likewise, that a nation exports doesn't say much about its economy. Instead, the question is *what* does it export and *why*. The economic risks in Saudi Arabia, where the primary export is a commodity with a finite supply, are very different from the risks in Japan, which makes complex manufactured goods for sale elsewhere. Some nations export because the home market is small relative to their productivity, and some export because they have no other choice. The exporter of a critical product may be able to set the invoice currency, but not always.

A nation's trade patterns will affect internal institutional structures, which in turn influence how the economy grows and changes. Japan, a net exporter, has a diversified economy and a wealthy, well-educated workforce. But that's not because Japan is an exporter, but rather because of the capabilities that it is able to apply to the goods that it exports. Many countries with large agricultural export economies operate under a quasi-feudal structure, with large concentrated landholdings, extreme income inequality, and a landless rural lower class. Mining often leads to a large workforce concentrated in a small geographic area, making disruptions possible if those workers hold wildcat strikes.

Similarly, countries that import may be vulnerable to disruptions in supply, or they may have an entire industry of commercial services necessary to make trade happen smoothly. These services can affect the locus of capital accumulation, strengthen the local business class, and create independence from government and foreign interference. In the United States, for example, imports of goods are financed by a large, sophisticated financial services sector.

There are many reasons why the cross-border movement of goods and services has increased over the last sixty years or so. Under numerous rounds of negotiations, under GATT and its successor WTO, tariff barriers to trade have repeatedly been reduced. Technology that has improved command, control, and communication has increased the span of management and allows the coordination of economic activity over large spaces. In effect, trade may increase as geographic space shrinks. That creates new industries and new investment opportunities in technology, transportation, and communication. Another way to shrink the practical space between trading partners is through multinational corporations that allocate operations to the nations that make the most economic sense but keep headquarters in stable, efficient locations. The apparent imbalances from trade often mask a strong internal economy, backed in part by foreign reserve holdings.

Pegged Currencies

Is currency a measure of sovereignty, a club, an identity, or simply a medium of exchange? That's the question that many small nations face when they decide whether to maintain their own currency or peg to another. But that relationship doesn't guarantee that a nation will take on the strength of the U.S. dollar—far from it. A currency relationship can create its own problems because the government may have to buy and sell reserves in order to maintain it. The medicine can be nasty, as Thailand found in 1997 when it could no longer raise enough funds to support the baht's peg to the rising U.S. dollar.

Over the years, some countries have pegged their currency to the U.S. dollar unilaterally, without permission and, of course, without their interests being taken into account when the Federal Reserve decides the appropriate setting of monetary policy. Panama doesn't even print its own currency, using the American greenback as its own. Thus far, only countries that have been admitted to the exclusive club have adopted the euro. (Monaco, San Marino, and Vatican City, which relied on currencies that preceded the euro, were granted exceptions.)

Some countries peg their currencies in order to keep their money in line with that of a major trading partner. In July 2005, the yuan's peg to the U.S. dollar was loosened, but even now the yuan appears to shadow the dollar, and its daily movement remains quite limited. It is not allowed to move on a daily basis against the dollar more than 0.5 percent (which itself represents a widening of the band in 2007 from the initial 0.3 percent band that had been announced when the peg was ostensibly broken in 2005) and is less movement than was allowed in some fixed exchange rate regimes such as Bretton Woods. Moreover, there have been periods, such as August 2008, when the pegged Hong Kong dollar moved more against the U.S. dollar than did the Chinese yuan.

Because intervention is one of the uses for reserves, pegged currencies are not candidates for reserve status. Although China's economic might is ascendant, its currency is tied to the U.S. dollar, and its government will manage the currency to keep it in line. If it were to let the yuan float, many observers—including apparently much of the U.S. Congress and many manufacturers—expect that it would appreciate, mostly as a function of its trade surplus.

Yet, as we have seen, trade balances do not really offer a reliable guide to currency movement. Contrary to conventional wisdom, some forces may actually see the yuan sink if officials tried to float it. For example, if the currency were to be convertible for capital and current account purposes, then foreign businesses would find it easier to repatriate earnings that have accumulated in China. And the upwardly mobile professionals being created in parts of the country would diversify some of their newfound wealth to overseas markets, as their counterparts do elsewhere. Speculators who had poured money into China to wager on managed currency appreciation would likely take their funds and look for a new game. Other considerations could potentially influence the movement of the yuan if it were freed, like the international appetite for risk or relative asset market performance.

Despite their verbal embrace of market forces, many critics simply want a stronger yuan, and more than they really want free markets. They would likely be just as contented if China's officials were to commit to a repegging of the yuan at a stronger level. It is easy to forget that most of the rapid economic growth and increase in living standards in the United States and Europe took place under regimes of fixed exchange rates. Floating exchange rates have different institutional requirements, but such arrangements and institutional capacity—like the strength of the financial system and market knowledge for traders, as well as officials—are necessary.

As nice as it might seem to have an economy that always chugs along with an exchange rate that is just right, that will never happen. Nor is it desirable. Disruptions are often due to technological or political changes that can make most people better off. Crisis creates stimulus for change. The crisis may be a shock that is a major unanticipated change such as a war that disrupts oil supplies or a higher-than-imagined default rate on subprime mortgages. Or it can come as pressure, a push for change or reform that is not unexpected but that makes the landscape a little different. Such pressure might come from a change in government policy limiting carbon emissions or a recession that makes all consumers, even credit-worthy ones, curtail borrowing.

Iceland's Saga

The Icelandic financial crisis of 2008 went far beyond a currency crisis, even though it is the biggest currency crisis since Thailand's collapse in 1997. Iceland went from being a trendy vacation spot and dealer in high-interest bank accounts to a spot on the United Kingdom's list of terrorist states. Inflation threatened to push the citizens back into the poverty of more than a century ago.

The issue is not that the financial system was too big to fail but that the balance sheets of the Icelandic banks were too big for the government to bail out—to say the least. Other nations had to rally to stop Icelandic losses. The assets of the three largest Icelandic lenders— Kaupthing Bank, Landsbanki, and Glitnir Bank—were worth around $126 billion at the end of 2007, which was about nine times the GDP of the country. (Iceland's population is just 300,000.) That limited the ability of the government to respond. Iceland's economy started to look like a hedge fund portfolio speculating on assets far beyond its borders.

The banks' deposits and loans spanned the globe, so a local crisis quickly turned into a major international crisis. Icesave, a division of Landsbanki, had collected about 4 billion pounds in deposits from British and Dutch consumers. Kaupthing Bank had a brisk lending business with some of the United Kingdom's biggest entrepreneurs and handled deposits for 150,000 Britons. The U.K. government tried to step in to minimize problems as part of its work to shore up U.K. banks; the first bank to fail in a long chain of global failures was Northern Rock, a U.K. institution, in September 2007. Alistair Darling, the U.K. chancellor of the exchequer, organized a taxpayer-funded recapitalization of Britain's banks to help settle nervous citizens. Then he and the British government used a 2001 law against terrorist states to freeze any Icelandic assets in Great Britain, arguing that the integrity of the country's financial system was at stake.

When banks face problems, they raise capital from savers, investors, or the government. By the end of October 2008, Iceland's government benchmark interest rate was raised to 18 percent to help attract foreign investors and strengthen the krona. Otherwise, almost all goods would become too expensive for people in a country heavily dependent on foreign trade. Even with the liquidity drawn by rate increase, Iceland faced a serious economic problem.

Had Iceland adopted the euro, it would have sacrificed its monetary independence. It would have lost the ability to manage its reserves and resources to keep its exchange rate in line with its economy. The competitive advantage that a currency depreciation may create, albeit short-term, would have been denied, which may have put even more pressure on the real economy and living standards. On the other hand, monetary independence may not be all that it is cracked up to be. In Iceland's case, the result was a total collapse; even until all the news about the country's banks came out, the krona fluctuated with the vagaries of the market. (It's also unlikely that a peg would have helped; it may have made the situation worse by forcing the Icelandic government to spend reserves in order to prop up the currency.) The question really is, who do a small country's officials want to set the price of their money—the European Central Bank, the Federal Reserve Bank, or impersonal and speculative market forces?

Until the banks failed, Iceland's Prime Minister Geir Haarde reassured everyone that Iceland was fine, the markets were wrong, and the pressure on the krona came from "unscrupulous dealers." That's no surprise; a common feature of currency crises is blaming the price action on speculators. In 1992, when France and Germany were trying to maintain the value of the French franc, Michel Sapin, the French finance minister, said, "During the French Revolution, such speculators were known as *agioteurs*, and they were beheaded."[8] Anonymous Swiss bankers the so called gnomes of Zurich—were the guilty parties in the 1960s and 1970s. George Soros was the boogeyman in the 1997 Asian crisis, and Zimbabwe's government blamed Western government sanctions for the 2008 hyperinflation.

Iceland's struggles shed light on the international role of the euro. The European Central Bank has been deeply involved in this crisis, but it did not want to assume Iceland's obligations or allow it into the eurozone without meeting the criteria. Although many market observers write and talk as if the euro is on the verge of supplanting the dollar as the chief reserve asset and the numeraire in the world economy, European officials in general and the ECB specifically do not appear particularly anxious for this to take place. The challenges managing the currency transitions within Europe and governing the growing and increasingly diverse economic and political region will occupy officials for years to come.

During the credit crisis, fissures within the monetary union became more apparent, though Martin Feldstein's claims that the monetary union might not survive its first recession will likely prove overly pessimistic.[9] Still, there will need to be institutional changes. The ECB, for example, will likely develop new policy tools that will allow it to better combat financial crises. However, at least one potential fissure lies at the very heart of monetary union and cannot be resolved by the crisis. Traditionally, some countries participating in the EMU, such as Italy and Greece but others as well, would devalue their currencies against the German mark to restore competitiveness that was lost to inflation or the relative increase in unit labor costs. That path is now closed. This would seem to put more pressure on governments to adopt more competitive policies. But the constellation of political forces may be aligned against such reforms, resulting simply in the continued loss of competitiveness. Over time, this may alter the cost–benefit analysis of participating in the EMU.

The Reality Is that the Dollar Is as Important as Ever

In an unstable world, capital will flow to places that are relatively more stable and can absorb the inflows. It's easy to look at the U.S. current account deficit and assume that the United States is unstable, but that ignores the strength and flexibility of the economy. For all the troubles that the U.S. economy had in 2008, it is still a more stable nation than many others. The size of the economic restructuring creates more bonds to be used for reserve holdings by nations looking for safety. The United States is able and willing to absorb the world's excess capital.

When the world financial markets swooned in September and October 2008, the U.S. dollar appreciated even though the U.S. markets were part of the problem. The trade-weighted dollar index was at 98.35 at the end of August. By the end of October, it had appreciated to 110.37.[10] The dollar looked like a safe haven when almost all asset classes declined in value and the world's economies seemed shaky.

Besides the strength of U.S. capital markets, one reason for the dollar's global popularity is that the United States is a leader in financial innovation. It is one of the nation's absolute advantages. That means creating new types of government securities of interest to international investors such as the Treasury's inflation-protected securities. National finance carries political freight. It is in America's interest to further engage Middle Eastern nations, which already rely on the dollar for exchange and the United States for their customer base and defense. One way to do that is to create new, Islamic-compliant securities. This is a golden opportunity for the United States to exercise its leadership and show its prowess in utilizing its soft power.

The sustained current account deficit, the advent of the euro, criticisms of U.S. foreign policy, or any number of supposed threats have essentially not affected the dollar's role as a reserve currency, as an invoicing currency, and as a metric for numerous commodity prices and national accounts. Therefore, there are good reasons to expect that the credit crisis with its epicenter in the United States will not dethrone the dollar. The attributes of the United States, with its large, flexible economy and the depth, breadth, and security of the Treasury market, have been more appreciated as the crisis became more acute. As counterintuitive as it may seem, the United States and the dollar may emerge from the crisis stronger than before.

Chapter Notes

1. Craig Karman, *The Biography of the Dollar: How The Mighty Buck Conquered the World and Why It's Under Siege* (New York: Crown, 2008).

2. Narodowy Bank Polski, "Swiss National Bank and Narodowy Bank Polski Cooperate to Provide Swiss Franc Liquidity." Press release, November 7, 2008.

3. Data from the International Monetary Fund COFER database, updated September 30, 2008

4. U.S. Bureau of Economic Analysis, "U.S. Net International Investment Position at Yearend 2007," June 27, 2008.

5. Ibid.

6. Department of the Treasury, "Treasury International Capital Data for August," October 16, 2008.

7. Annette Kamps, "The Euro as Invoicing Currency in International Trade." European Central Bank Working Paper Series, August 2006.

8. Cited in Roger Cohen, "Germany Backing Effort by France to Support Franc," *New York Times*, September 24, 1992.

9. Martin Feldstein, "EMU and International Conflict," Foreign Affairs, Nov-Feb 1997, (Vol. 76 No. 6).

10. Federal Reserve Bank of St. Louis, "Trade-Weighted Dollar Index" (http://research.stlouisfed.org/fred2/categories/105).

MYTH 7

Globalization Destroyed
American Industry

*A closer look at the evolutionary expansion strategy of
American businesses: Just what, exactly, has been
moving overseas all these years?*

To fully grasp the significance of the U.S. expansion strategy, one
needs to appreciate its origins. Some historians trace U.S. foreign
economic policy back to the Monroe Doctrine, which promised that the
United States would not insert itself in European affairs as long as Europe
did not establish new colonies in the Americas. The United States could
not enforce the document's claims, and to a large extent it depended on
Great Britain's commitment to a balance-of-power strategy. Nevertheless, the Monroe Doctrine reflected the traditional approach to foreign
affairs that carved the world into spheres of influence. Not until the end
of the nineteenth century and the beginning of the twentieth century did
the United States articulate an alternative vision and strategy.

The U.S. strategy begins with the Open Door Notes (1899–1900)
written by Secretary of State John Hay and sent to the other major
powers of the day (France, Germany, Italy, Japan, Russia, and the
United Kingdom). In the Spanish-American War of 1898, the United
States acquired its first and only colony, the Philippines. This (along
with a number of smaller islands acquired in the Pacific) gave the
United States the ability to project economic and political power into
China, which for more than a generation had captured the imagination
of American intellectuals, businessmen, and statesmen. The network

of coaling stations for steamships made the movement of goods and people possible.

However, America was late to the game. Britain, France, Germany, Portugal, and Japan were already in China and were busy carving the nation into various concessions—spheres of influence—that each nation would control. Hay considered the alternatives that the United States faced, including challenging some other country's sphere of influence or grabbing its own. Instead of these more traditional routes, Hay proposed something revolutionary: that the United States challenge the whole traditional sphere-of-influence approach to foreign affairs. The spheres of influence were tragically unstable because countries would go to war to enlarge their spheres. As an alternative to the fixed spheres, Hay proposed variable shares in the world economy. The shares would vary according to a country's economic prowess rather than political concessions or military might. That meant that the United States would be able to compete for all of China's business. This, in turn, necessitated the preservation of China's territorial and administrative integrity, which the United States vigorously defended.

It was as if the new kid on the block comes along and demands new rules. The Open Door Notes threw the weight of the United States on the side of the anti-imperialists of the time. Imperialism was associated with what U.S. Defense Secretary Donald Rumsfeld would infamously call "old Europe" a hundred years later. Hay's strategy was fundamentally global in scope, although the specific incident that led to its articulation was trade with China. It was essentially progrowth and prodevelopment and was perfectly consistent with Charles Conant's argument, which is explored in Chapter 3.

Hay set out a strategy for a rising power with an economically competitive economy, which was also good for the world. Out of the ashes of the great conflagrations of the first part of the twentieth century came the institutionalization of the Open Door on a global scale: the World Bank; International Monetary Fund (IMF); General Agreement on Tariffs and Trade (GATT), predecessor of the World Trade Organization; and the United Nations. These post–World War II institutions enable a type of globalization that promotes trade and capital flows, peaceful resolution of conflicts, and fiscal and monetary policies that are thought to nurture growth and development.

The U.S. government sometimes pursues policies that contradict the Open Door. The policies demanded by the multilateral agencies often seem to aggravate the very situations they are designed to address. Nevertheless, the type of globalization envisioned by Hay is largely in place, with varying degrees of success in different parts of the world. Trade in goods and services has increased significantly faster than world growth. Cross-border capital flows have increased faster than trade. Tariffs and barriers to trade in goods have generally fallen; now the WTO is pushing into new areas, such as agriculture and services, which tend to be more contentious.

During the Cold War, the Soviet Union and its sphere of influence were not integrated into the Open Door world. Neither was China nor the Middle East. Many other low-income countries were excluded. Over time, most countries joined GATT and the World Trade Organization, effectively committing them to the Open Door. China joined in late 2001, helping to signal that the Open Door world was going to survive the dreadful attack on the United States on September 11 of that year. Of the great and not-so-great powers, Russia remains remarkable by its absence. It had completed all the bilateral agreements necessary to join the WTO except with one country, Georgia, which was refusing to cooperate even before Russia invaded in August 2008.

Globalization

Businesses try to contain costs if they are to stay competitive and make profits. Businesses often perceive they have greater control of labor costs than the cost of capital or raw materials. The businessman and the class warrior agree: to become more competitive one needs to get more out of each unit of purchased inputs, including workers. In many cases, people are replaced with machines. Microsoft Office has replaced secretaries; ATMs have replaced bank tellers.

Scottish textile workers, who had taken market share from India, lost their market to Americans working in New England factories. New England mill workers lost their jobs to Southern U.S. workers. Then the weaving went to Mexico and on to China, always searching for cheaper places. Looking only at the textile industry, it would seem that America is completely uncompetitive, losing out to the rest of the world.

Much of the technology that made the move from New England to North Carolina, to Nuevo Laredo, and later to Nantong City came from the United States. If you walked into that textile factory in China, you'd probably see American machinery. If you walked through the town, you could see people wearing Nikes, listening to iPods, and headed toward McDonald's. If you stepped into a market, you could buy Coca-Cola, Pert shampoo, and Tylenol. Companies now look for global markets early in their corporate lives; such enterprises as Dell and Google are defined by globalization just as much as they are defining it.

In many parts of the world, globalization means Americanization, and it is something to be feared: the Great Satan, corrupter of traditional mores, destroyer of local business and culture. Walking down the street in Montreal, Mumbai, or Munich, it would be hard to argue that American influence is waning. Yet the big brands succeeded because they entered other countries from the perspective of fitting in rather than forcing U.S. standards on local tastes: Coca-Cola is sweeter in some markets than in others, and McDonald's serves fish sandwiches for breakfast in Japan and banana ketchup in the Philippines. Political scientists David Becker and Richard Sklar call those practices "postimperialism."[1] They argued that many multinational companies find it in their interest to be good local citizens.

Unlike the imperialist agents of earlier times, the agents of the Open Door and postimperialism understand that it is shortsighted to view commercial relationship as a sprint. It is a marathon; businesses have to know their customers. As astute business people know, it is much easier and cheaper to retain a customer than to get a new one. That requires cultural awareness and an appreciation of the needs of each market, which comes only by spending time in a place and working with local customers and employees.

There's Something Wrong with the Glass

There are various explanations for the persistence of the U.S. trade deficit. Some people argue that America buys more from the world than it sells because its companies are growing less competitive. Others blame the trade restrictions and labor policies of other countries that may make U.S. exports less competitive or give imported products advantages here. The problem is not that the glass is half full or half empty, but there is something wrong with the glass. The trade balance is no longer a valid scorecard for America's global sales and competitiveness. Given a choice, U.S. firms prefer to sell goods and services abroad through their foreign affiliates instead of exporting them from the United States. In 2005, the most recent year for which data are available, U.S. foreign-affiliate sales topped a staggering $4.2 trillion,[2] whereas U.S. exports—the common but spurious yardstick of U.S. global sales—totaled just $1.3 trillion.[3] Sales by these affiliates outstrip exports by a factor of four to one. How U.S. firms compete in world markets, in other words, goes well beyond trade.

American companies are more interested in establishing global footprints than in finding export markets. The world's largest nonfinancial transnational corporation, U.S.-based General Electric, has $442.3 billion in overseas assets, 63.4 percent of its total assets, through 785 foreign affiliates.[4] It's no surprise; General Electric isn't a big exporter. It makes its products all over the world, so it doesn't need to ship goods. Four of the ten largest nonfinancial transnationals—General Electric, ExxonMobil, Ford Motor Company, and Wal-Mart—are U.S. companies. Three of the ten are based in the United Kingdom (British Petroleum, Royal Dutch Shell, Vodafone Group), two in France (Total, Électricité de France), and one in Japan (Toyota Motor Corporation).

Trade erroneously remains the standard benchmark of global competitiveness. More worrisome, it is the most important factor shaping U.S. international economic policy. Overblown concern about the trade deficit, amid a weak economy and rising unemployment, could ignite a new round of trade protectionism in Washington, which could spark similar responses around the globe.

It's about the Footprint

One of the main characteristics of the U.S. expansion strategy under the Open Door is producing and selling locally. It explains, for example, why Ford Motor Company and General Motors have long owned affiliates in Europe and have recently entered such promising emerging markets as Brazil and China. The principle also underlies Dell Computer's direct-investment positions in Europe and Latin America, as well as those of Cisco Systems and Microsoft in China. Globalization of services has also seen a rapid expansion of affiliates of a broad range of U.S. service companies in areas such as finance, communication, logistics, and software development, creating a network of foreign-owned affiliates.

U.S. firms compete all over the world through both trade and foreign direct investment. They face multiple market opportunities, incessant technological advances, blurred industrial boundaries, and unrelenting global competition. Being an insider is increasingly critical in markets around the world. Unless a company is on the ground, it will often lose to other competitors. This is another benefit of a direct-investment strategy.

The United States had a $256.2 billion trade deficit with China in 2007.[5] Companies affiliated with foreign businesses account for roughly half of China's manufacturing exports. Incidentally, American private investors added $232.8 billion to the $2.1 trillion foreign direct investment in China in 2007, making the United States the largest single international investor in that rapidly growing country.[6]

Contrary to popular perception, foreign consumers' demands vary according to location, requiring firms such as Procter & Gamble, Gillette, and Coca-Cola to be close to their customers. For example, China's vastly diverse cultures, dialects, and, above all else, living standards demand that U.S. companies adapt their products to local tastes. Otherwise, Chinese consumers will purchase from a European or Japanese competitor willing to give them what they want. Chinese consumers, whether buying soft drinks, computers, or automobiles, are very brand sensitive. A local presence is crucial for building the brand recognition needed for success in the Chinese market.

Fierce competition for global market share compels U.S. firms to be close to their foreign competitors. How else can Procter & Gamble successfully compete in China against Japanese rival Kao? Wal-Mart cannot let its global competitor Carrefour of France enter key markets such as Brazil and Japan uncontested. At stake for all these companies are new customers, new resources, and new opportunities—and, by extension, long-term success—and their variable shares of the expanding world economy.

Global Heavyweights

Corporate America has some 23,000 majority- and minority-owned affiliates strategically positioned around the globe. In total, they rank among the world's largest economic producers, boasting combined sales of $8.3 trillion in 2006[7]—greater than the gross domestic products (GDPs) of most nations, including China, Japan, and South Korea combined. The strategic objective of most U.S. foreign affiliates is to produce and deliver goods and services to the host market. In 2006, roughly half of total affiliate sales were made to customers in the host nation. Yet as U.S. multinational corporations increasingly disperse different stages of production among different countries, their affiliates have also become world-class exporters of intermediate goods and components within their trading regions. A small fraction ends up back in the United States as well.

Critics often claim that U.S. multinationals export cheaper products from their overseas affiliates back to the United States, thereby contributing to the U.S. import bill and undermining American jobs and income. But, in fact, most U.S. affiliate exports do not go to the United States, and the majority of affiliate exports do not emanate from low-wage nations such as Brazil, China, and India.

Rather, nearly three-fourths of total affiliate exports come from high-wage industrialized nations such as Canada, the United Kingdom, and Germany. U.S. affiliates also stand among the world's top employers, collectively employing more than 9.5 million people in 2006,[8] a global workforce larger than that of most countries. Most Americans assume that the bulk of this workforce toils in developing nations under extreme and unfair conditions. But, in fact, corporate America's global workforce is concentrated in the high-wage developed nations. The largest number of employees working for U.S. companies abroad is in the United Kingdom (1.2 million), and almost half of all employees of multinationals (4.1 million) are in Europe. A mere 158,500 U.S. multinational workers are in the lowest-wage region of the world, Africa, and most of those are in the relatively affluent Republic of South Africa. Even in North America, more American multinationals hire people in Canada (1.1 million) than in Mexico, where they employ 889,800 workers. These same companies hire 21.9 million workers in the United States; meanwhile, 5.3 million Americans work directly for the U.S. affiliates of foreign multinational companies.

Location, Location, Location

Not only are U.S. affiliate sales significantly larger than U.S. exports, but also they are dispersed differently across the globe. Since the end of World War II, America's foreign direct-investment levels have soared.

Europe, notably the United Kingdom, has emerged as the favorite destination for U.S. multinationals. In 2007, U.S. companies invested $313.8 billion all over the world;[9] the largest share went to the European Union. Given the relative weakness of the dollar, many foreign companies invested in the United States that year, but the amount, $232.8 billion, was less than American investors sent out.

The post–World War II period provided powerful impetus to corporate America's direct-investment strategy. The dollar was relatively rich, purposely so to allow Europe and Japan to rebuild. Discriminatory trade practices were also tolerated. As Europe recovered from the ravages of war and moved toward creating a common market, U.S. firms seized the new commercial opportunities presented by peace and economic stability. By the 1960s, Europe accounted for almost 40 percent of total U.S. foreign direct investment, which gave rise to concern over the American invasion. In the following decade, the tilt toward Europe became even more pronounced: the region accounted for nearly half the value of American foreign direct investment, largely at the expense of Latin America and Canada. In the 1970s, meanwhile, Asia remained among the least-favored destinations for U.S. multinationals.

The first half of the 1980s proved to be a difficult time for U.S. multinationals. Courtesy of the 1979 oil shock, the global economy stumbled into recession. After reaching a postwar peak of $13 billion in 1980, U.S. direct investment in Europe plunged to just $3.5 billion in 1982. Investment flows to Canada turned negative in 1981–82 due to that country's adoption of restrictive policies such as the Natural Energy Program, which prompted U.S. companies to sell their existing assets in the politically charged petroleum and mining sectors. Meanwhile, Latin America's debt crisis and subsequent economic recession sharply curtailed U.S. multinational participation in that region.

Across the Pacific, talk of an "Asian miracle," compared to debt-ridden Latin America, protectionist Canada, and slumping Europe, inspired a friendlier view of Asia among U.S. firms. As a consequence, in the 1980s cumulative U.S. direct investment in Asia rose 71.5 percent from the previous decade, well ahead of the pace in Europe (64 percent), Latin America (37 percent), and Canada (–13.2 percent). More impressive still was the surge in U.S. investment to the developing nations of Asia, which rose to $14 billion in 1980–89 from $6.1 billion in the 1970s. Still, the region attracted only 8.1 percent of total U.S.

outflows in the 1980s, less than half the amount invested in trouble-prone Latin America.

Although the 1980s started with a gloomy investment climate for U.S. multinationals, the decade ended on a decidedly different note. In fact, the global investment backdrop at the end of the 1980s and into the 1990s was nearly perfect. Multiple forces, cyclical and structural, converged to produce one of the most powerful booms in global foreign direct investment, with American firms leading the way. Falling telecommunication and transportation costs allowed U.S. firms to broaden the geographic dispersion of their operations. The end of the Cold War opened new markets to U.S. firms, as did the proliferation of regional trading blocs such as the North American Free Trade Agreement, the Central American Free Trade Agreement, and the common market of the European Union. Moreover, low interest rates and surging equity prices around the world provided copious amounts of cash for global mergers and acquisitions.

All of these developments converged in the 1990s to trigger the most robust wave of U.S. foreign direct investment in history. During that decade alone, U.S. firms invested more capital overseas—$802 billion—than they had in the previous four decades combined. But the geographic preference of U.S. firms did not change, despite all the hype about new markets in central Europe, economic reform in India, privatization in Brazil, and liberalization in mainland China. The developed nations—by a wide margin—remained the biggest recipients of U.S. direct investment.

Around the turn of the century, U.S. foreign direct investment tapered off as the dollar fell in value. It became less expensive for foreign companies to invest here than for American companies to invest overseas. Still, in 2006, American businesses invested $153.2 billion dollars overseas, an increase of 17.8 per cent from the $130.1 billion invested in 2005.[10] Moreover, the declining dollar helped generate big profits from the investments that had been made in decades past.

A number of motives drive the global strategies of U.S. multinationals, but reducing the wage bill tends to be near the bottom of the list. More important are proximity of wealthy consumers, along with access to skilled labor and technology. These advantages reside in the developed nations, which accounted for two-thirds of total U.S. foreign direct investment in 2006.[11] Europe remained the preferred destination, accounting for 41.6 percent of the $153.2 billion total. Canada represented another 17.7 percent, attracting almost five times the U.S. investment of Mexico that year. Meanwhile, Asia's total share of U.S. investment during 2006 was 19.0 percent, not much more than Canada's. And even in the Asian-Pacific region, the most favored location of U.S. multinationals is Japan, one of the most expensive nations on Earth.

At the other end of the spectrum sits India. Although it is often viewed as one of the most promising emerging markets in Asia, with a massive and cheap labor force, India attracted just $1.0 billion in 2006, one of the smaller commitments in Asia. A dollar in India goes much farther than a dollar in the United Kingdom, but American businesses still see better opportunities in high-wage markets. If wage considerations were the main driver of direct investment, surely there would be a greater multinational presence (and development) in sub-Saharan Africa and Bangladesh, for example.

Tunnel Vision

While U.S. multinationals were enjoying their best decade ever, developing countries around the world were suffering successive economic crises. In 1995, Mexico fell victim to a currency meltdown. In mid-1997, it was Asia's turn. Russia rolled over the next year, followed by Brazil shortly thereafter. Each traumatic event set off a mad scramble on Wall Street to determine the collateral damage to the United States, using trade linkages as the standard benchmark.

As the Asian crisis unfolded, the flurry of attention surrounding U.S.–Asian trade linkages was understandable. Of the top fifteen U.S. export markets in the world, seven were in Asia. The region accounted for nearly one-third of U.S. exports in the year before the crisis, notably higher than the export shares of Europe (22.4 percent) and Latin America (17.8 percent). Using trade as the key variable, then, Asia factored heavily into the U.S. equation. But trade linkages were only half the story—if even that. Viewed from the lens of affiliate sales, the Asian meltdown was significant but hardly fatal to the U.S. economy, given that developing Asia accounted for only about 10 percent of total U.S. affiliate sales. (The credit crisis, by contrast, was driven almost entirely by problems in the circulation of capital. The nation that was affected the worst, Iceland, was hurt by investment commitments, not trade factors.)

The myopic focus on U.S. exports misunderstands the true picture of U.S. global competitiveness; so can a singular focus on imports. Many foreign companies compete in the United States the same way U.S. companies compete abroad—through affiliate sales rather than exports. Although American firms adopted foreign direct-investment strategies earlier and more aggressively than did their foreign counterparts, many Japanese and European companies have also begun to prefer affiliate sales over exports as their main approach to foreign markets. Most notably, BMW, Honda, and Toyota have chosen to make cars in the United States rather than ship them from Germany or Japan, putting a twist on the competitive problems facing U.S. automakers. Trade barriers were unable to protect the Detroit Three, and the Japanese companies didn't need subsidies on their end to compete here.

For many foreign multinationals such as Reuters, Royal Ahold, and British Petroleum, the answer to globalization was to plow billions of dollars into the United States, the growth champion and technological leader of the world. Companies cannot afford to ignore America's wealthy consumers and innovative workers. Indeed, foreign multinationals pumped $237.8 billion into the U.S. economy in 2007[12]; $144.9 billion of that came from companies based in Europe, and $108.1 billion of that went into manufacturing.

In 2005, U.S. imports of goods and services totaled $2.0 trillion. But as impressive as that number is, it falls short of the $3.4 trillion in sales by foreign-owned affiliates in the United States that same year. A fixation on imports ignores the extensive presence of foreign-owned affiliates in the United States, which numbered more than 9,700 at last count. It also overlooks that such affiliates contributed nearly $2.8 trillion in sales and employed around 5.3 million Americans in 2006. Businesses want to be here because they want access to the rich American market and the skilled U.S. workforce. Also, their sales are insulated from fluctuations in the exchange rate. The more a foreign company meets U.S. demand with local production, the lower imports may be, and this could reduce the trade deficit. American jobs may be created, and technologies, including ways of doing business, will be transferred. Hondas made in Ohio are domestic automobiles for trade accounting. The cars and jobs stay here; the profits go to Japan, though some are retained in the United States.

Beyond Trade

Foreign direct investment has changed the face of the international economy. Since the early 1970s, it has grown faster than either world output or global trade and is the single most important source of capital for developing economies. But America's foreign economic policy still centers on trade at the expense of investment. A trade spat with the European Union over beef and bananas, for example, risks America's large investment stake in Europe. And the suggestion of some to devalue the dollar to promote U.S. exports would only make it more expensive for U.S. affiliates to do business abroad while making it cheaper for foreign companies to buy American assets. An attempt to improve the trade balance, therefore, could actually hurt the foreign direct-investment balance.

Corporate America risks losing out on the best opportunities of the global marketplace if Washington continues to make trade its top priority in the world economy. The U.S. bilateral trade deficit with China is a cause of anxiety for many Americans, even though the real, more substantial penetration of the Chinese market by U.S. companies will likely come through direct investment and affiliate sales. This trend will only grow in favor of foreign direct investment. A continued fixation on trade, however, will divert attention from these more-promising investment opportunities in that fast-growing country.

The evolutionary strategy of U.S. multinational companies is increasingly being adopted by companies based elsewhere. The strategy is evolutionary in the sense that it has responded to the changes in the global political economy environment. Producing and selling locally provides natural insulation from dramatic swings in currency values that sometimes characterize the modern macroeconomy and that can overwhelm export-oriented strategies. Direct investment allows companies to be closer to their customers than they could be as exporters.

From a host country's perspective, direct investment is usually better than importing. Investment produces jobs; in many cases, those jobs pay more than other jobs in the host country. It leads to technology transfers. Direct investment also may generate what economists call *positive externalities*—unintended but real byproducts of an activity, in this case such as a pool of skilled workers, with a little bit of global trade expertise, who can later be employed in domestic businesses.

Direct investment is a sign of a longer-term commitment in the host country than buying a bond or shares of stock. The inflows are easier to manage within the domestic economy. Unlike a stock market investment, direct investment doesn't cause distortions from hot money inflows followed by inevitable outflows.

Employment and Output

The major transformations of the U.S. economy have had little to do with fluctuations in the value of the dollar or the state of global trade agreements. Instead, one key driver is technologic development and of a special kind in particular—labor saving and capital saving. The U.S. manufacturing sector illustrates the implication of this. It is larger than the entire Chinese economy even while employing fewer people.

But Americans have their own myths: that our jobs are being shipped overseas, stolen by people who will work for nothing, while our manufacturing output falls to a fraction of what it once was. The reality is different. Between 1939 and 2007, manufacturing employment declined as a percentage of the total private-sector workforce (see *Figure 7.1*).[13] Other than a blip during World War II, the proportion of factory workers has steadily declined, although the absolute number of manufacturing employees hasn't changed as much as is commonly believed. At the end of 2008, 13.1 million people held manufacturing jobs. This is down from a peak of 19.3 million in 1978, a year in which 72.8 million Americans worked in the private sector. By 2008, 113.5 million people were employed by private businesses, more than offsetting the declining number of manufacturing jobs.

Although manufacturing employment declined relative to the economy as a whole over the last seventy years, manufacturing output has not, thanks to dramatic improvements in the productivity of American workers. Between 1987 and 2006, manufacturing as a percentage of GDP fell from 27.5 percent to 19.9 percent (see *Figure 7.2*).[14] During that same period, manufacturing employment fell from 19.7 percent of the private workforce to 11.9 percent,[15] declining at a much faster rate than output.

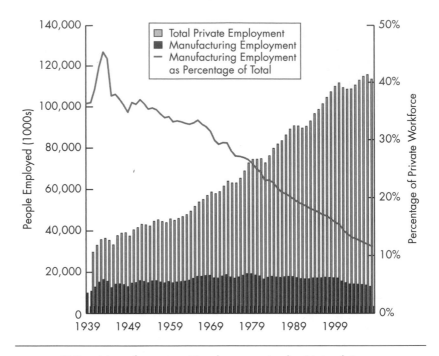

FIGURE 7.1   Manufacturing Employment in the United States, 1939–2008

Source: U.S. Bureau of Labor Statistics Database

Another way to look at the same data is to note that America's non-manufacturing workforce has grown faster than the nonmanufacturing output. This has implications not only for the American economy but also for how the United States approaches trade.

There may be a limit to how much productivity can be gained from service exports, though; most of the gains come in the form of low wage rates, 24-hour operations (with people in one time zone working while their colleagues elsewhere are asleep), or from exposure to new markets and new ways of doing things. But here's what one doesn't get: dramatic increases in output per hour. Thanks to a phenomenon now known as Baumol's disease,[16] service workers do not enjoy the same productivity gains as people in other sectors. A change in manufacturing plant design that allows a worker to make five times more widgets an hour increases productivity. A new computer system that

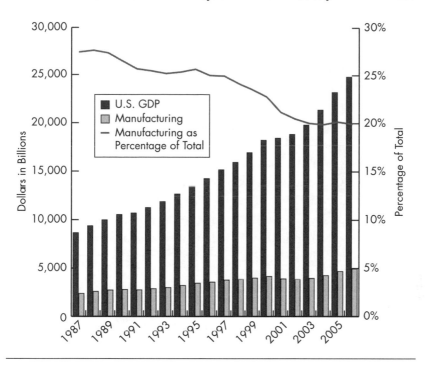

FIGURE 7.2   Manufacturing's Contribution to U.S. GDP

Source: U.S. Bureau of Economic Analysis Industry Accounts Database

lets a bank expand to twice the number of branches increases productivity. But if a first-grade teacher goes from having twenty students in class to one hundred, has her productivity increased? Probably not. Likewise, an orchestra can't perform a symphony with fewer people or in half the time without a serious decline in quality.

In the same way, companies find a limit to productivity gains from trade. The ability to import and export services has changed some of the assumptions about how global markets work. The importation and exportation of services may slow the growth of the trade deficit simply because of the lower productivity advantages, which limit the cost savings. It's not possible, at least not yet, to get a haircut remotely. A mammogram has to be taken on site, even though it can be read from an ocean away.

Globalization has not destroyed American industry. Output has increased, even as manufacturing jobs in the sector have declined in absolute and relative terms. More crossborder transactions involve people within the same corporate walls—as inventory is shipped from a manufacturing plant in Taiwan to a warehouse in the United States, for example, while software is shipped from the headquarters in the United States to the manufacturing plant in Taiwan.

And globalization slowed the transfer of finished products from the United States to elsewhere. Instead of an American firm shipping to a Mexican firm, the American firm ships to its Mexican subsidiary. Instead of the Mexican firm looking for an import agent in Brazil, it simply opens up its own office there. As travel and communications become seemingly cheaper and easier, remote operations may be more efficient and more profitable in the long run than importing and exporting between unaffiliated parties.

Capital Assets around the World

The U.S. Treasury reports that, in June 2008, private foreign investors including banks sold roughly $139 billion worth of U.S. securities. In the same month, foreign central banks bought $11.2 billion worth of mostly U.S. Treasuries and agency bonds. And in the three-month period through June, private investors and banks bought about $132.2 billion worth of U.S. securities, while central banks bought $30.7 billion.[17] Foreign central banks and private investors purchase U.S. securities month in and month out. Ironically, the most fickle investors are Americans themselves, especially U.S. hedge funds located in the tax havens in the Caribbean. They are more likely to trade these securities for speculative or short-term purposes rather than hold them until maturity. Moreover, foreign investors, both public and private, do not invest their savings in the United States out of altruism or generosity. They do it for an old-fashioned reason: money and security. The depth, breadth, and transparency of the U.S. capital markets, even during the credit crisis, know no rivals.

Although European bankers and some critics of the United States hoped that the advent of the euro would allow European capital markets to compete with the U.S., that hasn't happened. While there has indeed been some improvement, the European sovereign bond market is more like the U.S. municipal bond market, with various issuers, each issue being relatively small, and each country having different issuance and tax schedules. The secondary corporate bond market and the high-yield bond market are also small compared to those in the United States, which continues to lead in various financial innovations. As of early 2009, it is too early to see what the consequences are of the credit crisis in terms of financial innovation, but the implications would suggest more transparency, not less, more regulation and larger regulators, with better risk metrics and, perhaps, a better sense of the need for global cooperation, if not coordination.

Although many pundits seemingly never tire of repeating how the United States needs to import more than $3 billion each working day to finance its current account deficit, few recognize that a group of countries are, in fact, generating more than that in excess savings. As Conant realized a century ago, they must export the excess savings or face domestic crisis. Money has to be invested in order to generate a return. It would have been impossible for Europe and Japan to recover from the destruction of World War II without access to the U.S. market on favorable terms; likewise, the relatively open U.S. market for goods and its ability to absorb excess savings has been critical to the global recovery from the series of emerging market crises from Latin America to Russia to East Asia. Indeed, for some countries, their trade surplus with the United States accounts for a significant part of their economies' growth. Although domestic reforms in China since the late 1970s have been important, access to the U.S. market for both goods and capital provided the second pillar on which China's push for rapid development rests.

There are limits to the U.S. strategy of promoting foreign direct investment abroad and accepting investment dollars here. It is far from the ideal solution. But it is not obvious where those limits are. Some economic historians note that on the eve of World War I, the peak of an earlier version of globalization, the median current account imbalance of the major countries was more than 5 percent of their GDP. Now it is less than half that despite the incredible growth of crossborder movement of capital and goods. It is not clear if any other country has the capability or desire to replace or supplant the United States as the safety valve for the world's surplus capital. Nor do the numerous critics have a realistic alternative to the U.S. strategy. The development of capital markets, especially in Asia, and boosting world consumption to absorb the surplus savings may help, but it will take a long time because cultural as well as institutional changes are required. Moreover, the credit crisis, which put a premium on liquidity and safety, appeared to have stopped the development of a local currency bond market in Asia cold in its tracks.

The Fall of Bretton Woods and the Rise of the IMF

What ultimately made the first and only Bretton Woods successful was not just the two years of thought and planning that went into that summit. It was not just the caliber of leaders. It was not just that a major war had been fought that helped foster the spirit of cooperation. Indeed, the fiercest negotiations were between Harry Dexter White, representing the United States, and John Maynard Keynes, representing Great Britain. It was that the United States was the only major economy that was largely spared the destruction of the war. The United States had the preponderance of economic and military power at that time.

The United States was strong enough to largely dictate the key terms of the agreement. It held more monetary gold than the rest of the world put together. Many of those who embrace the hope of a second Bretton Woods see it as possible because the United States has been hobbled by two protracted wars in Iraq and Afghanistan, the second recession of the first decade of the new century, and a credit crisis of historic proportions. They hope that through a weakened United States and the collapse of Anglo-American capitalism, the world can once again re-create its financial architecture. And they are mistaken.

The United States still is the world's largest economy. American GDP is a little more than three times larger than Japan, the second largest economy. Its military spending exceeds the rest of the world combined. Yet the United States cannot dictate the outcome or impose a new international monetary regime as it could at Bretton Woods, nor does America want a sequel.

Some people seek to expand the authority of the IMF so that it would become the principle organization in charge of financial stability, with authority to monitor national regulators. This does not seem like a very promising route. The IMF lacks a certain legitimacy. Its reputation was tarnished by its handling of the 1997–98 Asian financial crisis, and it has limited enforcement powers. Many Asian countries, including Japan, China, and South Korea, are developing a network of swap agreements and reserve-sharing mechanisms that will allow them to bypass the IMF in a crisis.

One of the few political truisms is that any policy is a bad one if it cannot be enforced. It is one thing to tweak the interpretation of the IMF's charter; for example, the IMF now has the authority to monitor the foreign exchange market to ensure that countries are not unfairly manipulating currency, and, by all accounts, this initiative appears to have largely failed. It is quite another thing to give it enforcement powers.

Don't Sweat the Trade Deficit

The United States recorded a trade deficit for more than a quarter of a century, but it has not weakened it in any meaningful sense. The U.S. current account deficit (which measures the crossborder exchange of goods, services, and investment income) was $618.5 billion at the end of 2007[18]; it expanded by more than $1 billion a day to reach 4.5 percent of GDP.[19] Many economists worry that the huge trade deficit, which must be financed by foreign investors, could lead to a full-blown financial crisis if and when those investors become unwilling to fund the imbalance.

The credit crisis was not caused or even triggered by the feared capital strike against the United States—quite the opposite. The U.S. trade deficit bottomed in December 2005, whereas the broader current account deficit hit its low in the third quarter of 2006. The U.S. dollar did decline in the first year of the financial crisis. By the middle of 2008, and as the fuller nature of the crisis was becoming evident, the U.S. dollar soared against most currencies. The lone exception was the Japanese yen.

The leveraging and structural positions that been established in the first part of the twenty-first century were financed by borrowing dollars. They included hedge funds and banks in the United States and Europe and insurance companies, speculators, and investors in countries such as South Korea, Mexico, and Brazil. As the credit crises unfolded, they were forced to replace those previously borrowed dollars. As the dollar went up, more participants found themselves needing dollars. For example, corporations with foreign currency–denominated receivables might hedge them by buying dollars. Meanwhile, American investors sold overseas investments to take advantage of bargains in the U.S. markets. Momentum traders looked for a trend to participate in, hoping to make up for losses elsewhere, noticed the dollar. In combination, these factors made the dollar go up—and fast—even while other markets deflated. To a lesser extent, the yen, Swiss franc, and Hong Kong dollars were also used as financing currencies and tended to outperform during the crisis as previously sold positions had to be bought back.

Reality: America Is a World Leader in Productivity

In the realm of global economic competition and rivalry, the focus on trade is misplaced. It is only one dimension of America's role in the global economy, and it's hardly the most important. Under the conditions of the globalized Open Door, the direct-investment strategy of meeting foreign demand from local production rather than exports has proven to be successful, even if it hurts the trade deficit. Hence, the United States should shift the thrust of policy toward direct investment; anyone looking at world trade in order to make decisions should do the same.

This has clear implications for the dollar. The U.S. multinational strategy is relatively immune to the dollar's fluctuations by creating natural currency diversification. Corporate profits were strong in the second half of the 1990s when the dollar was strong. Corporate profits recovered cyclically after the early 2001 recession in a weak-dollar environment.

This also means that other considerations will dominate when making investment decisions. For example, conventional wisdom holds that in a weak-dollar environment, investments in large multinational companies should outperform more domestic-oriented companies. But the markets are more complicated and volatile. So, for example, Wendy's sales are more domestic than McDonald's, but the former outperformed during the periods of acute dollar weakness. The same is true for other company pairs, such as PepsiCo and Coca-Cola, John Deere and Caterpillar. Companies end up trading based on other fundamentals besides the dollar. McDonald's has proven that it can execute its strategy in any market, usually with local ingredients and always with local labor. Commodity prices are a concern for McDonald's investors; exchange rates are not.

This globalization of the division of labor has created a virtual factory. Companies move goods from place to place all the time, but when that trade takes place over national borders, even within the same company, it is counted as trade under our archaic national accounts system. This intrafirm trade accounts for half of the U.S. trade deficit. These are the synapses that connect the neurons. The command, control, and communication functions necessary to coordinate such production and supply chains are a competitive advantage, one that the United States owns. It's made possible by new technology. U.S. businesses tend to be faster at employing new technologies, and U.S. workers are used to the ongoing retraining that goes with their jobs, no matter where their titles fall on the corporate organization chart.

It is true that some low-skilled and low-paying work has moved abroad. This has not affected output because of technological applications that drive productivity. On the other hand, employment by overseas affiliates increases demand for services from the parent, and that creates different jobs. Evidence suggests that most countries are losing manufacturing jobs, even China; technology is the biggest threat to low-skilled or labor-intensive work, not offshoring.

Modern businesses look at the entire production process step by step, then cut it up into different pieces and distribute them wherever it makes economic and political sense. That sophisticated management expertise makes the United States a global manufacturing powerhouse, whether the work is done here or abroad. Before the credit crisis, the U.S. industrial output was higher than ever. This was accomplished with few man-hours of labor. This is *productivity,* and it is one of America's success stories that underpins its economic prowess.

Chapter Notes

1. David Becker and Richard Sklar, *Postimperialism and World Politics* (Westport, CT: Praeger, 1999).

2. U.S. Bureau of Economic Analysis, "An Ownership-Based Framework of the U.S. Current Account, 1997–2006." *Survey of Current Business,* January 2008 (Vol. 88, No. 1).

3. U.S. Bureau of Economic Analysis, "U.S. International Transactions: 1960–Present," December 15, 2008.

4. U.N. Conference on Trade and Development, *World Investment Report 2008: Transnational Corporations and the Infrastructure Challenge* (Geneva: UNCTAD, September 2008).

5. U.S. Census Bureau, Foreign Trade Division, Data Dissemination Branch.

6. U.N. Conference on Trade and Development, *World Investment Report 2008*.

7. U.S. Bureau of Economic Analysis, "Summary Estimates for Multinational Companies: Employment, Sales, and Capital Expenditures for 2006," April 17, 2008.

8. Raymond J. Montaloni Jr., "U.S. Multinational Companies Operations in 2006." *Survey of Current Business* (Washington, DC: Bureau of Economic Analysis, November 2008).

9. U.N. Conference on Trade and Development, *World Investment Report 2008*.

10. Raymond J. Montaloni Jr., "U.S. Multinational Companies Operations in 2006."

11. Ibid.

12. U.S. Bureau of Economic Analysis, "Foreign Direct Investment in the U.S.: Country and Industry Detail for Capital Inflows," September 17, 2008.

13. U.S. Bureau of Labor Statistics database.

14. U.S. Bureau of Economic Analysis, Industry Economic Accounts.

15. U.S. Bureau of Labor Statistics database.

16. The effect was first described by William Baumol and William Bowen in *Performing Arts: The Economic Dilemma* (Cambridge: MIT Press, 1966).

17. U.S. Treasury, Treasury Bulletin, September 2008.

18. U.S. Bureau of Economic Analysis, "U.S. International Transactions: Second Quarter 2008," September 17, 2008.

19. U.S. Bureau of Economic Analysis, "Gross Domestic Product: Third Quarter 2008," October 30, 2008.

U.S. Capitalist Development Prevents Socialism

Government and capitalism are partners, not opponents.

The University of Chicago may be home of some of the most ardent laissez-faire capitalists this world may have ever seen. Many economists affiliated with that university, such as Milton Friedman, believe that the discipline of the market is preferable to other means of distribution. Economic freedom, to them, leads to political freedom. Although the Marxists often are accused of being economic determinists, these students of capitalism are just as much so, if not more.

People don't want to use prescription medications with deadly side effects, so they'll choose to use drugs without them. It seems so simple, yet it only works if everyone knows in advance which drugs have deadly side effects and which ones don't. Because of the information gap, markets need regulations and tort systems, much to the dismay of the Chicago Boys. Government intervention makes it possible for companies to introduce new drugs successfully, for doctors to feel comfortable prescribing them, and for patients willingly to take them. It enables innovation and profit.

Americans like to think of their nation as a capitalist one, but it's really a hybrid system with enough government involvement to make the markets function. The credit crisis converted at least one ideologue, former Federal Reserve Chairman Alan Greenspan, who admitted to

133

Congress in October 2008 that deregulation had not worked as well as he had imagined.

U.S. culture is fundamentally individualistic and antistatist. The United States has its own brand of government support that fits its culture. Americans do want government involvement, especially when things are going wrong, they just don't like to admit it. Witness the fallout of the financial crisis. That crisis seems to be largely a function of market-based developments, as borrowers, lenders, investors, banks, rating agencies, and other actors responded to a myriad of incentives (the incentive structure itself was a mix of private and public negotiations). It was the type of event that appears to have emerged from within the market itself. However, the many people and businesses that suffered, the innocent as well as the guilty, clamored for the government's help.

The state has an important role in a capitalist economy, and both businesses and workers benefit. The government provides the structure that lets the invisible hand do the work, and it provides a safety net when that hand drops the ball. State involvement does not mean that a nation is sliding toward socialism; and if it were, socialism and capitalism can coexist. The credit crisis has tested capitalism, but it will not lead to socialism; it could lead to a more interesting hybrid of the two.

America, the Workers' Paradise

Over the last century, the American workforce has become more educated. Workers are mostly free from physical toil, enjoy more leisure time, live in larger and more comfortable residences, and live longer than ever before. They have the ability to instantly gratify every desire and whim at a declining cost in terms of time needed to work at average earnings. Through the various business cycles, compared with any other time, life for large swaths of the American public does not appear much different from how Samuel Gompers, founder of the American Federation of Labor, once defined socialism: More now.[1]

Even income inequality, which has widened in recent decades, masks dramatic improvement in family well-being. However, the gap between the consumption of the richest people in America and the consumption of the poorest people is much narrower.[2] Research by the Federal Reserve Bank of Dallas found that the top fifth of American households earned an average of $149,963 in 2006 and spent $69,863 of that. The bottom fifth of households earned $9,974, on average, and spent $18,153.[3] (That difference between income and spending was a function of savings and property sales, especially for retirees and people between jobs.) Although folks in the richer category are better able to save and pay taxes, the gaps in consumption do not appear as large as income and wealth gaps. That's because products that were once luxuries have become commonplace, made more affordable by mass production, mass distribution, and ongoing technological improvements.

Don't believe it? Well, a look at the costs of common items and the number of hours that the average American would need to work for them makes the case (see *Figure 8.1*).[4]

Not only has the median family gotten smaller, but the average house has gotten bigger. In 2007, the average new home was 2,479 square feet, compared to 1,750 square feet in 1978,[5] even though the average household has just 2.56 people.[6] The average American has achieved the dream of a "room of one's own." In 1970, the U.S. Census Bureau reported that 6.5 percent of households had incomplete plumbing; in 2007, just 1.1 percent of households did. Meanwhile, 86.4 percent of households had air conditioning in 2007, compared to just 35.7 percent in 1970.[7]

Inflation-adjusted per-capita income has nearly doubled since 1970, which may explain why so many more households have air conditioning. In 1970, the average worker brought home $15,139 in 2007 dollars; in 2007, that average income was $26,087.[8] But this too understates the improved living standard. W. Michael Cox of the Federal Reserve documented the decline in the work hours necessary to purchase common goods and services.[9] In 1956, for example, he found that it cost about sixteen weeks of work to purchase each one hundred square feet of a home. In 2000 (before the housing market bubble), it took about fourteen hours of typical pay to purchase each one hundred square feet of a home. In 1950, it took about thirty minutes of median wages to buy a cheeseburger. Now the cheeseburger can be purchased with just three minutes of work. It appears that only health care and college education require more work time to acquire.[10]

In 2007, there were more than 45 million Americans who did not have health insurance. It is a national embarrassment and a tragedy for

FIGURE 8.1   Cost of Consumer Goods in Terms of Work Hours in U.S.

Goods and services

	1972	1997	2007
Hand-Held Calcuator/price	$120.00	$10.00	$4.95
Hours/Minutes of Work	32 Hrs	50 Mins	17 Mins

Sharp 8-Digit Display Hand-Held Calculator (www.amazon.com)

	1978	2007
Videocassette Recorders (VCR)/price	$985.00	$59.95
Hours/Minutes of Work	175 Hrs	4 Hrs

Panasonic-4-Head VHS Hi-Fi Stereo VCR with Commercial Skip (www.amazon.com)

	1984	2007
Cell Phones/price	$4,195	$300.00
Hours/Minutes of Work	500 Hrs	18 Hrs

(Motorola RAZR V3xx)- Free with (–24.99) credit if with contract ATT

	1915	1997	2007
Phone call (San Franciso to NY)(3 mins)/price	$20.7	$0.40	$44.99
Hours/Minutes of Work	NA	2 Mins	2.6 Hrs

*Verizon freedom calling plans: Includes unlimited local, regional and long distance calling in the U.S.

	1967	1997	2007
Microwave/price	$491.04	$184.35	$69.99
Hours/Minutes of Work	176 Hrs	15 Hrs	4 Hrs

Sharp R-230KW 800-Watt 4/5-Cubic-Foot Compact Microwave (www.amazon.com)

	1940	1997	2003	2007
Big Mac/price	$0.30	$1.89	$2.65	$3.22
Hours/Minutes of Work	NA	0.15	0.17	0.19

*Big Mac Index, *The Economist*

	1919	1997	2007
Chicken (3 pounds)/price	$6.90	$2.31*	$1.49
Hours/Minutes of Work	2.3	11 min	5.5 seconds

(Per pound) for whole chicken/source* www.usda.gov (Chicken breast) . 79 cents/pound
http://usda.mannlib.cornell.edu/usda/ers/89007/table0097.xls

	1960	1997	2007
Video Camera (Bell & Howell)* with Kodak film/price	NA	$577.63	$349.95
Hours/Minutes of Work	58 Hrs	47 Hrs	20 Hrs

Sony DCR-DVD108 DVD Handycam Camcorder with 40x Optical Zoom

Goods and services

	1972	1997	2007
Seven-day Caribbean cruise/price	$193.80	$553.05	$499
Hours/Minutes of Work	51 Hrs	45 Hrs	30 Hrs

7 Day Eastern Caribbean from Miami, FL (Interior) http://www.carnival.com

	1930s	1997	2007
Automobile tire/price	$13.00	$75.00	$148.00
Hours/Minutes of Worka	NA	6 Hrs	8 Hrs

Good Year-Eagle ResponsEdge (carbon fiber reinforced sidewall) for Toyota Camry
www.discounttire.com 50,000 miles Warranty

	1927	1997	2007
Hart Schaffner & Marx suit /price	$42.95	$525.00	$795.00
Hours/Minutes of Work	NA	43 Hrs	47 Hrs

Hart Schaffner Marx Two Button Fancy Suit * http://shop.nordstrom.com

	1908	2007
Ford Taurus/price	NA	$23,245.00
Hours/Minutes of Work		1360 Hrs
	2 years of wages	34 Weeks approx 8.5 months

http://www.fordvehicles.com/cars/taurus/Ford Taurus 2007
(40 Hours) Full time a week taken to caluclate weeks and months

	1954	2007
12' Inches Color Television /price	NA	$317.00
Hours/Minutes of Work	3 months	19 Hrs

Sharp LC13SH6U 13" LCD TV (www.amazon.com)

	1997	2007
25' Inches TV (crystal clear picture w/ remote control)	$884.88	$723.35
Hours/Minutes of Work	3 days	42 Hrs

Samsung LNT2653H 26" LCD (High Definition) TV (www.amazon.com)

	1919	1950	1975	1997	2007
Half a gallon of milk/price	NA	NA	$0.76	$1.42	$2.19
Hours/Minutes of Work	39 mins	16 mins	10 mins	7 mins	8 seconds

.285 cent/second

	1920	1960	1997	2006
Median price for a new house/price				
	$4,700.00	$14,500.00	$140,000.00	$246,000.00
Hours/Minutes of Work			13,910 Hrs	14,386 Hrs

U.S Census Bureau Manufacturing, Mining and Construction Statistics
http://www.census.gov/const/uspriceann.pdf

(continued)

Goods and services

	1920	1956	1970	2006
Cost per square feet/price	NA	NA	NA	$85.44
Hours/Minutes of Work	7.8 Hrs	6.5 hrs	5 hrs	4.9 Hrs

Median and Average Price per Square Foot of Floor Area in New One-Family House
www.nahb.org/fileUpload_details.aspx?contentID=560

	1929	1957	1970	1997	2007
Twin mattress with box/price	NA	NA	$139.02	$294.96	$509.99
Hours/Minutes of Work	161 Hrs	78 Hrs	42 Hrs	24 Hrs	30 Hrs

Serta Blue Ridge Firm MattressSet
http://www.target.com/gp/detail.html/ref=sc_pgc_r_12_1_ 12945751/602-1278970-8286233?ie=
UTF8&frombrowse=1&asin=B000QDNEIQ

	1982	2007
Haircut	$6.00	$16.00
Hours/Minutes of Work	45 mins	56 mins

www.greatclips.com
Average price for haircuts

Source: Rab Jafri. Unpublished paper. New York: Terra K Partners, LLC, 2008.

many people. Yet in our grandparent's generation, health insurance was an exclusive purvey of the rich. Americans, like others in many countries, are living longer, are more active, and in less pain than previous generations.

With the advent of the Internet, cell phones, and BlackBerry-like products, one often feels as if one is always "on call." However, the length of the workweek has been reduced. In 1850, the typical workweek was six 11-hour days. By 1900, the workweek was more commonly five days and 53 hours. In 2000, the typical workweek was down to 42 hours.

As the workweek has decreased and the penetration of technology has reduced the time and drudgery of basic maintenance, Americans have more free time than ever. Robert Fogel, an American historian at the University of Chicago, estimates that in 1880, between the length of the workday and the time needed for such basic things as traveling and shopping, the average adult man had only 11 hours a week that could be considered leisure or relaxation. Fogel estimates that the average American male now has 40 hours a week of leisure, even though the demands of modernity may prevent us from experiencing it as such. There has been a dramatic increase in the working hours of the average American female, but Fogel estimates that women, too, have about 30 more hours of leisure now than they would have had a century ago.[11]

Studies by John Robinson of the University of Maryland and Geoffrey Godbey of Penn State University conclude that since 1960 the typical American has gained about 5 hours a week in free time, defined as time not under the compulsion of paid work or taking care of infants or doing household chores.[12]

Thanks to technological advances, those household chores take less time to complete even though the house itself is bigger. In 1900, 90 percent of American women spent at least four hours a day involved with primary housework (cooking and cleaning). Now more women than ever are working for wages, including two-thirds of women with minor children, but as a whole only 14 percent of all adult women (in 2000) spent four or more hours per day on primary housework.[13]

Ironically, it's hard to convince people of their economic success. In the United States, income and comfort levels have improved over the long run even while business cycles up and down. Perhaps it is the uncertainty and pace of change that contributes to people's anxiety, even though they are doing better by objective measures.[14] Americans are healthier, live longer, have greater income, and enjoy greater material pleasures while working fewer hours than at almost any time in the past. Even economic events that are bad for some, such as a decline in housing prices, are good for others such as first-time home buyers who could not afford the bubble prices. Even though Americans report unhappiness with the status quo, they know on some level that things are good enough that they do not seek radical change or the violent overthrow of the owners of the means of production. In fact, they are the owners of the means of production. To the extent change is embraced, there is a clear preference for gradual change.

The Role of the State

Too often, capitalism and socialism are thought of as simple polar opposites. On one side are markets, businesses, and freedom: capitalism. On the other side are the state, workers, and dictators: socialism. However, a quick look at the history of capitalism reveals a much more complicated relationship between the state and markets. It's not a simple either–or situation. In the United States, it's both–and.

The state was the midwife of capitalism as it emerged from within feudal society. Government action was needed to turn the factors of production (land, labor, and capital) into commodities that could be bought and sold. The nascent capitalists and their government helpers often encountered resistance, the same resistance that modernizers everywhere face. The Chinese call these the *Four Olds*: old habits, old ideas, old customs, and old beliefs.

The midwife stayed on to become a primary caregiver, fostering and supporting business activity. The corporate form of organization had to be created by the state with laws to protect property and establish boundaries. The state's power of taxation and regulation can have significant impacts on the incentive structure of economic activity. States intervene in markets on occasion to address what they perceive to be systemic risk.

Some scholars, such as Theda Skocpol, trace the origins of the modern welfare state to programs to support widows and orphans after the Civil War.[15] The Homestead Act of 1862 offered 160 acres of land to anyone who applied and who had not taken up arms against the Union, including former slaves. In exchange, the recipients had to make improvements, but almost anything qualified, including putting up a fence. This may have been among the first state-sponsored forays into promoting home ownership. Before the program wound down a little more than a hundred years later, 1.6 million homesteads covering 270 million acres were granted, representing about 10 percent of all the land in America. Although the U.S. government had long played a role in allocating resources, it took a larger one after World War II that was partly driven by an attempt to smooth out the business cycle. The bust before the war could not be repeated.

The partly conflicting and partly symbiotic relationship between capitalism and socialism does not simply take place between classes and institutions but within them as well. By looking at what each term actually means rather than equating capitalism with markets or businesses and socialism with the state or unions, the mix of the two economic organizing principles become clear. That characterizes the modern American political economy.

Consider the large modern corporation. Like politicians and workers, corporations want to smooth out boom and bust cycles. In practice, the managers try to escape the volatility of the free market. The centralized headquarters and the multiyear plan give the corporation an almost socialist feel. At the end of the day, there may not be as much of a difference between the government bureaucrat and the corporate bureaucrat.

Even the drive to globalization reflects this mix of capitalism and socialism. It is both an affirmation of the mobility of capital and an attempt to escape the omnipresent marketplace. Multinational companies internalize activities such as trade that previously took place between companies with separate legal identities.

When the financial markets broke hard in the fall of 2008, people around the world smirked over the comeuppance of Anglo-American capitalism, including leaders of capitalist nations following a more state-centered approach. Their cackles of glee were gratuitous. Free markets could not be dead because they did not really exist in the United States or the United Kingdom for that matter. And the differences between the Anglo-American style of capitalism and the continental European style were not sufficient to prevent their own credit crisis, which was only tangentially related to the U.S. subprime problems.

For a little more than half a century, the U.S. government has played a critical role in resolving a key problem at the core of the modern political economy: the surplus capital problem that Conant had diagnosed. The economy can produce more goods than consumers demand, which often contributes to the onset of economic crises. Savings grow in excess of profitable opportunities.

Before the expansion of government employment, the creation of new government departments, and the increase in federal spending by the George W. Bush administration, the U.S. government absorbed a little more than a third of all the goods and services produced in the United States (government expenditures as a percentage of GDP). The United Kingdom is near U.S. proportions, whereas continental Europe is nearer to 50 percent.

The significant size of the government before the credit crisis also leads us to another startling insight. In most modern capitalist countries, the part of the economy that is not driven by profit-maximizing considerations accounts for a majority. Consider the United States. Once the government, much of health care, many educational and research institutions, charities and foundations, and other not-for-profit companies are added together, one is stuck by the awe-inspiring revelation that more than half the world's largest economy is driven by something other than maximizing profitability. And this is well before the credit crisis, during which many pundits bemoaned the end of capitalism.

Noble Prize–winning economist Amartya Sen expressed a similar insight in an essay in early 2009:

> All affluent countries in the world—those in Europe, as well as the U.S., Canada, Japan, Singapore, South Korea, Australia, and others—have, for quite some time now, depended partly on transactions and other payments that occur largely outside markets. These include unemployment benefits, public pensions, other features of social security, and the provision of education, health care, and a variety of other services distributed through nonmarket arrangements. The economic entitlements connected with such services are not based on private ownership and property rights.
>
> Also, the market economy has depended for its own working not only on maximizing profits but also on many other activities, such as maintaining public security and supplying public services—some of which have taken people well beyond an economy driven only by profit. The creditable performance of the so-called capitalist system, when things moved forward, drew on a combination of institutions—public funded education, medical care, and mass transportation are just a few of many— that went much beyond relying only on a profit-maximizing market economy and on personal entitlements confined to private ownership.[16]

The government took a more active role during the credit crisis, but not much of its intervention used new techniques. Modern industrialized countries have experienced many banking crises over the last two generations. Along with producing things in a variety and scale unimaginable to any other generation, the modern economy generates financial excesses from time to time. It's an inherent feature of capitalism like the business cycle itself.

In bygone days, debtors would be imprisoned. Debt no longer carries a stigma, and it is used to expand the economy—usually. A combination of forces, such as the development of a service economy, better inventory management, and, of course, the modern state's intervention have smoothed out the business cycle. The United States experienced a total of seven quarters of negative growth in the twenty years between 1983 and 2008. The credit crisis snapped this run in dramatic fashion. It is far too early to know whether the cathartic nature of the credit crisis will once again put the economy on a sustained-growth footing.

The business cycle has not been repealed. It has been managed and mitigated. The amplitude of the swings has diminished, and the frequency and duration of the downturns have been reduced. That volatility instead was transferred to another set of shock absorbers, the prices of financial assets, including and especially the price of money itself.

Just as every business cycle is different, so too is every credit cycle, even though the cast of characters in the drama remains the same. There are always villains and crooks, heroes and Cassandras, and innocents and unfortunates. The abstract models that economists are so fond of are predicated on balance, and thus they and the policy makers that rely on them, knowingly or unknowingly, have ideological blinders that all too often prevent them from understanding the forces of instability.

Socialism and Capitalism

If capitalism can be defined as a type of society in which power is derived from the ownership of productive property, then America and other industrialized countries have something else. Many of the powers once drawn from the ownership of private property have been mitigated, limited, and redirected. That doesn't mean that these nations are now socialistic, but rather that they comingle capitalist and socialist forces.

Socialism is also about the extent of market forces. The basic characteristics of modern business, such as corporate ownership, management, employment, investment policy and revenue distribution, cannot be understood simply in terms of market forces. Public policy and pressure from various associational groups have helped shape the modern corporation and influence its operations and goals. This does not mean that power no longer emanates from the control of private property. Rather, the presence of socialist relations means that such power is tempered, checked, and sometimes even redirected.

To many people, any government involvement smacks of socialism. Socialism in America should not be confused with the fortunes of the Socialist Party. As an organized political entity, socialism had a colorful history in the United States. Few people joined the party, passed petitions, ran for office, or ever won. There's no Capitalist Party in the United States, either, but that doesn't mean the country is not capitalist.

The United States is hardly a socialist nation, but it has some features of socialism. One commonsense definition is that socialism is what socialists advocate. In 1980, Milton and Rose Friedman reviewed the Socialist Party platform of 1928 and were chagrined to find that most of the economic planks had been at least partially enacted.[17] The Socialist Party platform included calls for public unemployment insurance and employment agencies, health and accident insurance, old-age pensions, laws against child labor, and a shorter workday. It was also sensitive to environmental issues, calling for a national program of flood control and relief, reforestation, irrigation, and reclamation. Some of these advances have been rolled back over the past quarter century, but that doesn't mean that progress in a socialistic direction is impossible. On the contrary, it confirms it.

Peter Drucker, who studied and wrote about business and social theory, takes Marx seriously. In his book *Post-Capitalist Society*,[18] Drucker is explicit: under Marx's definition of socialism as "workers' owning the means of production," the United States is the world's most socialist nation while also being the most capitalist nation. Pension funds, of which employees are the beneficiary owners, have become the single largest owners of U.S. businesses, or the means of production. Mutual fund ownership is spread widely, with 44 percent of American households owning at least one.[19] These funds are among the largest owners of U.S. companies. Workers share in the earnings stream generated by capital. To the extent that worker ownership means socialism, the quest of U.S. citizens to be capitalists has delivered them to Karl Marx.

In the past, a company's chief executive was often a major shareholder, and his power derived from his ownership. That's not the case anymore. Capitalists themselves have become subject to the division of labor that they helped impose on the work process itself. Modern business is predicated on the separation of ownership and control.[20] Pension funds in America, for example, are the largest owners of the "means of production," with the beneficial owner being the American worker. Many American workers include the return on capital in their total income and pay taxes on it. They are owners, but exercise extremely little control.

Corporate power is not absolute. A corporation may still decide that redeployment of resources is required, for example. The socialist element insists on a voice for those who are affected and income protection, retraining, and outplacement services for those who lose their jobs. The redirection of power is also evident when businesses embrace noneconomic goals that reflect social values, such as non-discriminatory hiring practices, access and facilities for the physically challenged, transparency and accountability in transactions, and funding of the arts and educational institutions.

Although the economic theories of Friedman and company say that the only goal of the corporation is to maximize profits for shareholders ("the business of business is business"), corporate annual reports and Web sites are filled with flowery language to explain the company's noneconomic achievements in such fields as philanthropy, community development, environmental issues, and diversity. Moreover, the very ownership of the productive assets has increasingly been socialized through the public stock markets and defined-contribution pension schemes, by which equity ownership grows.

Capitalism in Crisis

Governments around the world intervened in their markets to an extent many found unimaginable to address the credit crisis. Many thought it marked the end of capitalism. Hardly. People have been declaring the end of capitalism almost since its beginning. Marx and his immediate followers anticipated the end of capitalism in short order. So did Lenin and his followers a half a century later. In 1926, John Maynard Keynes declared that capitalism had come to an end in his book *The End of Laissez Faire*.[21] That capitalism has a history is underappreciated—it changes over time. Its ability to integrate opposition, like blue jeans, rock-and-roll music, and organic food may help explain its longevity.

Booms are preferable to busts and have generally lasted longer. Economists have spent the last several decades studying growth. It became unfashionable to study crises. This will likely change going forward, as the credit crisis will provide a rich source of data to be mined for PhD dissertations.

There are two main schools of thought about modern crises. The first camp, the more orthodox one, sees the crises that end business cycles as happening outside of the market itself. Some external force interrupts capitalism's natural ongoing expansion: the Federal Reserve tightens too much; politicians sometimes propose policies that retard growth; wars and natural disasters throw an economy off its growth trajectory.

The second camp suggests that business cycles are like people. They don't have to be strangled by some outside force. They can die of old age. The causes of the end of a business cycle—the point when crises materialize—are laid out during the upswing. Crises are thus part and parcel of market economies.

Economists are famous for not agreeing on anything, so it shouldn't be surprising that the second camp itself has two factions. Hyman Minsky, an economist from Washington University in St. Louis who studied economic crises, represents the first faction. He argued that, in democracies, politicians seek to deliver prosperity: full employment, rising equity markets, and rising asset prices. But a prolonged period of that fosters speculative euphoria and what Minsky called "balance sheet engineering," in which companies look to add value in financial markets rather than from their core business.[22]

Sustained low volatility in and of itself encourages increased risk taking that often leads to unacceptable levels. Minsky noticed a self-reinforcing dynamic in speculative finance, in which decreasing debt quality leads to economic instability and crisis, with crisis being the acute form of instability. In other words, stability is temporary and leads to instability.

The other faction also sees crises as integral to capitalism. In true dialectic fashion, the crisis emerges not out of a market weakness but out of its strength. The economic elite is so successful at accumulating capital that this leads to excess investment and the building of excess capacity that leads to overproduction and causes downward pressure on prices. The current and potential supply of goods exceeds effective demand, and that can drive prices below the cost of production. Because of the high ratio of fixed costs to variable costs in the modern enterprise, businesses face little choice but to produce at a loss. That, in turn, exacerbates overproduction and eventually produces failures, concentration, and consolidation that destroy excess capacity. Charles Conant would fit into this camp, as would some scholars today, like James Livingston.[23]

This faction, a diverse group looking at the market from a range of angles, often depicts market economies as permanently in crisis. They are constantly transforming the labor process and revolutionizing production. Even though there is much interest in sustainable economic development, this faction argues that capitalism itself (not just finance) is unsustainable by its very nature. There is a nearly constant oscillation between booms and busts. The profound supply and demand disequilibrium is bridged by debt. And it is here that this second faction can make room for Minsky's minions.

It is true that the United States has had a different and lighter regulatory regime than Europe and many other countries. But the different regulatory regimes did not and will not avoid the excesses that can be built up during a protracted credit cycle. The regulatory regime provides the incentives for behaviors that shape and color the specificity of the credit cycle as it is expressed in different countries. The United States seemed to go overboard in the deregulatory push, as former Federal Reserve chairman Alan Greenspan and many others belatedly recognize. For example, in 2004, Henry Paulson lobbied the Securities and Exchange Commission to reduce capital requirements for broker-dealers. In 2008, when Paulson was secretary of the Treasury, he realized his mistake, though the proverbial horses were out of the barn, making it a bit late to close the door.

Nevertheless, the differences in U.S. and European regulatory regimes have been modest compared with their similarities. Subprime lending was not the cause of the global financial crisis. Leveraging was. And this practice knows no nationality. Rather, it knows all nationalities.

The unwinding of the foreign borrowing (mostly denominated in dollars and to a lesser extent Japanese yen, Swiss francs, and the Hong Kong dollar) by domestic businesses and banks drove the dramatic declines of various world currencies during the second part of the crisis, beginning most prominently in the summer of 2008. For example, individual investors in Japan lost significant chunks of their savings and pension money, and not because they engaged in subprime lending. Rather, the large losses that were realized were the result of unwinding leveraged short-yen carry trades, selling yen in order to get higher interest rates on foreign currency–denominated investments. For years, that helped Japanese households earn somewhat higher returns than were available in low-yielding Japanese government bonds, the poor-performing Japanese stock market, or the country's sluggish real estate market.

Surely U.S. deregulation and subprime lending cannot account for the collapse of Iceland's banking system and economy, perhaps one of the most spectacular implosions of modern times. Such other medium- and low-income countries as Hungary, the Ukraine, and Pakistan are being forced into the waiting arms of the International Monetary Fund like long-lost lovers. It's easy to blame the United States, but the responsibility of the crisis, like the crisis itself, was global.

Although it offers an outlet for plenty of frustration, blaming the Anglo-American capitalism for the financial crisis otherwise does little good and a great deal of harm. Pointing fingers at the United States prevents an appreciation of the global character of the crisis and personalizes what is a systemic issue described so well by Hyman Minsky. It encourages the externalization of one's domestic problems. It discourages the recognition of the real dangers of unchecked leverage. It fans the flames of an exclusionary type of nationalism. The spark may very well have emanated from the United States, but many countries had plenty of dry kindling that, if not the subprime, would have been ignited by some other (random or unpredictable) spark.

People elsewhere in the world have a tendency to blame the United States for the financial crisis, much in the same way that America was blamed for the Great Depression. Yet if the students of crises are right, capitalism is a global system. Hence no one, regardless of the regulatory environment or level of disdain for hedonistic consumer-oriented immediate gratification, is immune from the downside of the cycle.

What we have done with the business cycle we need to do with the credit cycle: accept that it is part of the modern political economy and develop the tools that allow it to be mitigated, elongated, and routinized. That isn't socialism; instead, it is asking the government to provide a regulatory and accounting framework to let this vital part of capitalism succeed. The result will be more transparent capitalism in the financial sector and, ultimately, a stronger economy.

Socialism, Capitalism, and More

The global economic crisis of the 1920s and 1930s had some disastrous fallout that now confuses discussions of government intervention— namely, it saw the rise of Communist Socialism and National Socialism. Governments in numerous countries, especially in the high-income countries, have responded to the credit crisis by extending their role in the economy in ways that have not been seen in at least a couple of generations and in a magnitude that appears unprecedented. Many observers, and not just unrepentant ideologues, are worried that capitalist practices and institutions are being abandoned in favor of socialism—but what type? A benevolent version featuring worker ownership that makes the United States both the world's leading capitalist country and the leading socialist one? A harsh version that stifles individual creativity in favor of government bungling like Communism? Or fascist dictatorship with some democratic trappings?

The socialist revolution in Russia in 1917 took place in an agricultural quasi-feudal society of mostly peasants. And it is Lenin and Stalin's violent, oppressive, totalitarian, statist regime that many now associate with socialism. But there was another type of socialism that was being articulated and implemented in the early 1920s. It was called fascism in Italy and Spain and later known as National Socialism in Germany.

Could it be that the second form of socialism is a greater threat than the first? In World War II, the Allies joined forces with the first type of socialism to defeat the second type. Although we often think of fascism as a racist and genocidal system, that was the situation primarily in Germany. In Italy under Benito Mussolini, fascism was totalitarian and fiercely nationalistic, but for the most part not as racist. Fascism was opposed to liberalism, individualism, and Communist socialism. The objectives and interests of the state were supreme; everything in the country was subservient to it.

The United States' and Western Europe's response to the economic crisis that spurred the advances of communism and fascism was to instead follow two economists of that period who offered strategies to bolster aggregate demand: Irving Fisher, who tended to emphasize a monetary response, and John Maynard Keynes, who advocated complementing monetary moves with fiscal policy. Nowadays, many pundits and bloggers confuse the Fisher and Keynes program with left-wing socialism, but at the time that the men were active, many thought their plans were closer to fascism—stripped of the ugly parts, of course.

Before former U.K. Prime Minister Tony Blair and former U.S. President Bill Clinton proposed a "third way" between the economic policies of the left and right wings in their countries, the fascists offered the same: a path between capitalism and socialism. If observers are correct and the United States and other high-income countries are becoming socialist, then is it the socialist or fascist variety? A key difference between the two is the type of institutional alliance that is the driving force. Under socialism, the state ostensibly is allied with workers, though in practice in the Soviet Union, China, and Cuba, the workers were miserably poor. Under fascism, the state was closely aligned with businesses, though the rights of property were conditional on use and closely regulated.

Since World War II, the United States and other high-income countries in the world have seen a permanent and significant increase in the role of the state in various aspects of the economy. To the extent that Keynes is associated with the use of fiscal policy to bolster aggregate demand, Nixon was right in saying we all have become Keynesians. However, in fairness, Keynes hoped that once an economy entered a self-sustaining upswing, the state-sponsored boost to demand would cease.

The size and role of the U.S. government increased regardless of the party affiliation of the president and Congress. The government has tried outsourcing a handful of functions such as operating prisons, schools, and some military activities. But those efforts have not been enough to curtail government growth. It has mostly kept pace with the growth of the economy. One of the outcomes of the credit crisis may be a quasi-permanent increase of the role of the state, not just in the United State but throughout the major industrialized countries.

How Governments Expand

A couple forces lead to an expansion of the government's role in the economy over time. The first is the engaged citizenry of a democracy. Over time, people want to receive more goods and services from the government that they elect and pay for. Perhaps in days of yore, the farmer or peasant would part with a substantial fraction of their produce to the sovereign or feudal lord, muttering under their breath that they were getting nothing for their hard work. But in the Age of Democracy, people expect the government to provide a growing range of goods and services that no feudal lord could dream of, let alone supply: excellent public schools from birth to graduate school, high-quality health care for the elderly, old-age pensions, insurance against bank failures, sound infrastructure, and, of course, a strong national defense.

The force behind the citizens for government expansion has been fed by another force in the years since the Great Depression: the modern economy can produce far more goods and services than it can consume. It is a function of excess investment, ongoing technological improvements, and accumulated productivity gains. In a financial crisis, we often hear that government, through its central banks, are the lenders of last resort. The government is also the consumer of last resort. Government spending can absorb excess economic capacity for corn, and it can absorb excess capacity for aerospace engineering. Of course, officials may rarely think in such terms, let alone admit that they do.

The government ensures sufficiently high utilization rates for capital and labor that allow for social stability. Although there are notable exceptions, the government's role in the economy tends to increase incrementally after a deep economic downturn. Government intervention is the go-to strategy for ending business cycle downturns. Modern governments, even nonrepresentative governments such as China's, want to deliver rising living standards to their people. Contrary to their ideological leanings, neither Reagan nor Thatcher managed to break that pattern. Critics of the expansion of the government's role have not proposed a viable alternative for maintaining adequate aggregate demand in the economy. And failure is not an option because social stability would be placed at risk, as has been the case historically.

Reality: Statism Does Not Equal Socialism

Imbalances drive modern economies, but they become unsustainable after a point. When the economy comes back into alignment, it is different and usually better. That creative destruction drives innovation, although it can leave a lot of pain in its wake. (What about the current account imbalance? Ah, but that's not a true imbalance but rather an artifact of an old understanding of global trade.) A major imbalance that drove the credit crisis was that between the financial industry's creation of newfangled financial products and investors' understanding of and commitment to them. There was another important asymmetry between the capabilities and activities of financial institutions and the regulatory regime (in the United States, as well as in Europe). In addition, the financial sector accounted for an unsustainably large share of corporate profits in America (and the United Kingdom), offsetting manufacturing and other services. Perhaps the most disturbing imbalance is that the price of the American dream—a house, a car, and college education for one's children—is often beyond the reach of good hardworking people, giving them little choice but to borrow now and hope for the best.

Just as finance capitalism drove rationalization in other industries, as it did with manufacturing in the 1980s and 1990s, it too will become rationalized. Because of technology, the economy has incredible financial capacity. In recent years, that capacity was used to promote products that were profoundly mispriced, considering their risk. The repricing of risk exposes the incompetent, inefficient, and unlucky. Industry consolidation will cull the excess capacity in a dramatic fashion. What will most likely emerge are fewer but stronger, more resilient, and more competitive financial institutions.

A fascist from the 1920s would find much of modern society that would be agreeable. The trains might not run on time, and people that Hitler would have killed may be helping to run the government and in other ways integrate into society, but the role of government itself would be familiar. The fascist "third way" emphasized corporate structures that included business, workers (who are also consumers), and the state.

Americans' belief in their nation's exceptionalism also fits the fascist mold. John F. Kennedy admonished Americans to "Ask not what your country can do for you, but what you can do for your country," while Bill Clinton noted "I don't understand how someone can say they love their country but hate their government." Franco, Hitler, or Mussolini could identify with those sentiments.

But the real issue isn't how much or what type of socialism a nation has. Instead, the concern is in whose interest things are being decided. There's an enormous difference between government policies that provide economic stability to voters and taxpayers and government policies that feed the megalomania of a madman. Both might fall into a loose category of "socialism" or "fascism" but with very different moral weights.

The United States currently has a growing disparity of wealth. The clichéd American dream of owning a car and a house and being able to afford to send one's children to college is increasingly out of reach for many American families based on their current incomes. That's a fundamental problem in our culture. Debt and the government have addressed this issue. After the credit crisis, debt is out. The government is in. What does that make America? Capitalist? Socialist? Fascist?

Perhaps, it simply makes the country pragmatic. Workers are also shareholders. Does that make them capitalists or socialists or simply innovative? Taxpayers want pensions. Does that make them socialists who want something for nothing or capitalists who expect a benefit for taxes paid?

Lord Acton said "power tends to corrupt, and absolute power corrupts absolutely." The American response is not to eschew power but to split it up and make it accountable. These are the famous checks and balances. Capitalist practices *and* checks on the power emanating from the ownership of private property, or socialism, codeveloped the United States in ways and to an extent that not one in a hundred people recognize or appreciate.

There is not a simple dualism between the state and markets. The relationship is significantly more complicated. A strong state is not antithetical to strong markets. One could not have markets without the state, and few would want to live in a state without functioning markets. The state's role as a consumer and investor helps mitigate the booms and busts of the real economy and manage what economists call *externalities,* the unintended consequences of business operations. Karl Marx expected socialism would appear where capitalism was the most advanced. And, as Peter Drucker observed, America is at once the most capitalist country and the most socialist country.

Chapter Notes

1. See http://www.nathanielturner.com/laborsproblemrealwages4.htm. Also cited in Martin J. Sklar, *The United States as a Developing Country: Studies in U.S. History in the Progressive Era and the 1920s,* page 144, footnote (Cambridge, UK: Cambridge University Press, 1992).

2. Presented in an op-ed article in the *New York Times* written by staff members W. Michael Cox and Richard Alm, "You Are What You Spend," February 10, 2008.

3. Ibid.

4. Rab Jafri, unpublished paper (New York: Terra K Partners, LLC, 2008).

5. National Association of Home Builders, *Single-Family Square Footage by Location* (Washington, DC: National Association of Home Builders, August 7, 2008).

6. U.S. Census Bureau, *Current Population Survey, 2007*. Annual Social and Economic Supplement (Washington, DC: U.S. Census Bureau).

7. U.S. Department of Housing and Urban Development and the U.S. Census Bureau, *American Housing Survey for the United States* (Washington, DC: U.S. Census Bureau, 2007).

8. *The Economic Report of the President, 2008*, Table B-29.

9. W. Michael Cox and Richard Alm, "How Are We Doing?" *The American*, July/August 2008.

10. See also Greg Easterbrook, *The Progress Paradox: How Life Gets Better and People Feel Worse* (New York: Random House, 2004).

11. Robert William Fogel, *The Escape from Hunger and Premature Death, 1700–2100* (New York: Cambridge University Press, 2004).

12. John Robinson and Geoffrey Godbey, *Time for Life: The Surprising Ways Americans Use Their Time* (University Park: Penn State University Press, 1999).

13. See Easterbrook, *The Progress Paradox*.

14. Cregg Easterbrook, "If Life is Good, Why Do We Feel So Bad?" *The Wall Street Journal*, June 13, 2008.

15. Theda Skocpol, *Protecting Soldiers and Mothers: The Political Origins of Social Policy in the United States* (Cambridge, MA: Belknap Press, 1995).

16. Amartya Sen, "Capitalism Beyond the Crisis," *The New York Review of Books*, March 26, 2009 (Vol. 56, No. 5) (www.nybooks.com/articles/22490).

17. Milton Friedman and Rose Friedman, *Free to Choose: A Personal Statement* (New York: MacMillan, 1980).

18. Peter Drucker, *Post-Capitalist Society* (New York: HarperCollins, 1993).

19. Investment Company Institute, *Trends in Ownership of Mutual Funds in the United States, 2007* (Washington, DC: ICI, November 14, 2007).

20. See Adolf Berle and Gardiner C Means, *The Modern Corporation and Private Property* (New York: Macmillan Co., 1932).

21. John Maynard Keynes, *The End of Laissez-Faire* (London: Hogarth Press, 1926).

22. Hyman P. Minsky, *The Financial Instability Hypothesis*. The Jerome Levy Economics Institute Working Paper No. 74, May 1992.

23. James Livingston, *Pragmatism and the Political Economy of Cultural Revolution (1850-1910)* (Chapel Hill: University of North Carolina Press, 1994). See also his blog (www.politicsandletters.com).

MYTH 9

The Weak U.S. Dollar Boosts Exports and Drives Stock Markets

Even if one had perfect foresight about exchange rates, it wouldn't help predict exports, the trade balance, or stock prices.

Pundits and policy makers often cite the chronic U.S. trade deficit as proof positive the dollar is overvalued. A marked dollar decline, they say, is integral to the reduction of the global imbalances that they believe pose a significant risk not only to the U.S. economy but also to the world's. The United States cannot continue consuming more than it produces. Herbert Stein, the chairman of the Council of Economic Advisors in the Nixon administration, once said that things that can't go on forever don't. Thus, some argue, there are only two outcomes for the dollar: an orderly decline or a disorderly one.

Although this may seem reasonable, it is wrong. The belief that the dollar has to decline because the trade deficit has to close eventually is counterproductive and may have unintended consequences. A weak dollar may not help boost U.S. exports or the earnings of large U.S. multinational companies. Nor is a weak currency a key to rising equity valuations.

Consider oil. It is one of America's largest imports. But the demand is relatively inelastic: it doesn't change much with the price. When gasoline goes up in price, people don't rush out to buy new, more energy-efficient cars, move to be closer to work, or refuse to go on road trips to see relatives for the holidays—at least not at first. They wait to see what happens, paying up at the pump in the meantime. It takes a large increase in prices in a relatively short time to produce a change in behavior, judging from the oil boom that ended abruptly in the middle of July 2008. Since oil prices are largely denominated in dollars, most oil-consuming nations need to acquire dollars to buy oil. The higher the cost of oil, the more dollars are required. This is called transactional demand.

Yet, as oil prices surged in the second half of 2007 and the first half of 2008, the U.S. dollar was sold to extreme lows. And as oil prices collapsed after mid-July 2008, the dollar rallied. Clearly, other forces that drive the foreign exchange market can overwhelm the transactional demand for dollars. For example, higher oil prices can make the trade deficit widen even though the dollar weakens. It's the opposite of what's supposed to happen. The standard relationship taught in Economics 101 is that a weak currency reduces the trade deficit by lowering export prices and increasing import prices.

Make no mistake about it. The United States remains a formidable export player, sending $1.2 trillion worth of goods around the world in 2007.[1] Still, exports aren't the key source of revenue for most U.S. multinationals. Instead, multinationals earn their overseas revenue in ways that are relatively impervious to the movement of the dollar. When PepsiCo makes beverages in India and sells them to Indians, a U.S. company profits, but there's no change in imports or exports. The relative strength of the dollar may affect PepsiCo's reported revenues, but it won't affect the price or demand in local markets.

As we saw in Chapter 2, a weak dollar in and of itself is neither good nor bad. It is a trade-off. There are winners and losers. A weak dollar, as opposed to a falling dollar, may help bring in some types of investment and tourist dollars, for example. However, a dollar kept intentionally weak through fiscal and monetary policy in the hopes that it will improve markets for U.S. exports is another matter entirely. It is folly.

What Drives American Trade?

Of the $1.2 trillion in goods shipped out of the United States in 2007, 38.4 percent were capital goods and 27.2 percent were industrial supplies.[2] The import mix was a bit different; in 2007, the United States took in $2.0 trillion in imports. The largest segment of that, 32.4 percent, was industrial supplies, with the next-largest segment, consumer goods, making up 24.3 percent of the mix. Within the industrial supplies category, U.S. exports are widely diversified, with the largest segment being chemicals. The imports in that category, by contrast, are concentrated on petroleum and energy products. We're taking in different goods than we're sending out, which means that supply and demand is driven by more than just currency values.

The United States also buys and sells from the same countries. Our largest export buyers are our closest neighbors. Canada took in $248.9 billion in U.S. goods in 2007, or 21.4 percent of our exports. Mexico took in another $136.5 billion, or 11.7 percent. The United States then purchased $313.1 billion from Canada, 16.0 percent of the total, and $210.8 billion from Mexico, a 10.8 percent share. Thanks to the North American Free Trade Agreement (NAFTA), much of the trade among the United States, Canada, and Mexico is within companies because businesses have integrated continental production. Canada is America's largest export market and its second-largest source of imports. China accounts for $321.5 billion of U.S. imports, or 16.5 percent of the total. China received about $65.2 billion or 5.6 percent of U.S. exports, ranking it third behind Canada and Mexico.[3]

The United States buys cheap—from China—and sells dear—to more developed nations. However, the relative price isn't determined by the currency but rather the value of the goods being bought and sold. Capital goods (any goods used to produce other goods), a U.S. export specialty, add significant value to the manufacturing process and thus are priced based on the features and benefits. Basic consumer goods, whether they are socks or toys, tend to be in more competitive markets where price is paramount.

In fact, demand for U.S. exports is more sensitive to growth in trading-partner income than the fluctuations of the dollar itself. One of the goals of NAFTA was to open Mexico's markets to U.S. and Canadian companies, which would allow for the reorganization of business for the entire continent. It was also understood that a more stable and prosperous Mexico was in the United States' commercial and political interests.

Likewise, if India's economy expands, the nation will take in more U.S. exports regardless of the exchange rate. The nation will need more capital equipment and industrial supplies. The long-term increase in income will do more to stimulate Indian demand than short-term fluctuations in currencies. That means that the best way to promote

U.S. exports is to encourage policies that boost the world's growth, not reduce the value of the dollar. That will also stimulate the market for American products produced and sold in local markets, helping U.S. companies even if the trade deficit does not change.

Imports and exports are not driven only by list price. Instead, their markets are affected by the availability of substitute products, utilization rates, and economic development policies. Demand for some products is more price-sensitive than for others. That's why U.S. consumption is relatively insensitive to the price of gasoline, at least in the near term. Clothing prices, on the other hand, are very sensitive to price. Traditionally they are labor-intensive products, which is why production often moves to places with cheaper labor rates. As Chinese workers want higher wages, more production may move to Vietnam.

American companies are known for their innovations in technology and design. Europeans didn't switch their operating systems to Microsoft Vista software because it was cheaper when the dollar weakened against the euro; they switched because they wanted to keep their computers up to the latest standards. Japanese folks didn't buy Beyoncé CDs because the weak dollar made the royalty embedded in the price cheaper; they bought the CDs because they liked the pop sensation's singing.

Terms of Trade

In 2007, the United States purchased $348.8 billion in crude oil, fuel oil, other petroleum products, and natural gas from abroad, which made up 17.8 percent of total imports.[4] These products, denominated in dollars, are a significant factor in U.S. trade and in foreign policy; major oil exporters, including Venezuela, Saudi Arabia, and Nigeria, do not always have the same interests in the world as the United States does. The value of the dollar has not been a key issue. Oil prices are typically more volatile than the dollar on a trade weighted basis and recently the two tend to move in opposite directions, with a weaker dollar coinciding with higher oil prices (see *Figure 9.1*).[5]

But as important as it is to the American lifestyle, oil is just one of many commodities on the market that are denominated in dollars. Energy and industrial commodities, precious metals, and most foodstuffs and fibers are denominated in U.S. dollars. And most of those that are not denominated in dollars are denominated in British pounds. Current account deficits be damned.

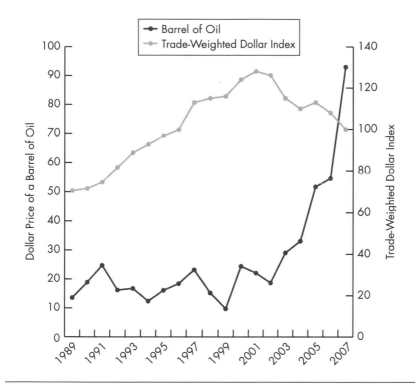

FIGURE 9.1   Oil Prices Per Barrel versus Exchange Rates,
1989–2007

Source: U.S. Department of Energy, Energy Information Division, *World Weighted
Average Oil Prices;* Federal Reserve Bank of St. Louis, "Trade Weighted Exchange
Index"

Over the years, most of the past commodity booms have been
preceded by a sharp dollar decline. The dollar's depreciation is often
associated with global inflation. Also, there are times, as during the
credit crisis, that some investment advisers caution against the debase-
ment of paper assets in general and find that buying things that "hurt
when you drop them on your feet" is a prudent alternative.

The number of mortuaries in a city is highly correlated with the number of churches, but the relationship is not causal. Both are correlated
with a third factor: population size. The seemingly strong correlation at
times between commodity prices and the dollar are often transitory and
most of the time don't appear causal in nature. Agricultural prices may

move sometimes in tandem with the dollar, but both respond to such additional factors as strong world growth.

One of the key relationships that shape the contours of the world economy is that between the price of raw materials and finished goods, yet hardly any Wall Street economists or policy makers appear to include it in their analyses of the global economy. The importance of commodity prices in terms of manufactured goods is so subtle that, although it lies at the heart of development theories, the International Monetary Fund, the World Bank, and the U.S. Treasury often ignore it when making policy prescriptions. It is so powerful that the last quarter of the twentieth century would have been completely different if the relative prices remained constant through the period.

If non-oil commodity prices had remained constant relative to the price of manufactured goods, the United States would have had smaller current account deficits. After all, America exports grain and other commodities all over the world. Had that happened, the U.S. trade deficit may not have exploded. Conversely, Japan, which has relatively few natural resources and little agricultural land, would not have experienced such large trade surpluses. At the same time, resource-rich Latin America would have avoided many of its debt crises because its imports would have been more easily financed by its primary product exports.

Throughout the twentieth century, raw material prices fell relative to manufactured goods prices. Peter Drucker, in a seminal essay in *Foreign Affairs* in 1986, noted that international raw material prices fell at an average annualized rate of about 1.2 percent.[6] A more recent study by José Antonio Ocampo and María Angela Parra, conducted under the auspices of the Economic Commission for Latin America and the Caribbean, concluded that, over the course of the twentieth century, raw material prices lost 50 percent to 60 percent of their value to manufactured goods.[7] It's no surprise; the design and manufacture adds more value to the commodities themselves.

There are other reasons why non-oil commodities fell relative to manufactured goods prices. Productivity growth in agriculture boggles the mind. Although demand for foodstuffs rose, output increased even faster. Between 1945 and 1994, the U.S. crop yield grew threefold. Agricultural output rose by a third in the 1972–85 period alone, with a declining number of work hours. Through various other applications of science, animals can become more efficient in converting grains to protein. Consider the chicken. In 1900, the average hen laid thirty eggs a year. Now a hen can lay 250 eggs or more a year. In 1900, it took 16 weeks for a chicken to become suitable for frying (weight of 2 pounds). Today a 4-pound roasting chicken is ready in just 6 weeks. In 1930, it took more than 6 pounds of feed to yield 1 pound of broiler meat. By 1940, it required 4 pounds of grain. Today, less than 2 pounds of feed are needed. In the 1920s, according to Michael Pollan in *The Omnivore's Dilemma*, an average acre of American farmland could produce 20 bushels of corn.[8] Today, an acre yields more than ten times the amount. Now that is productivity. The sharp spike in food prices in late 2007 and early 2008 prompted U.S. agricultural companies like Monsanto to promise another green revolution.

Manufacturers, too, are more efficient users of industrial raw materials. New synthetic, plastic, and ceramic materials replaced more expensive industrial raw materials, especially metals. The most successful steel mills use scrap steel. Increasingly, the metals in ubiquitous electronic products are being recycled. And for good reason: a ton of computers has more gold than a ton of gold ore. Governments, especially in Europe, are forcing manufacturers to make more of their goods recyclable.

As with agriculture, reducing waste boosts efficiencies and flatters profits. Increasingly, businesses aim to reduce their waste and find other uses for it. In addition, the manufacturing sector of the large, advanced industrialized countries has fallen steadily as a percentage of GDP as the role of services has expanded. The less dependent an economy is on commodities, the lower the impact of commodity price swings. As the environmental issues began to rise in the public's conscience and commodity prices bubbled, a more serious effort was made to find uses for one's own waste products and by-products such as heat. This holds out the promise of giving another boost in manufacturing productivity, which may become more apparent on the other side of the credit crisis.

If the twentieth century was marked by the decline in real values of commodities, the twenty-first century may be marked by the reverse. In the early part of the first decade, commodity prices rose relative to those of manufactured goods. There is not enough data available yet to call the end of this century-old trend, but if that is indeed the case, it will have far-reaching implications for global trade imbalances.

There are several factors that may drive the terms of trade reversal. Increased productivity in the manufacturing sectors of the United States, China, and India has helped turn many manufactured goods into, well, commodities. Even items as complex as computers sell into ruthlessly competitive markets. In early 2009, India announced as a national goal to produce a $20 computer. The sheer economies of scale available in China and India have also lowered the per-unit cost of many manufactured goods, colorfully illustrated by a number of automobiles with sticker prices of less than $10,000 available in many parts of the world. Tata Motors offers the Nano for 100,000 Indian rupees, which is about $2,500. At the same time, China's voracious demand for raw materials in its rapid modernization program helped drive commodity prices sharply higher. Some observers warn that the ecological damage from the rapid industrialization in China may force the country to become a major importer of foodstuffs in the coming years.

The ease by which a commodity can be accessed influences the cost and price they can command. People have already picked the "low-hanging fruit" as it were. The minerals that were close to the surface are already gone. To get more oil, for example, we have to go into deeper waters or denser rocks such as the tar sands in Alberta. As extraction becomes more aggressive, it can do more damage to the ecosystem. Environmental action has thus raised the cost of exploration and production.

Some commodity prices have been kept artificially low. Many advanced industrialized countries, including the United States, subsidize and otherwise promote with government money the production of numerous agricultural goods, which encourages excess production and distorts prices. These practices are being challenged slowly but surely before the World Trade Organization. Claims against U.S. cotton subsidies and European sugar subsidies are making their way through the bureaucratic system. If the WTO rules against the subsidies, this could break through the logjam of a particular kind of protectionism and price distortion of some agricultural goods.

If raw materials prices increase relative to manufactured goods, then countries that rely on commodity exports will enjoy a strong economic boost and could assist in development efforts. Although manufacturing has migrated to developing countries, it is highly concentrated within nine—Hong Kong, Singapore, South Korea, Taiwan,

Indonesia, Philippines, Malaysia, Thailand, and China—that account for more than three-quarters of the developing countries' manufacturing exports. Brazil, which produces manufactured goods from cell phones to airplanes, is also among the world's largest producers of foodstuffs and fibers. That makes it particularly well positioned, for example, to benefit from a sustained shift in the terms of trade.

Economic Value and Accounting Value

Although it's clear that foreign sales are important to the health and well-being of major American corporations, reported international sales figures may be a bit misleading. When companies serve local markets, they receive the revenues in local currency. When the dollar is weak, as it was in 2007, local currency represents more dollars when it is translated for accounting purposes and therefore boosts revenue. A weak dollar may boost corporate earnings without actually changing the level of economic activity.

How much the dollar affects reported earnings is not only a function of the value of the dollar relative to whatever currencies were used in the company and its strategy for reducing currency exposure through hedging, but also the accounting method that the company uses. Under generally accepted accounting principles, companies have a choice of different accounting methods (the temporal-rate method, the current-rate method, and the monetary–nonmonetary method) for foreign currencies, depending on how business is conducted. These have different effects on the income statement and balance sheet. This means that two companies in the same industry could show very different profit effects from currency when earnings are reported even if they were affected equally.

Because translation exposure affects the income statement, and because the income statement is a reflection of the firm's operations, it is easy to confuse translation exposure with economic exposure. There's a key difference: economic exposure affects a firm's actual value, not just its accounting value. This is a serious matter for corporate managers. They have to understand how exchange rates affect their operations if they are to run an international business successfully.

Corporate treasurers can accept accounting exposure to currency fluctuations. In fact, trying to manage accounting exposure to exchange rates can have disastrous consequences for the rest of the financial statements. However, they typically don't like too much economic exposure. Financial officers view economic exposure as a risk that needs to be managed. How they do that varies.

Some companies hedge a currency exposure as soon as they send out an invoice, selling the value in the forward market in order to lock in the exchange rate. Some companies hedge anticipated receivables from export sales with currency purchases in the forward market. One advantage of the foreign direct-investment strategy and the servicing of local demand with local production is that it reduces the economic exposure to exchange rates. Companies create natural hedges for foreign subsidiaries using such local currency expenses as wages, supplies, and rent so as to minimize the exposure to currency-induced revenue changes.

Because a weak dollar may inflate translated revenues, there's a perception that a weak dollar helps the U.S. stock market. The data on that are not clear, but at best the dollar and the S&P 500 have moved in tandem for extended periods of time, which is the opposite of what would be expected in an export-oriented economy.[9] In the last fifteen years, the two have decoupled to the extent that it's difficult to tease out any meaningful relationship (see *Figure 9.2*), though tortured statistics will confess to almost anything.

Hedging, or taking action to offset a currency risk, can itself be a source of reported profits. Under the Financial Accounting Standards Board's Statement 133, approved in 1999, companies can post gains and losses from exact hedges—those that match the amount of cash coming into or going out of the foreign currency market. Savvy financial managers have been able to use this to protect economic profits while generating a little bit of extra funds for the income statement. For investors, this further weakens the relationship between currency and corporate profits.

Another reason that the relationship between exchange rates and the stock market may not be that close is that most cross-border portfolio flows involve bonds and other fixed-income products much more than equities. Foreign investors, as we have seen, prefer sending their excess savings to the United States, and they typically prefer fixed-income investments to equities. American investors, by contrast, prefer equities to fixed income when they invest abroad.

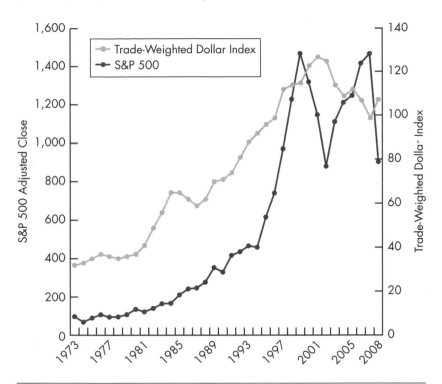

FIGURE 9.2   The Dollar versus the S&P 500

Source: Federal Reserve Bank of St. Louis, "Trade Weighted Exchange Index"; Bloomberg L.P.

The Dollar and Intrafirm Trade

Although a typical U.S. multinational corporation tends to service international customers with local production rather than via exporting it from the United States, it also engages in plenty of import and export activity. When this trade takes place within the firm, it is not affected by exchange rates over short and intermediate terms, even if it takes place across borders.

If a razor company makes razor blades in the United States and then sends them to an affiliate in Mexico for assembly and packaging, the Mexican subsidiary has "purchased" them. The volume that it "purchases" will be affected by the demand for new razors throughout North America, not by the strength of the peso relative to the dollar. When the Mexican assembly plant ships finished razors back to the

United States for sale, the U.S. parent "purchases" them at a higher price, but once again no cash changes hands. It is largely an accounting entry. The exchange rate effect is nil.

The focus on exports is wrong from the get-go. As we have seen, U.S. companies do not primarily service foreign markets by exporting. That multinational strategy had evolved ever since the end of World War II, when the dollar was strong and industrial centers in Europe had to be rebuilt. Barriers to trade raised the costs of import–export strategies, while lower transportation costs, improved communications, better supply chain management tools, and volatile foreign exchange values made it both easier and more important for companies to operate locally. U.S. intrafirm trade was enough of an issue in the early 1960s that the Commerce Department's Bureau of Economic Analysis decided it needed to keep track of these activities. In 2005, sales made by the majority-owned affiliates of U.S. multinationals were more than triple U.S. exports at $4.2 trillion compared to $1.3 trillion.[10]

Policy makers, investors, and students should look at foreign sales in addition to exports to get a fuller sense of how the United States competes in the world economy. In 2007, 45.8 percent of the sales of S&P 500 companies, some $2.3 trillion dollars, was outside of the United States,[11] an increase from the 43.6 percent reported in 2006. In some cases, the numbers were enormous. ExxonMobil had $269.2 billion in total 2007 international sales. General Motors sold $47.1 billion just in Asia—the company's problems are related to long-term liabilities embedded in U.S. labor contracts and erosion at its customer base, not to the underlying demand for its vehicles outside the United States. Meanwhile, companies in the S&P 500 paid $123.6 billion in income taxes to foreign governments, making them important contributors to the revenue of numerous governments in addition to their own. Because not all companies in the index break out their international sales, the actual sales are higher than those reported by Standard & Poor's.

Another way to consider the role of the United States in world markets is to look at how much value its affiliates, built and acquired through foreign direct investments, add to the economies of their host countries (see *Table 9.1*). It can be significant in the case of small nations heavily dependent on tourism such as Barbados—or in the case of nations that welcome international operations like Ireland and

TABLE 9.1   Role of the U.S. in World Markets

Country	GDP ($ in Millions)	Value Added ($ in Millions)	Value Add/GDP (Percentage)
Barbados	3,739	2,773	74.16
Ireland	258,600	48,594	18.79
Singapore	161,300	16,560	10.27
Canada	1,432,000	114,247	7.98
Nigeria	166,800	12,538	7.52
United Kingdom	2,773,000	154,813	5.58
Switzerland	423,900	22,714	5.36
Hong Kong	206,700	10,637	5.15
Belgium	453,600	22,219	4.90
Costa Rica	26,240	1,261	4.81

Source: *CIA World Factbook;* U.S. Bureau of Economic Analysis, "U.S. Multinational Companies: Operations in 2006," *Survey of Current Business,* November 2008.

Singapore.[12] Even for a large country like the United Kingdom, the dollar value and share of GDP that affiliates of U.S. multinationals produce is nothing to sneeze at.

Although the weak dollar may not have a big effect on most exports, total foreign sales, or the stock market, it may affect demand for other assets. Anecdotal reports suggest that foreign purchases of U.S. real estate increased when the dollar was falling in 2007 and into 2008, until the credit crisis overwhelmed everything. Tourism also tends to increase whenever an otherwise stable country experiences a dramatic decline in its currency. When tourists come to the United States, some of their spending, but not all of it, is recorded as a service export. In 2007, tourism was the source of almost a fifth of the $497.2 billion in U.S. service exports.[13]

Foreign direct investment also increases as foreign companies move more production and sourcing to the United States. The dollar's decline from the start of the decade until late 2007 and early 2008 coupled with generally strong productivity gains in the United States means that unit labor costs are relatively cheap from foreign producers' vantage points. Some studies suggest U.S. unit labor costs have declined by as much as 30 percent between 2000 and 2007 against most other major industrialized countries, making it attractive for foreign companies to hire workers here, although the credit crisis needs to be resolved before many businesses can contemplate such expansion strategies.

Increasingly, foreign companies are meeting the demand of their American customers with local production, like the Japanese auto manufacturers. This puts them inside a wall of protectionism, able to take advantage of the protracted periods of a weak dollar and strong yen, and closer to their customers, the largest middle class in the world. Foreign companies operating in the United States accounted for about 5 percent of private-sector employment in 2007, another 5 percent indirectly, and 6 percent of GDP.

Dangers of a Weak-Dollar Strategy

The dangerous myth is that a major dollar decline is required so the United States not only stops running trade deficits but also can run a sustained surplus to reduce the mountains of debt it has accumulated—forget about the rest of America's global strategy. But driving the dollar down low won't help exports and may hurt other sectors of the economy.

The evolutionary strategy of U.S. multinationals is built more on foreign direct investment than trade per se. Keeping the dollar low exaggerates the importance of the role of trade flows at the expense of capital flows. A weak dollar makes it more expensive to pursue the multinational evolutionary strategy of building locally and selling locally because it increases the dollar cost of the foreign direct investment. It makes it more expensive for a U.S. company to acquire an international competitor, expand a factory in a developing market, or hire local professionals who understand how to reach a new customer group.

Depending on other economic factors, a depreciating dollar may boost U.S. interest rates. That's because investors, both domestic and foreign, may want a premium to offset the risk of currency depreciation. A weak dollar policy also may discourage portfolio investment in the United States if investors fear it will debase its currency.

A weak dollar can influence crossborder mergers and acquisition strategies and how they are financed. A weak dollar may offer foreign investors a fire sale of U.S. real assets and fan the protectionist sentiment that often lurks not far below the surface. It may cost the country some iconic brands: Anheuser-Busch became part of a Belgian brewing combination in the middle of the credit crisis, when the dollar was near historic lows.

If the political goal of dollar depreciation is to score points with workers by making the goods they produce less expensive, it could backfire by making all companies inexpensive to foreigners, coupled with higher interest rates and slower growth. A depreciating dollar may also lead to slower world growth under certain macroeconomic conditions. It may lead to a tightening of monetary conditions on U.S. trade partners, for example, thereby weakening the demand for U.S. products and services. Countries typically do not depreciate their way to prosperity, and that includes the United States.

Moreover, the real or threatened use of the dollar for trade advantage, what economists call "beggar thy neighbor" polices, would likely be responded to in kind by trade partners. It's a lot of risk to take in the hopes of stimulating exports, which seem more dependent on foreign growth than the price of the dollar in the first place.

It may seem that a decline in the dollar would make U.S. financial assets cheaper in foreign currency terms. The behavior of investors suggests otherwise. Since most currency pairs are more volatile than bonds, the currency component often accounts for the bulk of the return on an unhedged portfolio of international bonds. Investors therefore often prefer to invest in a foreign country's bonds, in which the currency is appreciating. A depreciating currency often offsets in full or more the interest rate differential that may attract funds, which is one of the reasons that carry trades can be so destructive when they go bad as seen, for example, in the second half of 2008.

In recent years, the concern has been that the dollar will be weakened intentionally—not to help the trade balance, but to reduce the U.S. debt burden. Debasing a currency can feel like a stealth default to an investor. For example, suppose an investor in Switzerland buys $1,000 for 1,200 Swiss francs and puts it in a dollar account at a local bank. He then buys a $1,000 2-year U.S. Treasury note direct from the Treasury through its online noncompetitive auction. The interest is wired into his account. At the end of the two years, he gets a check from Uncle Sam for $1,000. But in the meantime, the dollar has declined, so that $1,000 only buys 1,000 Swiss francs. That's a

20 percent loss. Because U.S. Treasury bonds are popular with international investors, the state of the dollar may impact the demand for the bonds.

And this is why the strong dollar policy first articulated by Treasury Secretary Robert Rubin in 1995 was popular with overseas buyers of U.S. bonds. Rubin's predecessor, Lloyd Bentsen, appeared to threaten Japan with a weaker dollar unless it made some trade concessions. Eight years earlier, James Baker was Treasury secretary, and it appeared that he threatened Germany with a weaker dollar unless it made a policy concession and cut interest rates. When that threat comes from the world's largest debtor, investors quake. There were violent market reactions both times. Rubin's mantra became that a strong dollar is in America's overall national interest. All his successors have repeated that, although not always as convincingly.

After 1995, Rubin authorized U.S. intervention in currency markets once. That was in a joint operation with Japan to sell dollars. Rubin's handpicked successor, Lawrence Summers, also authorized intervention once and it was also to sell dollars. It was part of the multilateral operation in 2000 to support the euro. George W. Bush was the first president since the end of Bretton Woods not to sanction intervention in the foreign exchange market, though the massive currency swaps the Federal Reserve offered to a number of central banks during the credit crisis may have preempted pressure to intervene by providing dollars for the obviously short market.

Nevertheless, the strong dollar policy is not just a hollow slogan. It sends a very important signal to foreign investors and officials that the United States will not intentionally seek a weaker dollar to reduce its debt burden or manipulate it for trade purposes. As the dollar fell in 2007 and the first half of 2008, the president of the European Central Bank, Jean-Claude Trichet, often noted with appreciation that the U.S. Treasury secretary reiterated the importance of a strong dollar on U.S. interests.

Consider the damage that could have been done had the Treasury secretary said the opposite. If a U.S. Treasury secretary came out and said, "After much consideration, we have decided that our critics have been right and U.S. interests would be better served by a weaker dollar," it would undoubtedly trigger a run on the greenback by investors.

Reality: A Weak Dollar Doesn't Boost Exports

If the world were still following the trade models of the start of the twentieth century, then a weak dollar would make U.S. exports cheaper than German exports and help American companies pick up market share in the world. In the decades since, companies have changed their approach to international trade. Many of the largest multinational companies, especially in the United States but also many in the United Kingdom and Japan, compete in local markets through direct investments, which offer some insulation from the volatile swings in the currency market that floating exchange rates entail. In fact, a weak dollar makes it more expensive for U.S. multinationals to do what they do best: establish and expand local operations all over the world.

An intentionally weak dollar may scare off foreign investors who put their savings into U.S. government bonds. In the face of growing currency risk, investors often demand a risk premium, and in the debt markets, it means higher interest rates. It means that interest rates may be set by different considerations from what the economy needs at that moment. If the dollar falls in value relative to investors' home currency, their safe investment return may be wiped out or even turn into a loss.

It is not particularly helpful or profitable to try to deduce equity market movement from currency movement. On occasion, currency does affect equity portfolios, but the relationship does not appear consistently significant enough that investors can rely on it. The proper level of analysis is the company level—its approach to servicing foreign demand and its management of the currency exposures that naturally arise.

The largest multinational companies receive revenues from a diverse range of countries, naturally neutralizing part of the currency risks. A weak dollar does not always lead to the outperformance of companies that enjoy a higher share of global sales. Also, analysts and investors appear to look past the impact of translating foreign earnings back into dollars.

In the late 1990s, the United States enjoyed both a strong dollar and a bull market in stocks; the potential of new technologies offset the higher prices of American exports. From the second quarter of 2003 through late 2007, U.S. shares trended higher while the dollar entered a bear market of its own. As that bear market ended and the dollar strengthened, equity prices collapsed.

It is also not particularly helpful to think about currencies as shares of stock in a country. Since the exchange rate is the price of a currency in terms of another currency, it is not always clear which side of the equation is the driving force. Was the price action in the second half of 2008 best characterized by the surge in the dollar or by the collapse of the sterling, euro, Australian dollar, and other currencies?

Chapter Notes

1. U.S. Census Bureau, *U.S. International Trade in Goods and Services, Annual Revision for 2007* (Washington, DC: Department of Commerce, June 10, 2008).

2. Ibid.

3. U.S. Census Bureau, *Top Trading Partners—Total Trade, Exports, Imports* (http://www.census.gov/foreign-trade/statistics/highlights/top/top0712.html).

4. U.S. Census Bureau, *U.S. International Trade in Goods and Services, 2007*.

5. U.S. Department of Energy, Energy Information Division, *World Weighted Average Oil Prices*; Federal Reserve Bank of St. Louis, "Trade Weighted Exchange Index" (http://research.stlouisfed.org/fred2/categories/105).

6. Peter F. Drucker, "The Changed World Economy." *Foreign Affairs*, Spring 1986.

7. Jose Antonio Ocampo and Maria Angela Parra, *The Terms of Trade for Commodities in the Twentieth Century* (http://129.3.20.41/eps/it/papers/0402/0402006.pdf).

8. Michael Pollan, *The Omnivore's Dilemma: A Natural History of Four Meals* (New York: Penguin, 2006).

9. Federal Reserve Bank of St. Louis, "Trade Weighted Exchange Index"; Yahoo! Finance.

10. U.S. Bureau of Economic Analysis, "Ownership-Based Framework of the U.S. Current Account," *Survey of Current Business*, January 2008.

11. Standard & Poor's Corporation, "S&P 500: 2007 Global Sales," July 30, 2008.

12. *CIA World Factbook;* U.S. Bureau of Economic Analysis, "U.S. Multinational Companies: Operations in 2006," *Survey of Current Business*, November 2008.

13. U.S. Census Bureau, *U.S. International Trade in Goods and Services, 2007*.

MYTH 10

The Foreign Exchange Market Is Strange and Speculative

There are known unknowns.
—DONALD RUMSFELD

The dollar has been a de facto global currency for so long and America is such a large country that Americans are less concerned with foreign exchange than people in other parts of the world. Sure, the value of the dollar writes headlines at times, but there is little accompanying context. Foreign exchange seems like a scary thing that involves people with brightly colored jackets waving their hands in trading pits in downtown Chicago.

Yet the foreign exchange market itself (also known as *forex*) is the largest financial market in the world. Money itself has become a commodity. The relationship between the symbol, money, and the signifier, value gets more and more tenuous as the vast amounts being traded are little more than electronic blips. Every day, people trade money, sometimes for profit, sometimes for convenience. And trading rarely takes place on the floor of an exchange these days. The market is different from the stock or bond markets, though. A stock goes up when earnings are strong and investors are optimistic. A currency sometimes goes up because of strong underlying economic growth, but not always. The dollar strengthened dramatically in the second half of 2008 as the recession deepened. Strong U.S. growth from early 2003 through the first half of 2006 coincided with a weak dollar (2003–04), a strong dollar (2005), and a weak dollar again (2006).

Many factors influence the foreign exchange market, and growth rates are just one of many variables—and not an especially strong one at that. Sometimes high interest rates coincide with an appreciating currency. That was the case with the Australian dollar, which appreciated for several years leading up to and well into the credit crisis. Yet if high interest rates were really a sign of a strong currency, there wouldn't ever be devaluations. In fact, economists traditionally see high interest rates as a sign of a fundamentally weak currency. High interest rates are not offered because a country is generous. They are demanded by investors to compensate for inflation, political risk, or poor policies.

A currency crisis in Ireland before the advent of the euro colorfully illustrates these points. In 1993, Ireland enjoyed favorable macroeconomic conditions—low inflation, a small budget deficit, and a growing current account surplus. Yet after a massive depreciation of the British pound, Ireland was facing a dramatic loss of competitiveness. Rumors of a devaluation circulated. Overnight interest rates reached a spectacular 1,000 percent. However, this was an annualized rate, hardly sufficient protection on even a small depreciation, let alone the 10 percent devaluation that was delivered.

The foreign exchange market is enormous: every day, $3.2 trillion of currency trades all over the world.[1] This is a mind-boggling figure that can only be appreciated in some kind of context. The turnover in a little more than a fortnight is sufficient to finance world trade for a year. In less than a month, the turnover in the foreign exchange market is enough to buy the annual output of the world. Capital flows swamp trade flows and the world output of goods and services. Importers, exporters, investors, speculators, and ordinary tourists need to convert one form of money into another in order to get through the day.

Very little of this trade takes place at an airport currency exchange desk. Instead, it takes place through banks and often involves different financial instruments, including, though rarely, simple coins and notes. Some trades are transactional: a computer company in the United States wants to buy semiconductor chips from a company in Taiwan, so if the invoice is the local currency instead of dollars, it has its bank exchange U.S. dollars for Taiwanese dollars and then send the payment to the vendor's bank account. Other trades are placed to hedge or fix a price today for a future payment. In order to ensure the exchange rate on Taiwanese dollars when the invoice is due, a U.S. company may use a forward contract to lock in the price for a payment due to the chip maker in forty-five days. The "rolling out" of that forward position each day (for the term) also helps account for part of the large daily turnover.

Trading turnover is also boosted by raw speculation, the doppel-gänger of gambling. For a price, speculators assume the currency risk that others do not want. They are purposely taking on currency risk with the goal of managing that risk profitably. A hedge fund looking at the relative differences in value between the euro and the dollar, for example, may decide to borrow as many euros as possible, exchange them for dollars, and then invest the money in U.S. Treasury bills in hopes of being able to exchange the dollars for even more euros when the loan is due.

Investors, including many professionals, tend to underestimate the significance of the foreign exchange market. As noted earlier, the price of money has two dimensions: *interest rates,* or the cost of borrowing money; and *foreign exchange,* or the price of one currency in terms of another. Globalization requires that businesses and investors take the second dimension as seriously as the first. Prudent investing requires appreciating the risk and returns generated by the fluctuation of the price of money. This fluctuation can affect interest rates, prices, and opportunities for people, even if they've never converted money in their entire lives and don't plan on beginning now.

Where Currency Gets Its Value

Although the dollar's value is often quoted in the news and appears prominently in the financial press, it may be the least understood of all the capital markets. How is the foreign exchange price of the dollar determined? The quick answer is "supply and demand," but there is more to it than that. When one purchases a stock or a bond, one acquires a claim on a future income stream that can be modeled. An analyst can sit down and determine how much revenue a company should get next year, what its expenses are likely to be, and what dividends it can pay and then calculate the current value of that dividend and others in the future.

In their pure form, currencies do not have an income stream, so there is nothing to project or discount. They no longer represent a claim on gold or silver. Valuation, then, is much more elusive in the foreign exchange market than other asset classes. It doesn't help that money rarely has a physical presence in the modern world.

Under the Bretton Woods agreement, the value of money for most industrialized nations was tied to the price of gold indirectly through the dollar. Some folks agitate for a return to the gold standard, but that would not be in most countries' interests, including the United States. Nor is it very practical. Given the magnitude of trade and capital flows, there simply is not enough gold in the world to support modern money.

A new gold standard today would induce a major global deflation and depression that would have the potential to make the credit crisis appear as a poor dress rehearsal. It would potentially reverse the transgenerational increase in living standards. The antigrowth bias of a gold standard goes against the underlying and historic progrowth thrust of U.S. economic policy (not that it always gets it right).

Ironically, one of the most famous speeches in American history was a warning precisely about the dangers of a gold standard. In his 1896 "cross of gold" speech, William Jennings Bryan celebrated the first of what was to be three nominations as the Democratic candidate for president by warning the Washington insiders of his day: "You shall not press down upon the brow of labor this crown of thorns, you shall not crucify mankind upon a cross of gold."[2] He understood that the gold standard would undermine America's economic prowess. It would today, too.

Purchasing Power Parity

Many contemporary economists focus almost exclusively on price these days instead of value. Traditional theories of exchange-rate valuation concentrate on how exchange rates fluctuate to bring other macroeconomic measures into equilibrium, such as interest rates or inflation. If exchange rates are fixed, then economic disruptions may generate pressure to change the fixing level. Floating currencies, by contrast, are consistent with the Open Door view of the world even though they could not have been imagined when John Hay was thinking about how best to trade with China more than a century ago. With floating currencies, changes in one country's currency relative to another may affect macroeconomic policy, which is the reverse of how it works in the fixed exchange-rate system.

One common theory of exchange-rate valuation is *purchasing power parity* (PPP). In its absolute form, PPP states that the cost of goods in one country should be exactly the same in another country after the currency is exchanged. That rarely happens in the real world. However, another form of PPP, the *relative* form, looks at changes in income and inflation levels to estimate a fair value for a currency. Over the years, economists have developed more complicated models that include a role for international balances as well. Purchasing power parity, economists say, is the level that currencies ought to gravitate around in the long run. There is another level that currencies also gravitate around: *a long-run moving average.* In fact, a 10-year moving average often serves as a fairly accurate estimation of PPP for the major industrialized countries, regardless of what is actually happening to income and prices. Although there are plenty of examples of a currency moving toward its PPP rate, there are also a number of examples—most notably the Japanese yen—in which PPP rates appeared to have trended toward the currency's nominal price.

Although purchasing power parity can be used as a mile marker to gauge a dimension of valuation, currencies are more volatile than the prices of goods, services, or unit labor costs that go into PPP. One of the challenging characteristics of the foreign exchange market is the number of variables that can influence the price of a currency in short and intermediate terms. Floating currencies have deviated from levels suggested appropriate by even the most sophisticated models of PPP by sufficiently large magnitudes and for sufficiently long duration that only rarely are they useful to investors and traders, as we will see shortly.

Drivers of Price

The myriad of factors in the intermediate trend can overwhelm investors and policy makers. An appreciation for the general environment can often be achieved by simplifying the variables to two: monetary and fiscal policy. What we are interested in is their effect in combination. The policy mix that is associated with an appreciating currency is tight monetary policy and loose fiscal policy. It is as if the central bank has its foot on the brake, the government has its foot on the accelerator, and the currency gets squeezed up. This is essentially the policy mix that Ronald Reagan and Paul Volcker pursued in the early 1980s that helped fuel a dramatic multiyear dollar rally. Germany followed a similar strategy after the Berlin Wall fell. The leveraged buyout of the East by the West and the subsequent fiscal stimulus was accompanied by a tight monetary policy that produced the "übermark" of the early 1990s, in turn helping to stiffen Europe's resolve for economic and monetary union.

The opposite policy mix—tight fiscal policy and loose monetary policy—is often associated with a depreciating currency. The combination of President Clinton's 1993 tax hikes and an accommodative monetary policy to help blunt the headwinds from the savings and loan crisis and the early 1990s recession pushed down on the dollar. The combination of the German policy mix and the U.S. policy mix helps explain what was an incredible move in the foreign exchange market at that time in which the German mark overshot while the dollar undershot.

Although the policy mix may help identify the intermediate term trend, it does not explain all the volatility, or variability, of prices. Other factors drive near-term movement. These can simplify the challenge of assessing currencies as well, but the purpose here is not to provide a comprehensive list or to suggest trading or investment tools but to offer an overview of some of the macroeconomic variables that can impact prices.

To illustrate the motivations and conditions that drive currency prices, it may be helpful to consider the basic trading strategies. There are three core strategies in the foreign exchange market: carry trade, momentum strategy, and mean reversion.

In the carry trade, traders and investors borrow a currency with a low interest rate and sell it to buy a currency with a higher interest rate, or they might use that currency to buy assets that are expected to return an amount in excess of the interest rate being paid on the currency that was borrowed. To realize the "carry" in any meaningful way often means that speculators or investors with a short time horizon do not use this strategy.

Certain macroeconomic conditions contribute to making this strategy attractive or not. Often a strong appetite for risk is needed to induce buying a high yield, which often means, by definition, higher risk. Interest-rate differentials generally need to be wide and stable. Carry trades also work best when currency markets are not particularly volatile. These conditions generally existed in the years before the credit crisis.

As the precise opposite conditions emerged during the crisis, the opposite of carry trade, dubbed the *risk-aversion trade,* became common in the forex market, but it tends to blend into the second core strategy, the *momentum* or *trend follower* strategy in which traders looking for profits buy a currency in hopes of selling it at a higher price within a matter of minutes, hours, days, or weeks, depending on their time frame. These trend followers jump aboard what they expect will be a train leaving a station.

Momentum traders may react to a headline about or rumors of macroeconomic developments that either justify or contradict the trend in prices anticipating a change in trend. They typically want to buy what is going up and sell what is going down. Various measures of market psychology may be employed. Momentum traders often rely also on technical tools, which essentially are used to help identify trends, quantify risk (where one admits one is wrong and limits one's loss), and project price objectives. They study past price action to predict future price action rather than analyzing macroeconomic variables the way an economist does. At its extreme, this strategy almost seems to border on numerology.

The third and final core strategy, *mean reversion,* is based on the belief that the price of a currency will move toward purchasing power parity or some other measure of value. It is as if the virtual elastic that connects currency prices to this "value" can only be stretched so far, although we do not and cannot know precisely how far. Rather than buy what is going up, as a momentum strategy requires, in mean-reversion trades, one buys what has been depressed and others are selling.

Some traders use some shorter-term mean, like a 100-day moving average, or build bands measured in standard deviations around a moving average. This allows more frequent trading opportunities. Mean-reversion strategies based on PPP are rare because they require that prices be extreme. By definition, that does not happen often. It did happen, though, in late 2007. The dollar's decline had reached such proportions that never before had it been so inexpensive relative to PPP measures against the euro (and the mark before it), sterling, the Canadian dollar, and the Australian dollar.

With the benefit of hindsight, it is clearer that the widespread use of the dollar—and to a lesser extent, the yen—as a financing currency, in various permutations of the carry-trade strategy, which was part of the excesses leading to the credit crisis, led the dollar to trade at extremely inexpensive prices. Ironically, as the credit crisis unfolded, beginning in late 2007, but especially beginning in July 2008, most of the major currencies moved back to PPP levels by the end of that year.

Several macroeconomic considerations may influence the direction of foreign exchange prices. We can categorize and remember them as the "Four Rs": risk, recession, rates, and resources.

People who participate in the foreign exchange market at their discretion to speculate on trends are willing to accept more risk at some times than at others. In a more risk-averse climate, speculators are less interested in returns and more interested in security. Stability is relative: in the credit crisis, the dollar strengthened even though the problems were particularly acute in the United States. Switzerland, always thought of as a safe haven, tends to have a softer currency than the rest of Europe when leveraging and risk taking are all the rage, as was the case in the run-up to the crisis.

The forces leading a country into a recession and the policy response may weigh on a currency. As an economy slows, the central bank may cut interest rates, which may lead or coincide with a currency decline, depending on the context. There is less economic activity, and a weaker currency acts as a transmission mechanism for monetary policy. However, often when the U.S. economy slows in absolute terms and relative to some of its main trading partners, the U.S. trade deficit has shown improvement, which many want us to believe is good for the dollar.

Interest rates do matter in the foreign exchange market, but the relationship does not appear to be linear. That is why one cannot deduce currency direction simply from interest rates. Nearly everything important is relative in the foreign exchange market. Interest rates in and of themselves do not mean nearly as much as what rates are relative to those of other countries. And even there, much of the sophisticated quantitative work shows the interest-rate differentials are not good predictors of currency movement. That is because in certain parts of the business or credit cycle there appears to be a stronger correlation between the two than in other parts of the cycle.

The resources part of the analysis gets one to think about a country's endowments of land, labor, and capital. It includes an appreciation for the terms of trade and reflects what a nation has and how it uses it. This is the economic prowess that determines the variable share of world trade that a country gets in the Open Door world. And it's not just about commodities. It includes things that we have looked at before such as how long it takes to open a business, how hard it is to register property, and how transparent and fair are the legal system and property rights. When it comes to natural resources, many, if not most, countries that depend on basic commodity extraction or production tend to be poor with generally weak or volatile currencies. Oil-producing nations in the Middle East, which peg their currencies to the dollar, are a notable exception.

The Players and Their Impact

The significance of the foreign exchange market outstrips its impressive size. It is an important part of the return on foreign investments. Academic studies suggest that the variability of currencies can account for almost a third of the return over time of a portfolio of international equities and almost two-thirds of the return on a portfolio of global bonds. For that matter, investors in U.S. blue-chip multinational companies take on currency exposure, albeit indirectly, too.

It is ironic, but prices in the currency market—not only the biggest of the capital markets but also the one at the heart of this version of globalization—may not be set the way we might assume they are, with profit-maximizing buyers and sellers duking it out over them. That's because many, if not most, of the folks trading those trillions of dollars every day are not trying to maximize their profits in the foreign exchange market. They simply don't see currencies as an asset class, as an opportunity for profit, but only as a risk that needs to be hedged, a cost that needs to be made certain, or a transactional vehicle needed to purchase another asset, which is more likely what one is trying to maximize return on.

Corporate treasurers are hedgers. Currency exposure is an uncertainty, and uncertainties are often costly. Companies find it difficult to succeed in growing earnings by increasing productivity, client servicing, and the like, but executives are loath to risk earnings on what appears to some to be little more than a bet on a currency direction. Moreover, the incentive structure appears to be such that the decision to hedge when not necessary is much more forgivable than not hedging when one should have. For these investors, currency risk is best managed in a disciplined and deliberate fashion. But it is not a profit opportunity.

Equity investors tend to see currencies as little more than the transactional vehicle necessary to buy foreign shares. Some international equity funds hedge all or some of the currency risk embedded in their portfolio, but for the most part they seem to be in the minority. Fixed-income managers more typically hedge out the currency risk of a foreign bond purchase in the swap market or another derivative market; they simply want to capture the interest rate potential and capital gain of the bond, not the value of the currency the bond is denominated in. Central banks also operate in the foreign exchange markets, but they operate under political and economic motivations that should not be confused with profit-seeking behavior.

Trading Currencies

The subset of foreign exchange market participants who view the forex market as a potential profit opportunity appears to be rather small. It is largely limited to speculators, hedge funds, and dealers and proprietary traders at banks. Although foreign exchange trading can be very lucrative, banks typically may not make as much money outguessing the market as one might imagine. Instead they make money the old-fashioned way, relying on the spread between the bid, or purchase price, and offer, or sell price, and access to superior and private information, such as their clients are doing (that is, the *order book*).

In the U.S. equity market, client activity is inside information, and it is illegal to trade on it. However, the foreign exchange market is mostly unregulated. (Banks have to comply with applicable capital regulations, and listed currency derivatives contracts are regulated.) If bank traders do not use information generated from the clients' activities to influence their own assessment and risk taking for the bank, then they are not maximizing the opportunity of their position. Their performance will likely reflect that.

The currency market may hold out the promise of lucrative profit opportunities for those who are willing to take the time to learn how to trade foreign exchange because many other participants are not looking to maximize profits in that space. However, because of the nature of the foreign exchange market, retail investors seem to be at a distinct disadvantage. The information asymmetries are profound and significant.

Retail investors have access to public information, and it is relatively inexpensive. This includes news, macroeconomic developments, government data, and even market-positioning data from the futures exchanges. Prices are also readily available. What retail investors do not have is information on who is buying and selling and at what levels. Bank dealers do have access to some of this information. Their order book is an important source of proprietary information and contributes to discovering profitable trading opportunities.

Not everyone can dissect and digest the public information that they receive. Banks hire hundreds of economists, analysts, quantitative programmers, and financial engineers. These often include former Federal Reserve and Treasury Department officials. Alan Greenspan became a special consultant to Deutsche Bank in his retirement from the Fed. How one analyzes even public information is private information. Without access to this kind of analysis, retail forex traders may be experiencing another type of competitive disadvantage.

There is yet another way that the retail forex trader is vulnerable. Proprietary traders at hedge funds, banks, and other financial institutions often have knowledge of and access to a range of financial instruments and risk management tools that small investors simply will not know about or have access to, even if they can comprehend them. Many retail investors face an additional handicap. They don't have the deep pockets needed to sustain positions and ride through the high volatility of the foreign exchange market. They are capital-shy, like the short stack in a poker game.

However, retail investors are often seduced by the amount of leverage offered by some electronic trading platforms. There is much variance among the business models in this space. Some platforms granted 100 to 1 leverage—or more—to qualified retail investors before the credit crisis. That kind of leverage is suicidal; even savvy hedge funds won't take it. That's not even gambling—where the risk of ruin is to be avoided as it is in trading—it is buying a lottery ticket.

Even at a 50-to-1 leverage, a 2-percent adverse move wipes out one's entire capital. On top of that, some of the foreign exchange platforms may trade currencies for their own account. The buy and sell orders they receive in aggregate become part of *their* private information. Their interests may not always be the same as their clients' interests.

In some ways, these electronic platforms represent a democratization of the capital markets. In the 1970s, forex trading was the purview of banks, financial institutions, and large corporations. By the late 1970s, the Chicago Mercantile Exchange traded futures on foreign currencies, alongside the pork bellies and live cattle futures. Currency options trade on the Philadelphia Stock Exchange, now part of Nasdaq. That daily turnover on the currency futures is higher relative to open interest (the number of futures contracts that are open at the end of a session) than in the currency options suggests that currency futures are more a speculator's market, whereas the option market may be more a hedger's market.

In recent years, new currency products have been introduced that trade like equities. Among the more successful are Rydex's suite of CurrencyShares Trust exchange-traded funds that make it easy for retail investors to participate in the currency markets. There are CurrencyShares for major foreign currencies, including the euro, sterling, and yen, as well as for some secondary currencies such as the Swiss franc and Swedish krona and some emerging-market currencies like the Mexican peso and Russian ruble. As equities, the leverage on an exchange-traded fund is the 2 to 1 allowed by the 50-percent margin set by the Federal Reserve. There are options available on the CurrencyShares for the more sophisticated or adventuresome. Recently new exchange-traded currency products have been introduced that grant somewhat more leverage.

Retail investors outside of the United States also are known to trade currencies. Their activities sometimes influence overall currency trends. Japanese retail investors became involved in foreign exchange trading to try to beat low yields and low stock market returns at home. The Nikkei has long been an underperforming stock index, even when Japan had a weak currency and record corporate profits. Hence, retail investors in Japan became involved in the yen-carry trade, selling the yen and buying higher-yielding currencies such as the New Zealand and Australian dollars, the South African rand, and the U.S. dollar.

As seems to be the case in other instruments as well, there is no substitute for disciplined risk management in the foreign exchange market because any set of macroeconomic and technical conditions are consistent with a wide range of prices. No matter how sure one is, there is someone on the other side of the trade who may be just as convinced of the opposite. Because of the asymmetries of information, the volatility of currencies, and the typically undercapitalized position of the retail forex trader, discipline is all the more critical.

Currency and Crisis

The current stage of globalization has been going through waves of birthing pains. The first was the series of financial crises in Mexico during 1994–95, Asia from 1997 to 1998, Russia in 1998, and then

Argentina in 2001–02. To a large extent, these were currency crises as the fixed exchange rate regimes in Latin America, Asia, and Russia moved abruptly to somewhat more flexible "dirty" float regimes. The second was the end of the technology bubble of the late 1990s, which gave birth to a more intensive globalization of production and distribution of goods and services. As Thomas Friedman observed in *The World Is Flat*, fiber-optic networks lowered the price of globalization.[3] Suddenly, it seemed that many white-collar workers in the United States could lose their jobs to people in India willing to work at a fraction of the wage, a profoundly disruptive idea.

The credit crisis that began in 2007 marks the third wave. On some levels, these financial woes appeared to be a classic garden-variety bust-follows-boom crisis described so well by Hyman Minsky: a world of persistent and sustained asset price increases produces the opposite. Sustained stability is itself the source of financial instability, mispricing risk, and its own irrational exuberance and excesses.

Yet this is the first financial crisis that appears to be largely rooted in those markets that were heralded as an evolutionary step for finance: credit derivatives, residential mortgage-backed securities, and leveraged loans. These innovations were supposed to spread risk more evenly to encourage economic growth; instead, they concentrated risks in ways that were unimaginable. CDO-squared, where a collateralized debt obligation is composed of other collateralized obligations, epitomizes such developments.

Despite these waves of crises, the global economic and financial system has shown remarkable resilience. The markets quickly recovered from past problems, with new record highs set in many equity markets following collapses. Implied volatility, especially in the equity and currency markets, spiked higher but quickly came back off. Many had come to see these occasional bouts of turbulence to be short-lived, countertrend phenomena. When investors and speculators saw weakness, they viewed it as a buying opportunity and snapped up assets at low prices (helped by ready leverage), which brought prices back up to higher levels. And it worked until it didn't.

The credit crisis marks an important watershed. There wasn't the buying that cushioned earlier market declines, in part due to the lack of credit and in part because the financial institutions that were often leading the buying charge were the most bloodied by the collapse.

Although many were slow to recognize it as such, the credit crisis was the materialization of systemic risk—a low-probability, high-impact event. Just as important as it is to understand the cause of the credit crisis and the conditions that allowed it to metastasize, it is also important to recognize that *it was not a currency crisis.* The dollar was not having a disorderly and destabilizing decline. If anything, after the middle of 2008, it was not the dollar's weakness that prompted policy action. It was the dollar's strength, reflecting a severe shortage of dollars and that the Federal Reserve sought to address through those extensive currency swaps with foreign central banks.

Currency and Diversification

One of the most compelling arguments against a broad decoupling of world asset markets from the U.S. market is also a significant challenge for investors and asset managers. That's the strong correlation within and between asset classes. In financial theory, diversification should allow investors to receive a higher rate of return for a given level of risk than they could receive by investing in any one asset. Investors should look for assets with as little correlation as possible; the idea is that the ups and downs of the different assets will cancel each other out.

Easier said than done. One of the elements of globalization has been the deeper integration of the market for capital. Diversification was elusive and the credit crisis exacerbated this. By the end of 2008, everything, it seemed, was going in the same direction—down—and by almost unimaginable amounts.

In 2000, Morgan Stanley Capital International's (MSCI) benchmark Europe, Australasia, and Far East index (EAFE) index moved in the same direction as the S&P 500 only about a third of the time. As the decade passed, the five-year rolling numbers for EAFE showed a 93-percent correlation with the Standard & Poor's 500 Index. That's higher than the 91-percent correlation between the S&P and the Russell 2000 Index, both of which are concentrated in the United States. U.S. stock investors won't find much diversification in either EAFE or the broad Russell index.

At the end of 2008, the MSCI Emerging Market Index's correlation with the S&P 500 was nearly 70 percent, whereas Brazil's Bovespa index had moved in the same direction as the S&P 500 on a weekly basis more than 75 percent of the time. Emerging markets weren't offering investors much in the way of diversification, either.

Even in the alternative investment space, diversification is difficult to find. The correlation between equity hedge funds—which promise absolute return, not just beating an index in order to justify the lucrative fees—and the S&P 500 has almost tripled since 2000 to about 90 percent by the middle of the decade. To achieve diversification and augment returns, some asset managers have begun looking for opportunities farther afield. The S&P Frontier Markets Index, which tracks markets in the Middle East, Africa, and other places that lag behind the emerging markets of Brazil, India, and China, has tracked the S&P 500 less than a quarter of the time. Since 2000, the Frontier Index has returned nearly three times as much as the MSCI Emerging Markets Index, whereas the S&P 500 has changed little. But these markets are very tiny, so they are not practical for most investors. Furthermore, looking at the performance of all markets between the United States and the frontiers at the end of 2008, it seems only a matter of time before the African and Middle Eastern markets have 80-percent correlation or so with the S&P 500. Foreign exchange exposure may be one of the last ways to diversify a portfolio.

The U.S. dollar entered a cyclical bear market in 2000–01. Within the bear market, there was a countertrend improvement in the dollar in 2005. Some observers tied in part to a tax holiday that allowed U.S. businesses to repatriate their foreign earnings at a tax rate close to 5 percent rather than the normal tax rate of about 30 percent. Although several hundred billions of dollars may have ultimately repatriated, according to some accounts, the impact on the dollar may have been exaggerated. U.S. corporations often keep the bulk of their foreign earnings in dollar-denominated securities. In any event, the dollar's downtrend resumed by early 2006.

The dollar's multiyear decline against most of the major foreign currencies may also be understood as an unwinding of the dollar's gains registered in the late 1990s. Yet again with the advantage of hindsight, part of the dollar's decline was not benign. It appears that part of the dollar's decline was a function of the global leveraging that was built to astronomical levels by 2007.

One point that the data seems unequivocal about is that the dollar's decline was not a function of the diversification of central banks' reserves. As we saw previously, there is no compelling evidence that this took place on an aggregate level. The dollar's decline was not a function of the decline in the competitiveness of the U.S. economy. By a number of macroeconomic measures such as gross domestic product per capita and productivity growth, the U.S. economy remained highly competitive. The dollar's decline was not a function of a widening of the U.S. trade deficit. The trade deficit had been narrowing even as the dollar's decline reached a fevered pitch in 2007 and early 2008.

It turns out that businesses, banks, and individuals in places as disparate as Europe, South Korea, Brazil, and Russia borrowed dollars and reinvested them domestically. The growth in European bank balance sheets now appears to have been financed with largely U.S. dollars. Hedge funds' investments in commodities and emerging markets often were financed with dollars. U.S. investors themselves sold dollars when they chased the higher returns seemingly available abroad by pouring money into international mutual funds, American depositary receipts, and foreign companies listed on the U.S. exchanges. At its peak, it was estimated that 20 percent to 25 percent of U.S. equity investments were in foreign markets.

All these activities represent the downward pressure on the U.S. dollar. The dollar declined, for example, as oil prices rose, not for the macroeconomic or structural reasons commonly cited at the time. There was a relationship: many large investors used short dollar positions to finance purchases of oil and other commodities, the euros, and a host of other investments. Some analysts recognized the correlation between say the euro and oil and often offered a causal narrative. The two were correlated, but correlated to a third factor: the use of the dollar as a financing currency.

The dollar's dramatic recovery as the credit crisis became more acute was largely a function of that leveraging process put in reverse—violent, dramatic, and persistent deleveraging. There was an aspect of the crisis that was like a large margin call. The dollar was lifted, as were other financing currencies such as the Japanese yen and, to a lesser extent, the Swiss franc and Hong Kong dollar as previously sold positions were covered.

Why was the dollar such an important financing currency? Some analysts attribute it to the exceptional and prolonged accommodative monetary policy pursued by the Greenspan Fed. Although it clearly played a role, it was not simply caused by domestic U.S. considerations. The Fed raised interest rates well before the excesses mounted. Long-term interest rates, which the Fed has little control over, were also lower than economists would anticipate for the prevailing macroeconomic conditions. This was the Greenspan "conundrum."

Bernanke explained the conundrum through surplus savings, which in turn highlights an international dimension to the credit crisis. After the 1997–98 Asian financial crisis, many countries in the region began running large current account surpluses. In addition to export revenues, there was also foreign capital pouring into local equity markets. Central banks, sovereign wealth funds, and private-sector institutions recycled the savings that could not be absorbed domestically.

That other currencies were used as financing currencies and that other countries appeared to have their own asset bubbles, sometimes with higher interest rates than the United States, lends support to arguments that there was much more to the credit crisis than U.S. monetary policy and subprime mortgages. Moreover, the Federal Reserve has the greatest influence over short-term interest rates and began to tighten policy in the middle of 2004. By the middle of 2006, the Fed funds target was at 5.25 percent, which is above its 10- and 15-year averages.

Reality: Foreign Exchange Offers Investment Opportunities

The currency market is larger than any other part of the capital markets. Trillions of dollars of currencies exchange hands every single day all over the world; each month, enough currency trades to buy the goods and services that the world produces in a year.

Although many people use trade accounting as a measure for the strength of a currency, this belies the reality that trade is only a small part of currency markets. The trade deficit doesn't explain why the United States continues to have a strong economy (the credit crises and recession are exceptions, though obviously significant); the nontrade component of the turnover in the foreign exchange market suggests the direction of the answer. People buy and sell currency as part of their investing activities. Nations buy and sell currency as part of their reserve activities. Corporations buy and sell currencies to hedge the exchange-rate risk of their local market investments.

Despite so much activity, currency trading seems exotic. It can be in the hands of a hedge fund that uses leverage to arbitrage between the currencies, using second- and third-generation derivative products. But most currency-market activity is mundane. Currency trading has become popular with individual investors (although maybe that trend itself was part of the conditions that led to the credit crisis), many of whom do not appear to appreciate that the currency playing field is anything but level.

Besides, trading currencies directly, individuals can assume currency exposure through the purchases of major U.S. companies with global businesses, international stock, bond, and money market mutual funds, commodity trading advisers, currency-based exchange-traded funds, and foreign currency bank CDs. These may provide the diversification benefits of the large and powerful foreign exchange markets.

Chapter Notes

1. Bank for International Settlements, "Triennial Central Bank Survey," December 2007.

2. Speech audio and transcription available at http://historymatters.gmu.edu/d/5354/.

3. Thomas Friedman, *The World Is Flat*, 3rd ed. (New York: Picador, 2007).

Summary and Some Thoughts on the Way Forward

The dollar is just fine.

There is much to worry about in the financial markets, and the world economy in general, but the U.S. trade deficit and the value of the U.S. dollar should be low on the list. Is that a surprise? It wouldn't be if the conventional wisdom about trade and trade accounting had kept pace with the rapid changes in the world economy and the management of multinational corporations. As we look at the realities of foreign trade and the complex network of international economic relations and activities, it's obvious things have changed. At one time, powerful nations exported, weak nations imported, and investors kept funds within their own borders unless they were especially enamored of risk. However, as we've seen in the previous pages, global trade doesn't work that way at all in the twenty-first century. But unless investors and people in government realize that, their decision making will be flawed, producing counterproductive policies.

Opinion appears to be coalescing into two camps: those who think America has begun a long-term decline and those who don't. The triumphalism at the end of the Cold War has given way to a profound concern among friends and enemies alike that America has either lost its way or that others are catching up. The credit crisis, and the large levels of debt that the U.S. government is taking on, fan those fears.

Using the old measures of economic success, the United States may appear to be in decline. But those metrics are out of date. The United States remains the largest and most powerful economy on Earth. What emerges from the arguments in this book, individually and collectively, is a nuanced picture of how the U.S. commercial expansion strategy works. It does work, producing wealth and better living standards.

The Trade Deficit and the Dollar

The traditional measure of economic success is whether a country exports more than it imports, even though Adam Smith argued specifically and compellingly against such views more than two hundred years ago. The U.S. trade balance has been in deficit for a generation. It has become a structural component of the world economy as it has evolved and been molded since the end of the 1970s. It is as given as any certainty in this probabilistic world that when the United States reports its trade balance, it will be a deficit.

Yet the real meaningful gap, in per-capita GDP and productivity, has grown in the United States' favor. The United States remains a vibrant and innovative country despite the severe credit crisis. U.S.-headquartered businesses continue to occupy many of the commanding heights of the global economy. It is now the world's only military superpower, even though the wars in Iraq and Afghanistan tax its resources.

During the global financial crisis, U.S. leadership has been critical. The depth and breadth of its asset markets are second to none. Despite the purported U.S. blemishes, the Treasury market once again provided a safe harbor during the most tumultuous and violent times of the credit crisis. Throughout the credit crisis, and in past crises, U.S. officials often took measures that arguably sacrificed some short-term American interests to prevent a more virulent systemic crisis. In addition, the Federal Reserve's extensive currency-swap arrangements with a number of central banks in both major and developing countries during the credit crisis helped alleviate a destabilizing shortage of dollars.

Investors and policy makers need to think about money and trade in a different way. To start, policy makers should look more carefully at an ownership-based framework of trade rather than the traditional balance-of-payments calculations that focus exclusively on the movement across national borders. Substantial work has already been done in this area. The Bureau of Economic Analysis issues a report annually that supplements the traditional balance-of-payments accounts. It documents two important aspects of America's corporate evolutionary strategy: produce and sell locally and the in-sourcing trade. It keeps the focus on ownership rather than simply the movement of goods and services over a national frontier, which makes good sense given the globalization of production and distribution.

The supply and demand of money for trade is important, but trade is not the only reason, or even a major reason, for trade in a currency. Crossborder movement of capital far and away outstrips trade flows globally. Exports are not the primary way in which U.S. companies service foreign demand. Sales by foreign affiliates of U.S. multinational companies exceed exports by a factor of four. Japanese car producers rely on a similar model to service the U.S. market. Yes, Japan exports cars and car parts—but the sales of cars made in the United States and assembled by American workers is the primary way that U.S. demand is met.

A large part of the trade that takes place occurs within the same company. In the case of U.S. companies, this activity is often between different stages in the production process, like parts that need to be assembled. Exporting parts and importing finished goods characterizes the U.S. trade patterns under NAFTA as production was organized on a continental scale. Typically, trade between the foreign-owned affiliate operating in the United States provides distributional and marketing services for the parent importing finished products. This intrafirm trade may not be as sensitive to fluctuations of currencies as trade between arm's-length parties. It also does not appear to require the same offsetting movement of capital because it is often an accounting entry.

These two features are central to the evolutionary strategy of U.S. companies and, increasingly, other multinational companies: they require the free movement not only of goods but also of capital. The credit crisis may reinforce these trends if governments adhere to their treaty obligations and verbal reassurances to avoid a retreat to protectionism. The volatility of the currency market during the crisis reached levels that approached twice that experienced around 9/11. The build-local, sell-local strategy offers natural diversification of currency exposures and positions a company against potentially protectionist actions by foreign countries. It also leads to development of host countries through the transfer of technology and the creation of jobs in a way that the traditional export-oriented approach to meeting foreign demand simply can't accomplish.

The malaise associated with the collapse of Bretton Woods, the second oil crisis in the late 1970s, and stagflation was a symptom of a serious breakdown of the post–World War II economic order. For three years starting in 1978, three people rose to power who personi-fied the unleashing of new forces that rebuilt and replaced that which had broken down. Deng Xiaoping rose to power in China, representing the integration of not only the People's Republic of China but many other emerging markets into the world economy. In 1979, Margaret Thatcher became prime minister of the United Kingdom; and then, in 1980, Ronald Reagan was elected president of the United States.

The world they ushered in featured steadier economic activity— generally booms or busts in the business cycle that were not as large. It was as if the volatility of the business cycle was transferred to interest rates, foreign exchange rates, and asset prices. The increased impor-tance of the service sector and corporate practices, like better manage-ment of the inventory cycle, also contributed to what economists have dubbed the "Great Moderation."

In what may be seen as a new phase in the globalization of the Open Door, the U.S. economy was opened up in a way that had not been done previously. The United States became the banker for the world. Rather than competing in the export of surplus capital, the United States became the recipient, the safety valve, for the lion's share of the world's surplus savings. It kept some of the capital in the United States and recycled the remainder, sometimes to the same countries that were bringing their savings to the United States in the first place. This, in turn, produced large and unstable imbalances that were dangerous from an economic point of view and unacceptable from a political point of view.

It is possible that the credit crisis and the associated deep reces-sion will call into question this approach. Yet a closer look suggests to the contrary: the institutional consequences of the crisis will likely be more of the approach rather than less. The disintermediation was not as extensive as it was portrayed. The capital markets were not as trans-parent as was claimed. Greater transparency and greater disintermedia-tion will likely be the results of the credit crisis. Many risk-management tools were rendered obsolete and will have to be replaced. This will ultimately allow the United States to more efficiently absorb and manage the world's surplus savings.

One lesson from the credit crisis is that the volatility that was transferred to the prices of financial variables can create a negative feedback mechanism that could hit the real economy. The credit cycle needs to be smoothed out. This will likely require different regulations and regulators that address the way business and finance are conducted in the twenty-first century. It may help make the postcrisis capital markets more stable if the incentives and temptations Minsky warned of can be checked by consistent enforcement. There always will remain the risk that the scar tissue heals and the prudence of one generation gives way to a new generation that once again needs to learn that markets mean more than the pursuit of unbridled greed and that strong rules are needed.

Contrary to what is often suggested, a stronger regulatory regime is not antithetical to America. In fact, it is perfectly consistent with and a logical extension of the American contribution to political theory. The republican theory of the Founding Fathers did not reject power because its use could be corrupting. Rather, it accepted the necessity of the exercise of power; yet cognizant of the dangers, it held that power needs to be divided, must be kept in check by a countervailing power, and has to be held accountable. In the face of the power of capital, especially in light of its increased mobility and complexity, classic American political philosophy requires a countervailing power, like regulation, to keep it in check and accountable.

An economy that has productive uses for funds can take them from anywhere in the world. The key is that the uses have to be productive. In the near term, though, even productive uses sometimes create deficits. Outmoded accounting definitions exacerbate the imbalances. The definition of savings does not include such things as employer-sponsored retirement savings contributions (considered to be income) or gains on those investments. It also considers spending on higher education to be consumption rather than an investment in the student's future economic success. That understates the level of savings in the U.S. economy and overstates American consumption.

The crisis will not threaten another source of U.S. economic prowess: its innovativeness. In 2008, the United States recorded 157,774 patents, a slight increase over the 157,284 recorded in 2007.[1] IBM alone registered 2.7 percent of those patents, or 4,486. That single U.S. corporation is responsible for more patents in 2008 than those of all companies in China combined. China may demonstrate impressive economic prowess in manufacturing, but the workers are making items designed elsewhere—mostly in the United States.

America's most important investment is in people and ideas. In an open economy, people gain status through accomplishment, not last name. That creates an incentive to get an education, start a business, and develop new ways of doing things. The diversity of America may also prove to be an enduring strength after the crisis ebbs. America is a land of immigrants. People from different cultures, religions, and social classes regularly rub elbows in the workplace. The constant challenge of having to get along with others who are different, and the cross-fertilization of ideas can animate the creative and competitive process. "In no other country on Earth is my story even possible," Barack Obama has said,[2] and that's true; as president, he joins a long line of patricians and rednecks alike, including patricians who pretended to be rednecks.

Businesses, especially during expansion phases of an economic cycle, tend to argue that government intervention will destroy capitalism. Capitalism has so many forms. A progressive tax rate or universal health insurance or regulations that limit the degree that a bank or hedge fund can be leveraged don't really mark the end of capitalism. The dialectic relationship between the state and markets was always more complicated than the simple dualism often implied by many protagonists. There could not be and weren't markets before the state.

The state created markets and sanctioned a market for the factors of production (land, labor, and capital); in doing so, it turned traditional (feudal) society on its head. Markets, as aggregators of information and opinions, are invaluable for modern policy makers. The state's role and involvement in the economy grew during the credit crisis. There will likely be a backlash against it in the immediate aftermath of the crisis. Yet it seems unlikely that the state will completely return to pre-crisis proportions. The government's demand for goods and services accounted for a little more than one-third of U.S. GDP and around half of continental European GDP before the crisis. It was already an essential force supporting what economists call *aggregate demand.* Without it—or if it were to cease, as in the fantasy of some extreme libertarians—can there really be any doubt but that society would be significantly worse off?

As a mechanism to distribute scarcity, markets can be ruthlessly efficient in the purest of economic senses. This is acceptable when it comes to the color of automobiles, whether hemlines will be higher or lower, or whether neckties will be narrower or wider. But there may be other areas in which market mechanisms may be somewhat less acceptable, such as the distribution of health care, water, education, and justice. A society may have other goals in addition to economic efficiency such as fairness and diversity.

The state has always played an integral role in American capitalism. Laissez-faire never really existed. Yet it seems that every generation mourns its death. The government's response to the credit crisis, some people claim, marks the end of capitalism. Some argued that Franklin Roosevelt and his New Deal spelled the end of capitalism. In 1999, Milton Friedman and his wife, Rose, bemoaned that most of the important economic planks of the Socialist Party platform in 1928 had largely been implemented. Keynes had declared the end to laissez-faire in a book with that title in 1926.

Different cultures have different capitalist styles. Some grant more power to the corporation and others the state. In every case, the notions of private ownership of the factors of production and compensation for investment risk hold. It's not surprising that different cultures would approach business differently. China, India, and Russia are timely examples because they have moved beyond so-called socialist practices and adopted very different forms of capitalism accompanied by very different styles of governance.

U.S. capitalism has been so successful that buyers and sellers all over the world rely on the dollar as their default currency. In early 2009, the Swiss National Bank, a bastion of independence and prudence, backed by one of the largest current account surpluses among advanced industrialized countries, announced it would begin issuing short-term debt instruments (like T-bills) denominated in U.S. dollars.

The dollar is almost universally embraced for investment, trade, and global reserves. The United States still can boast of the largest economy that is typically fairly stable, the credit crisis not withstanding. This, coupled with its stable political system, creates a range of investment opportunities and safe places to which the world's excess savings are attracted. People prefer dollars regardless of whether they are buying or selling U.S. goods or their own goods. Observers and policy makers who focus nearly exclusively on a trade-centric worldview generally do not appreciate that role of the dollar in the world economy and in the halls of finance.

The obsession with the trade balance often shifts to the role of U.S. manufacturing, which is widely perceived to be in decline. That might be the case for those who can't see past the dashboard of a Chrysler, Ford, or GM car. However, U.S. manufacturing output has grown even though the absolute number of manufacturing jobs has shrunk. American workers are more productive than ever. U.S. manufacturing prowess illustrates another strength of America's that is also lost in the gallons of ink spilled on deindustrialization. The significance extends well beyond the direct employment in manufacturing. It's from the ability to make more things, better, and with fewer people.

That is the expertise that U.S. companies export when they move manufacturing abroad. At the end of 2007, General Motors had a 10-percent market share in China. The company has had a long string of problems, but being competitive overseas is not one of them. Globalization transcends the traditional emphasis on the movement of goods over national frontiers, which tends to be rather shallow. Direct investment is a deeper type of economic integration, and it can help companies improve market share and manage risks better than they could with export-oriented trade.

Many American workers participate in the stock market. Although few individuals purchase shares directly, many do so as beneficiaries of mutual funds and pension plans. In some industries, especially technology, the use of employee stock options gives people at all levels of the firm a stake in the success of the enterprise and a tangible incentive to see the business thrive. That makes for an interesting irony: the world's most capitalist nation is also the most socialist one. Ownership has been socialized, and workers are the beneficiary owners of what the Marxists call the means of production. As we have seen, the ownership function has been decoupled from control, and it is that dialectic between ownership and control that promises to be an interesting space, with potential for realignment in the wake of the credit crisis. Profits and control cannot remain privatized if losses and what economists call *negative externalities* are socialized—that is, shouldered by society.

Some people have argued that a weaker dollar lifts equity markets. The data show otherwise. In the past, there may have been a closer relationship between the equity market performance and the dollar, but that tie appears to have been broken for almost two decades. Perhaps it is, at least partly, because the typical U.S.-based multinational corporation is simply not constrained by demand in the U.S. economy and relies less on exports to meet foreign demand. Instead, it serves local customers where they are, making goods and selling them in faraway lands rather than shipping them from the United States. That insulates companies from many of the economic effects of currency fluctuations, reducing the changes in profits from the dollar that might lead to changes in stock market performance.

This strategy that has evolved by American businesses to compete in a world in which tariff barriers to trade are largely at negligible levels; capital flows freely, generally speaking; and currencies fluctuate dramatically. It is based on producing goods locally and selling them locally. Although some corporate functions have been outsourced, American multinational businesses have insourced trade. The strategy allows U.S. companies to compete when the dollar is strong as in the second half of the 1990s or declining as it was from 2001 through 2007. This strategy will most likely survive the credit crisis and economic contraction.

Some economists and policy makers advocate a significant dollar decline to reduce the trade deficit. Yet there is little evidence that a devaluation strategy works. There has been sharp depreciation of the dollar against the Japanese yen over a couple of decades, and still a substantial bilateral deficit exists. There does not appear to be strong correlation between the U.S. trade performance and exchange rates.

Consider the Chinese yuan, which seems to have eclipsed the yen for the dubious honor of attracting the attention of policy makers and economists. In 2005, Nicholas Lardy and Morris Goldstein, two highly respected economists at the renowned Peterson Institute for International Economics, used state-of-the-art economic techniques and estimated that the yuan was 20-percent to 25-percent undervalued. This was near the middle of the range of estimates that were discovered by a couple of U.S. senators as they drafted legislation that year seeking the appreciation of the yuan.

In July 2005, China ended its peg against the dollar, and the yuan had appreciated by the middle of 2008 by nearly as much as Lardy and

Goldstein advocated. And the Chinese trade surplus with the U.S.? It doubled over the intervening years. Lardy and Goldstein? They were calling for another 10-percent to 20-percent appreciation of the yuan in early 2009 to eliminate China's trade surplus.[3]

It is not just that a weaker dollar does not achieve the anticipated desirable results that its proponents advocate, but a devaluationist strategy actually inflicts material harm. A weak dollar makes it more expensive for U.S. companies to pursue their foreign direct-investment–led strategy while at the same time making it less costly for foreign business to adopt the same strategy. Purposely seeking a weaker dollar may also interrupt capital markets by calling into question America's commitment and ability to absorb the world's excess savings. To the extent that the U.S. official stance of backing a strong dollar means that it will not purposely seek to depreciate the dollar to reduce the country's debt burden, the strong dollar policy is also likely to survive the credit crisis.

When businesses approach international markets, they are looking at supply and demand. That's how all markets function. A consumer products company making an investment in the Vietnamese market may be thinking about very long-term demand rather than making big profits right now. But supply and demand affect sales of shampoo in Hanoi, and they also affect the exchange rate between the dong and the dollar. Investors increasingly need to understand the foreign exchange market. A basic understanding of it can give people more confidence in recognizing investment opportunities.

In fact, foreign exchange exposure may offer a better source for portfolio diversification than international equities. Global stock markets are moving more in sync, making diversification harder to achieve. The currency exposure can create the kind of noncorrelated returns that financial advisers and investment professionals often look for. Financial innovation—which is also unlikely to have been killed by the credit crisis, even if, going forward, greater transparency is demanded—has, through the securitization and equitization process, created a growing number of equity vehicles that allow individual investors to access the foreign currencies on an exchange platform.

In many ways, though, the full impact and consequences of the credit crisis on the constellation of political and economic forces discussed in this book remain indeterminate. One major unknown is the dimensions of the new financial architecture that will be built to reconstruct the sector. Regulation had not kept pace with changes in financial products and the globalized nature of finance; hence, securities that needed more oversight did not receive it, while other types were regulated to the point of inflexibility.

The clear risk is that the economic challenges prove too great and countries will try to retreat from the global economy and insulate themselves through various nationalist and protectionist measures. Institutional rigidity and nationalism toppled the globalization of the nineteenth century; those same forces can effectively close the Open Door.

Nevertheless, there is some reason to expect that stronger and more transparent institutions emerge. The evolution of the junk bond market may offer a glimpse into the future. In the late 1980s, junk bonds, also known as high-yield corporate bonds, were popular and seemed to trade readily. But they didn't. The market was rigged and run almost entirely by one trading desk at one brokerage firm, Drexel Burnham Lambert. When the firm collapsed, it seemed that the junk bond market would collapse with it. However, many companies needed that type of financing, and many investors were attracted to the return opportunities. A real market developed around the need, and now these high-yield bonds trade freely in a market that is well covered and well researched by a range of analysts, with investors committed to that asset class.

Not only are there those who adapt and succeed but also there are some evolutionary dead ends. Some products will die off in this market restructuring, and that may be a good thing. Distortions caused by securities that were not well understood by anyone, from the issuers to the buyers, led to a massive mispricing of risk. Some structured investment vehicles, auction-rate bonds, and mortgages made with no down payment and no income verification are likely to disappear from the market and should. The practice by which one company originates loans and another company owns the loans creates all sorts of destabilizing incentive structures. Their legacy may also be more simplicity, transparency, and maybe even greater prudence in finance.

The United States enjoyed a large, variable share of the world's economy based on its economic prowess under the fixed exchange rate and limited capital mobility regime of Bretton Woods. That regime was also conducive to the rebuilding of Europe and Japan. The United States also enjoyed a large, variable share of the world economy under an international monetary regime characterized by floating currencies and great capital mobility. The expansion strategy that has evolved allows U.S. companies to compete in both strong- and weak-dollar environments. The new rules that emerge from the credit crisis will undoubtedly create new incentives and disincentives; in turn, these could influence the contours of the expansion strategy. Nevertheless, the ability and flexibility of American markets, the innovativeness of the American people and policy makers, and the nation's pragmatic ideology suggest the dollar will remain the numeraire for years to come.

Chapter Notes

1. IFI Patent Intelligence, press release, January 14, 2009.

2. Barack Obama, speech at the 2004 Democratic Convention, July 27, 2004 (http://www.washingtonpost.com/wp-dyn/articles/A19751-2004Jul27.html).

3. "Economics Focus: Burger-Thy-Neighbour Policies." *The Economist*, February 7, 2009.

Bibliography

Albert, Michel. *Capitalism vs. Capitalism: How America's Obsession with Individual Achievement and Short-Term Profit Led It to the Brink of Collapse*. New York: Basic Books, 1993.

Bacevich, Andrew. *American Empire: The Realities and Consequences of U.S. Diplomacy*. Cambridge, MA: Harvard University Press, 2004.

Becker, David, Jeff Frieden, Sayre Schatz, and Richard Sklar. *Postimperialism: International Capitalism and Development in the Late 20th Century*. Boulder, CO: Lynne Rienner, 1987.

Berle, Adolf. *Power Without Property: A New Development in American Political Economy*. New York: Harcourt, 1959.

Berle, Adolf, and Gardiner C. Means. *The Modern Corporation and Private Property*. New York: Macmillan Co., 1932.

Chandler, Alfred D. *The Visible Hand: The Managerial Revolution in American Business*. Cambridge, MA: Belknap Press, 1993 (original edition released in 1977).

Conant, Charles. *The United States in the Orient: The Nature of the Economic Problem*. Port Washington, NY: Kennikat Press, 1900 (reissued 1971).

De Soto, Hernando. *The Mystery of Capital: Why Capitalism Triumphs in the West and Fails Everywhere Else*. New York: Basic Books, 2000.

Dicken, Peter. *Global Shift: The Internationalization of Economic Activity*, 2nd ed. New York: Guilford Press, 1992.

Doremus, Peter, William Keller, Louis Pauly, and Simon Reich. *The Myth of the Global Corporation*. Princeton, NJ: Princeton University Press, 1999.

Drucker, Peter F. *Post-Capitalist Society*. New York: HarperCollins, 1994.

Easterbrook, Gregg. *The Progress Paradox: How Life Gets Better While People Feel Worse*. New York: Random House, 2004.

Ferguson, Niall. *Empire: The Rise and Demise of the British World Order and the Lessons for Global Power*. New York: Basic Books, 2003.

Ferguson, Niall. *The Cash Nexus: Economics and Politics from the Age of Warfare through the Age of Welfare, 1700–2000*. New York: Basic Books, 2002.

Fogel, Robert William. *The Fourth Great Awakening and the Future of Egalitarianism*. Chicago: University of Chicago Press, 2000.

Fogel, Robert William. *The Escape from Hunger and Premature Death, 1700–2100*. Cambridge, UK: Cambridge University Press, 2004.

Friedman, Thomas L. *The World is Flat: A Brief History of the Twenty-First Century*. Waterville, ME: Thorndike Press, 2005.

Friedman, Thomas L. *The Lexus and the Olive Tree*. New York: Farrar, Strauss and Giroux, 1999.

Friedman, Milton, and Rose Friedman. *Free to Choose: A Personal Statement*. New York: Harcourt, 1980.

Gilpin, Robert. *U.S. Power and the Multinational Corporation: The Political Economy of Foreign Direct Investment*. New York: Basic Books, 1975.

Greenspan, Alan. *Age of Turbulence: Adventures in a New World*. New York: Penguin Press, 2007.

Hall, Peter, and David Soskice, editors. *Varieties of Capitalism: The Institutional Foundations of Comparative Advantage*. New York: Oxford University Press, 2001.

Hampden-Turner, Charles, and Alfonso Trompenaars. *The Seven Cultures of Capitalism: Value Systems for Creating Wealth in Britain, the United States, Germany, France, Japan, Sweden, and the Netherlands*. London: Piatkus Books, 1994.

Hellman, Rainer. *The Challenge to U.S. Dominance of the International Corporation*. Translated by Peter Ruof. New York: Dunellen Publishing, 1971.

Hobson, J. A. *Imperialism*. Ann Arbor: University of Michigan Press, 1965.

Karmin, Craig. *Biography of the Dollar: How the Mighty Buck Conquered the World and Why It's Under Siege*. New York: Crown, 2008.

Keynes, John Maynard. *The End of Laissez-Faire*. London: Hogarth Press, 1926.

Laswell, Harold. *Politics: Who Gets What, When, How*. New York: Meridian Books, 1964.

Lenin, V. I. *Imperialism: The Highest Stage of Capitalism*. Beijing: Foreign Languages Press, 1973.

Livingston, James. *Pragmatism and the Political Economy of Cultural Revolution (1850–1910)*. Chapel Hill: University of North Carolina Press, 1994.

Livingston, James. *Origins of the Federal Reserve System: Money, Class, and Corporate Capitalism (1890–1913)*. Ithaca, NY: Cornell University Press, 1986.

Mann, Catherine. *Is the U.S. Trade Deficit Sustainable?* Washington, DC: Institute for International Economics, 1999.

Polanyi, Karl. *The Great Transformation: The Political and Economic Origins of Our Time*. Boston: Beacon Press, 1971.

Pollan, Michael. *The Omnivore's Dilemma: A Natural History of Four Meals*. New York: Penguin Press, 2006.

Quinlan, Joseph P. *Global Engagement: How American Companies Really Compete in the Global Economy*. New York: Contemporary Books, 2000.

Ricardo, David. *Principles of Political Economy and Taxation*. New York: Cosimo Classics, 2006.

Robinson, John, and Geoffrey Godbey. *Time for Life: The Surprising Ways Americans Use Their Time*. University Park: Penn State University Press, 1999.

Rubin, Robert, and James Weisberg. *In an Uncertain World: Tough Choices from Wall Street to Washington*. New York: Random House, 2004.

Skocpol, Theda. *Protecting Soldiers and Mothers: The Political Origins of Social Policy in the United States*. Cambridge, MA: Belknap Press, 1995.

Servan-Schreiber, Jean-Jacques. *The American Challenge*. New York: Penguin Press, 1969.

Sklar, Martin J. *The Corporate Reconstruction of American Capitalism, 1890–1916: The Market, the Law, and Politics*. Cambridge, UK: Cambridge University Press, 1988.

Sklar, Martin J. *United States as a Developing Country: Studies in U.S. History in the Progressive Era and the 1920s*. Cambridge, UK: Cambridge University Press, 1992.

Smith, Adam. *An Inquiry into the Nature and Causes of the Wealth of Nations*. New York: Oxford University Press, 2008.

Wade, Robert. *Governing the Market: Economic Theory and the Role of Government in East Asian Industrialization*. Princeton, NJ: Princeton University Press, 1990.

Williams, William Appleman. *Tragedy of American Diplomacy*. New York: Dell, 1972.

Williams, William Appleman. *Contours of American History*. Cleveland, OH: World Publishing, 1961.

Index

About the Author

MARC CHANDLER is a senior vice president and global head of currency strategy at Brown Brothers Harriman, which he joined in 2005. Previously, he was the chief currency strategist for HSBC Bank USA and Mellon Bank. He has been involved in the global financial markets for more than twenty years and is a prolific writer and speaker. Chandler contributes to TheStreet.com and Seeking Alpha, *Active Trader, Currency Trader,* the *Financial Times, Barron's,* and *Fund Strategy.* He appears on CNBC, Bloomberg Television, *Nightly Business Report,* and ABC and NBC national news reports, as well as on Canadian and Chinese television. Chandler is also a frequent speaker to business groups, investors, and universities.

Chandler's current research projects include global imbalances, Islamic finance, and the relationship between savings, investment, and growth. Since the early 1990s, he has taught classes on international political economy at New York University at the Center for Global Affairs, where he is currently an associate professor. He holds a master's degree in American history (1982) from Northern Illinois University and a master's in international political economy from the University of Pittsburgh (1984). He lives in New York.

About Bloomberg

BLOOMBERG L.P., founded in 1981, is a global information services, news, and media company. Headquartered in New York, Bloomberg has sales and news operations worldwide.

Serving customers on six continents, Bloomberg, through its wholly-owned subsidiary Bloomberg Finance L.P., holds a unique position within the financial services industry by providing an unparalleled range of features in a single package known as the Bloomberg Professional® service. By addressing the demand for investment performance and efficiency through an exceptional combination of information, analytic, electronic trading, and straight-through-processing tools, Bloomberg has built a worldwide customer base of corporations, issuers, financial intermediaries, and institutional investors.

Bloomberg News, founded in 1990, provides stories and columns on business, general news, politics, and sports to leading newspapers and magazines throughout the world. Bloomberg Television, a 24-hour business and financial news network, is produced and distributed globally in seven languages. Bloomberg Radio is an international radio network anchored by flagship station Bloomberg 1130 (WBBR-AM) in New York.

In addition to the Bloomberg Press line of books, Bloomberg publishes *Bloomberg Markets* magazine.

To learn more about Bloomberg, call a sales representative at:

London:	+44-20-7330-7500
New York:	+1-212-318-2000
Tokyo:	+81-3-3201-8900